Jesus
Is Not A
Republican

Jesus
Is Not A
Republican

THE RELIGIOUS RIGHT'S WAR ON AMERICA

EDITED BY CLINT WILLIS AND NATE HARDCASTLE

THUNDER'S MOUTH PRESS | NEW YORK

JESUS IS NOT A REPUBLICAN:
The Religious Right's War on America

Published by
Thunder's Mouth Press
An Imprint of Avalon Publishing Group Inc.
245 West 17th St., 11th Floor
New York, NY 10011

AVALON
publishing group incorporated

Compilation copyright © 2005 by Clint Willis and Nate Hardcastle
Introductions © 2005 by Clint Willis

First printing October 2005

Library of Congress Cataloging-in-Publication Data is available.

ISBN: 1-56025-763-6
ISBN 13: 978-1-56025-763-9

9 8 7 6 5 4 3 2 1

Book design by Paul Paddock
Printed in the United States of America
Distributed by Publishers Group West

For the Religious Left

CONTENTS

INTRODUCTION

Jesus and I go way back. When I was four or five years old, I dreamed that I was crucified at a Baptist church on St. Charles Avenue in New Orleans. As I grew older, I lay in bed nights and vowed to live a perfect, sinless life—to be more like the Jesus I imagined back then.

Jesus as I know him remains my creation—a mix of dreams, stories, desires, fear . . . and also things I cannot name or describe even to myself. My relationship to this Jesus of mine is like the relationship of a spiritual seeker to a teacher. My Jesus is a gate to something greater that lives in both of us.

My Jesus is not entirely real, even to me. I have invented him from what I know and from what I don't know—from wishes and aversions, from fantasies and shortcuts. Still, I believe that this made-up Jesus is partly real, and he aims to bridge the gaps between all of us.

The Religious Right in recent years has allied itself with the Republican Party. The party's leadership in turn has allied itself with the most powerful institutions among us—in particular, the huge multinational corporations that increasingly shape and even dominate our culture and our lives. Together, certain Christian fundamentalists, Republican politicians and corporate leaders have worked hard to impose their versions of Jesus on the rest of us; they exploit the name of Jesus, making it a marketing tool for power and profit.

This radical Republican version of Jesus also is composed of stories. These stories sometimes suggest that Jesus is an angry and self-important character. Such a Jesus would be worse than useless to me. An angry Jesus cannot teach me how to be happy. I don't want to live in his kingdom, where revenge matters more than forgiveness and where judgment is stronger than compassion. It is a kingdom of fear and of hatred; it sounds like hell to me.

The Bible can't settle this matter for us; we must find Jesus for ourselves. The Gospels offer us more than one version of Christ—including the angry and self-righteous versions. This reflects the fact that the men who wrote the Gospels lacked the spiritual maturity of their subject, as well as the fact that they had their own personal and political agendas.

Fortunately, the Gospels also offer a Jesus who can teach us much of what we need to know.

I wish I had a photograph of Jesus. I would frame it and hang it on my office wall and look at it from time to time, as I look at other pictures there—for reminders and for solace.

I lack such an image, so I consult my stories about him. These stories are composed of passages from the Bible and other books, and from my own imaginings—which include my experience of Jesus as a friend. Our friendship has evolved; my notions of Jesus have sunk into me like grass cuttings into soil, so that I begin to see that I have no need of the man—what lived in Jesus lives in me.

Our political discourse and political doings should be guided by our wish to be happy, the impulse that lies at the heart of any spiritual pursuit. We often confuse happiness with the achievement of some aim, but it is in fact a state of awareness that dissolves the boundaries between us. If we cultivate this wish for happiness, for connection, we can build a community that sustains all beings—not merely our friends, but our supposed enemies.

What do I mean when I say that Jesus is not a Republican? I mean that Jesus as I imagine and know him would not support policies that profit the strong at the expense of the weak.

—Clint Willis

JESUS IS NOT
A KILLER

*with quotations from Jesus;
and cartoons by Aaron McGruder, Ruben Bolling and Pat Oliphant*

Republicans lately have spoken of a culture of life, by which they seem to mean a culture that pursues these policies:

• It withholds resources and distorts information (about condoms, for example) that could save millions of potential AIDS victims and stop unwanted pregnancies that lead to abortions.

• It prevents young, ignorant and poor girls and women from having safe abortions, but does nothing to sustain or protect their children once they are born.

• It spends huge sums keeping a brain-dead person alive, but next to nothing to provide basic health care to poor children.

• It executes a young or mentally disabled person.

• It trains young men and women to kill strangers, and abandons them when they return from their missions.

• It kills civilians by the thousands in pursuit of political ends that are at best murky.

• It does almost nothing to save the thousands of children who needlessly die of starvation or illness every day in developing nations.

What would a culture of death look like?

"You have heard that it was said, You shall love your neighbor. But I tell you, love your enemies, do good to those who hate you, bless those who curse you, and pray for those who mistreat you, so that you may be sons of your Father in heaven; for he makes his sun rise on the wicked and on the good, and sends rain to the righteous and to the unrighteous.

"For if you love only those who love you, what credit is that to you: don't even the tax-gatherers do the same? And if you do good only to those who do good to you: don't even the Gentiles do the same? But love your enemies, and give, expecting nothing in return; and your reward will be great, and you will be sons of the Most High, for he is kind even to the ungrateful and the wicked. Therefore be merciful, just as your Father is merciful."

—from *The Gospel According to Jesus Christ*, edited and translated by Stephen Mitchell

"Love your enemies, do good to those who hate you, bless those who curse you, pray for those who abuse you . . . Be merciful, even as your Father is merciful."
—Luke 6:27–8, 36

Sister Helen Prejean, best known as the author of Dead Man Walking, *is a Catholic nun and an activist who campaigns against the death penalty. Here is a letter she wrote to Pope John Paul II in 1997.*

from *Death of Innocents* (2005)
Sister Helen Prejean

Dear Holy Father,

The very first words I write in this new year are to you. May the Spirit of Christ continue to strengthen you and give you joy in your awesome vocation and responsibilities.

Thank you for raising your voice on behalf of Virginia death row inmate, Joseph O'Dell. Though it is hard to point to exact causality, there is no doubt in my mind that your intervention helped to save his life. He was not executed on December 22. On December 17 the U.S. Supreme Court, which as a matter of course these days refuses to hear death penalty cases, unanimously granted a stay of execution and voted 8 to 1 to review Mr. O'Dell's case. Joseph O'Dell is alive, though still in grievous trauma from his ordeal. He cannot control his tears. "They tried to kill me," he keeps saying. While awaiting his turn to die, he watched two others, one a close friend, be taken to their deaths. Just across from his cell was the shower stall, and he watched in mute horror as his fellow inmates were forced to shower and put on "execution clothes" shortly before being led to their deaths. Joseph had asked me as spiritual advisor to accompany him to his death, and I kept looking at my airline ticket to Richmond as the days and hours ticked by bringing him to the brink of death. Thank God I did not have to use that ticket. I have already accompanied three men to their deaths in Louisiana's electric chair, and I have "seen with my eyes and touched with my hands" the suffering face of Christ in the "least of these" as they went to their deaths. I have seen the practice of the death penalty close up and have no doubt that it is the practice of torture. What all of the men I have accompanied have said when at last they died was, "I am so tired." Conscious human beings anticipate death and die a thousand times before they die, no matter what the "humane" method of death may be, even lethal injection, which is supposed to just "put you to sleep."

Interestingly, the lone dissent in the Supreme Court decision to hear the O'Dell case came from Catholic Justice Antonin Scalia, who is relentless in his pursuit of legalizing executions, even of juveniles and the mentally retarded, and who expedites the death process in the courts in every way he can. He seems to have no trouble squaring executions with his Catholic faith, and in this he is no exception. For fourteen years I have been speaking to groups all across the United States about the death penalty, and, for the most part, find Catholics, including many priests, religious educators, and teachers supportive of government-sanctioned executions. Rarely is the death penalty questioned from pulpits at Mass, and "pro-life," as it turns out, most often means pro-innocent life, not guilty life. The death penalty is very much a poor person's issue (99 percent of the 3,100 souls on death row in the U.S. are poor), and I have found that as a general rule those involved with justice for poor people readily oppose the death penalty, whereas those separated from poor people and their struggles readily support it. They are more prone to see poor people as the "enemy" and to be willing to inflict harsh punishments to "control" them.

Your words on the death penalty in *Evangelium Vitae* have come as a fresh breeze. Your strong words on behalf of life even of violent offenders encourage church leaders to be more courageous in voicing gospel values in opposition to the death penalty and hopefully these words will make their way into classrooms and pulpits. Especially welcome were your words upholding the dignity of human life, the "sacred and inviolable character" that each human life possesses. In contrast, the U.S. Supreme Court in *Furman v. Georgia* upheld that retribution, even in its most extreme form, execution, is not "inconsistent with our respect for the dignity of men." How can one possibly subject human beings to torture and to death and yet respect their dignity?

Unfortunately, however, when in *Evangelium Vitae*, paragraph 56, you uphold the state's right to execute in cases of "absolute necessity," some pro-death penalty advocates such as Catholic district Attorney of New Orleans, Harry Connick, Sr., use those words to justify their vigorous pursuit of the death penalty. As the death penalty is practiced now, Mr. Connick has stated, the death penalty is "all too rare," so he feels that every death penalty that he succeeds in getting is an "absolute necessity." As Amnesty International has amply documented, whenever governments around the world punish criminals by killing them, they claim to act out of "absolute necessity." By way of contrast, one of the first acts of the Constitutional Court of South Africa was to unconditionally forbid state executions. The leaders of South Africa understand all too well that when governments are given the right to execute their citizens, invariably the deepest prejudices of the society exert full sway in the punishment of those considered the "dangerous criminal element." The United Nations Universal Declaration of Human Rights states in clear, unequivocal terms every human being's inalienable right not to be killed (Article 3) nor "subjected to torture" (Article 5). From the time of St. Augustine of Hippo, one of the first to argue that the "wicked" might be "coerced with the sword," we Catholics have upheld the right of governments to take life in defense of the common good. But, as you point out in *Evangelium Vitae,* the development in societies of penal institutions now offers a way for societies to protect themselves from violent offenders without imitating the very violence they claim to abhor. How can any government, vulnerable to undue influence of the rich and powerful and subject to every kind of prejudice, have the purity and integrity to select certain of its citizens for punishment by death? Even in a so-called developed country such as the U.S., for example, we are discovering how much the status of the victim plays a part in the decision to seek death as a punishment. The vast majority of people on death row in the U.S.—85 percent—are chosen for death because they killed white people; whereas, when people of color are killed (fully 50 percent of all homicides) not only is the death penalty seldom sought, but often there is not even vigorous prosecution of such cases. A society and its government would have to care equally about the life of all of its members to be entrusted with the death penalty, and we know that on this earth no society can make that claim.

I pray for the day when Catholic opposition to government executions will be unequivocal. I say this because I know that words of the law and words in church teachings can be used to justify and pursue the death penalty, and I have watched as these words become flesh in front of my eyes as I have watched human beings die at the hands of the state. "I just pray that God holds up my legs," each of the condemned said to me as they were about to walk to their deaths, and from the depths of my soul, from Christ burning within me, I found myself saying to them, "Look at me. Look at my face. I will be the face of Christ for you." In such an instance the gospel of Jesus is very distilled: life, not death; mercy and compassion, not vengeance. Surely, Holy Father, it is not the will of Christ for us to ever sanction governments to torture and kill in such fashion, even those guilty of terrible crimes. . . .

In the United States there is presently an initiative to gather and motivate Christian communities, Catholic and Protestant, across the country to become active in abolition of the death penalty. In the first Abolition Movement to abolish slavery in the U.S., Christian churches played a key role. Now the time has come to summon Christian churches to participate in the Second Abolitionist Movement to abolish state-sanctioned death. As I mentioned earlier about widespread Catholic support for the death penalty, surely there is much work to he done to enlighten hearts and awaken consciences. But I am full of hope. Over these past fourteen years of talking to groups I have found that when people are brought to a deeper level of reflection on the gospel of Jesus and can get real information about the death penalty, not just rhetoric from politicians or sound bites from media, overwhelmingly they reject the death penalty and choose life. A steering committee, of which I am a part, is planning national conference[s] for Christian churches. It would be wonderful if we could get vigorous and wholehearted participation of the Catholic community in this effort. Whatever you can do to encourage the Catholic Bishops to participate in this new initiative will be warmly welcomed.

In closing, Holy Father, again, thank you for helping to save the life of Joseph O'Dell. I so appreciate your willingness to stand with the "least of these" as Jesus did. I so appreciate your close identification with the poor and struggling ones of earth. What a large heart and what strong faith in Christ you must have not to be overwhelmed by the sufferings of so many that you constantly encounter. May Mary, who brought Jesus to the world, comfort and sustain you as you continue her holy birthing task, bringing Jesus to our hungry, suffering world. My earnest prayers are with you . . .

"And he began to teach them, and said,
'Blessed are the poor in spirit, for theirs is
the kingdom of God.
'Blessed are those who grieve, for they
will be comforted.
'Blessed are those who hunger and thirst
for righteousness, for they will be filled.
'Blessed are the merciful, for they will
receive mercy.
'Blessed are the pure in heart, for they
will see God.
'Blessed are the peacemakers, for they
will be called sons of God."
—from *The Gospel According to Jesus Christ*,
edited and translated by Stephen Mitchell

TOM the DANCING BUG

BY RUBEN BOLLING

HE'LL GO EIGHTEENTH CENTURY ON YOUR BUTT!

JUDGE SCALIA

This Week: "KIDS THESE DAYS"

JUDGE SCALIA WAS ENJOYING HIS DAY OFF, OBSERVING THE EXECUTION OF A TEENAGER, WHEN--

I LOVE THAT NEW BOOSTER SEAT FOR THE CHAIR...!

JUDGE SCALIA!

THE COURT IS CONSIDERING THE CONSTITUTIONALITY OF THE EXECUTION OF MINORS!

IN NO TIME...

CRASH

WHAT'S THIS I HEAR ABOUT KILLING KIDS?

SCALIA! WE THINK IT'S "CRUEL AND UNUSUAL PUNISHMENT!"

BUT HERE ARE THE FOUNDING FATHERS--THEY **WROTE** THOSE WORDS!

AND WE SAY A PUNK IS A PUNK ... IN ANY MILLENNIUM!

COME ON, SCALIA! YOU KNOW THAT ONLY **YOU** CAN SEE THEM!

AND MANY PEOPLE TODAY OPPOSE THE EXECUTION OF MINORS!

ONLY IF YOU COUNT PINKOS, SUBVERSIVES AND FOREIGNERS! IF YOU ONLY COUNT **REAL** AMERICANS, **EVERYONE** FAVORS IT!

YOU'RE TOO LATE, SCALIA! WE HAVE A MAJORITY!

NOOOooOOO!

Next Week: JUDGE SCALIA GETS HIS REVENGE, IN THE TEN COMMANDMENTS CASE!

I'LL HAVE "THOU SHALT NOT KILL" ENGRAVED IN EVERY COURTHOUSE IN THE LAND!

William H. Willimon, Dean of Chapel and Professor of Christian Ministry at Duke University, delivered this sermon on Palm Sunday.

No More of This!

from CFBA.info (4/4/04)

William H. Willimon

The story of Jesus' Passion ends in high drama, and not just in the movies. At last the moment comes for the soldiers to arrest Jesus.

And at that moment the disciples ask Jesus a curious question: "Lord, shall we strike with the sword?" (Luke 22:49). Curious, because well, these are the disciples, the ones closest to Jesus. What of that which Jesus taught or did up to this point would lead the disciples to think that now they should "strike with the sword"?

Here's a somber irony. When Jesus is arrested the soldiers have swords. (No irony in that, all soldiers have swords. This is the way governments keep afloat, with swords. This is the way we attain national security, with swords. As you pay taxes this year, for the largest military budget in the world, you all know that "In God we trust," is a lie. In a pinch, give us a good sword.)

The irony is that Jesus' own disciples have swords. Matthew, Mark, and Luke don't name the disciple with the sword. John says that the sword-swinging disciple was none other than Peter, the rock, the church, us.

All of that Jesus talk about turning the other cheek, about not resisting evil, was fine for sunnier days, back on the road, when Jesus was popular and spiritual. But when it's dark, as soldiers come with swords, it's time for the church to be responsible, realistic, take matters in hand, take up the sword. Church, let's roll.

Here are the people who heard every of word Jesus spoke, and still ask, "Lord, shall we strike with the sword?"

Of course we know that violence is not the way of Jesus. Jesus' way was love, justice, and other sweet spiritualities. But sometimes you have to forget all that and take matters in hand. I remember those armchair campus liberation theologians who, while not thinking that violence was a good idea, particularly violence worked by the state, thought that the violence worked by Sandinista righteous revolutionaries in behalf of the poor was OK. Violence is wrong—unless it is in the interest of justice, which makes it right.

Michael Moore told me that the day that two spoiled young men opened fire on fellow students at Columbine High, the Clinton administration and NATO dropped the largest number of bombs in one day on Bosnia, destroying a hospital and a school.

Violence is bad, when worked by terrorists, but violence is good, when worked against terrorists. Which makes all the more amazing that even at this point, when Jesus' life is threatened, when his movement is faced with its extinction, even then, to our question about perfectly justified self-defense, Jesus replies, "Put away your sword . . . everyone who takes up the sword will die by the sword." (Matthew 26:52) These are the last words, the very last words, that the disciples hear before they flee into the darkness. Put away the swords.

Surely, if there were a moment in human history when

violence is justified, it is here when the Son of God is being so unjustly attacked. But then come the words of Jesus; No more of this. Elsewhere Jesus suggests: "consider the lilies," "blessed are the peacemakers." Here he commands with no equivocation, put away your sword! It is not only that Jesus' followers are not allowed to kill to protect themselves; they are not even to defend him.

Perhaps it is a savvy strategy. We know that violence begets violence. Violence against the Palestinian terrorist produces more terrorists. Bush Senior's war to end all war in Iraq produces a more costly second Bush war in Iraq. The soldier trained to right the wrongs in Iraq through violence comes home to Fayetteville and works violence within his own family. As Jesus said; those who take up the sword die by the sword. Over eleven thousand Americans died with guns last year, far more than in Iraq or Iran where almost no one claims to be following Jesus.

But this is beyond astute pragmatism. Jesus is against swords, not as a matter of astute strategy, because of something Jesus knows about God. The authorities have their swords to prop them up. Jesus has nothing to support his "kingdom" but God. When we draw the sword, there is no difference between the Empire and us. The state is careful to identify its enemies, to get conclusive evidence against them, as justification for its violence. Jesus commands us to love our enemies, to take our swords and beat them into plows.

At this, his final word to them, his last command, the disciples of Jesus scurry into the dark. And Jesus is left alone, to go head-to-head with the powers, like a lamb to the slaughter. And the Christian faith claims that this is the way God wins God's victories!

Last year, during Islamic Awareness Week, we had a panel. There was an Imam from Chicago, a local Rabbi, and me (representing all Christians everywhere, even though you didn't vote for me). During the discussion, the Imam said, "Islam is a very tolerant faith. In the Holy Koran, if an unbeliever attacks a believer, I am under obligation to punish the unbeliever. If my brother here, the Jew, is attacked by an unbeliever, the Holy Prophet commands me to punish the attacker."

The rabbi seemed pleased by this. For my part, I said, "Gee, I wish Jesus had said that. I got people that I want to punish, folks who need killing. Unfortunately, even when we tried to defend Jesus, he cursed us!"

It may be possible to have a good debate over the virgin birth of Jesus—Mark, Paul, never mention it. It may be possible for us to have a real fight over whether or not the Bible really condemns homosexuality; the texts are few and some are conflicted.

Alas, there is no debate over whether or not Jesus condemned violence for any purpose, in any cause, noble or not.

During the last presidential election, there was debate about Senator Lieberman. "He's a devout Jew," some said. "He keeps Kosher. If we have a national crisis and need to go to war on a Saturday, could we count on Lieberman?"

Nobody said, "George Bush is a Methodist, Al Gore is a Baptist, don't these Christians have some funny ideas about violence? Can we count on them to kick butt when we need it?"

Nobody asked because, well, when it comes to such issues, you can't tell the worshippers of Caesar from the devotees of Jesus. In the dark, they've all got swords.

I don't know what to do about this. America is built on, bathed in, blood. I, and my family, are the beneficiaries of blood, as are you.

I took a palm branch, joined the happy troupe behind Jesus, parading into the city, shouting "Hosanna!" But at this point, as we move toward an unjust, horribly suffering death and defeat on a cross, I begin to lag. Do you?

On Thursday, when the disciples gather with Jesus in the Upper Room, at the table, Jesus makes a curious remark. He says, "Now, the hour of darkness. Now Satan has entered. Now let him who has no sword buy one." And the disciples reply, "No problem. We've got two swords right here."

Why would Jesus urge his disciples to have swords when, just a few moments later, when the soldiers come and we try to use the swords, he rebukes us, tells us to put them away?

I don't know. One of my teachers, Paul Minear, said that he thinks these two swords may relate to the requirement, back in the book of Deuteronomy, for two witnesses to convict someone of a capital crime. You couldn't be convicted of a serious crime without two witnesses. Two.

See? Jesus asks, "When I sent you out earlier, I ordered you not to take a sword, or an extra pair of shoes, or fat wallet, so that you might rely only on God to preserve you. Did you disobey me?"

And we say, "Sure, and we've got these two swords to prove our disobedience. The power of God is fine, but just in case this messiah thing didn't work out, we kept a couple of Smith-and-Wessons in the glove compartment."

And Jesus says, "It is enough. My betrayer is at hand."

I'll say. His "betrayer" is right here at the table with him.
Us. With our swords, our defense programs, our guns and
vengeance and all, you don't have to look far to find the
betrayers of Jesus.

On the cross, his crucifiers screamed, "He trusted God,
let God deliver him." We can't. We may say, on our money,
"In God we trust," but when push comes to shove, we ask,
"Lord, is now the time to strike with the sword?"

In just a short time, we are going to see that, when Jesus
says, "In God I trust," he means it. God only knows what
God now does with us and our disobedient bloody,
bloody mess. Let go the swords and watch. Only God
knows.

*Our Republican rulers often invoke religion in pursuit of aims
Jesus would abhor.*

Leo Strauss's Philosophy of Deception

from AlterNet.org (12/7/04)

Jim Lobe

What would you do if you wanted to topple Saddam
Hussein, but your intelligence agencies couldn't
find the evidence to justify a war?

A follower of Leo Strauss may just hire the "right"
kind of men to get the job done—people with the intellect, acuity, and, if necessary, the political commitment,
polemical skills, and, above all, the imagination to find
the evidence that career intelligence officers could not
detect.

The "right" man for Deputy Defense Secretary Paul Wolfowitz, suggests Seymour Hersh in his recent New Yorker article entitled "Selective Intelligence," was Abram Shulsky, director of the Office of Special Plans (OSP)—an agency created specifically to find the evidence of WMDs and/or links with Al Qaeda, piece it together, and clinch the case for the invasion of Iraq.

Like Wolfowitz, Shulsky is a student of an obscure German Jewish political philosopher named Leo Strauss who arrived in the United States in 1938. Strauss taught at several major universities, including Wolfowitz and Shulsky's alma mater, the University of Chicago, before his death in 1973.

Strauss is a popular figure among the neoconservatives. Adherents of his ideas include prominent figures both within and outside the administration. They include *Weekly Standard* editor William Kristol; his father and indeed the godfather of the neoconservative movement, Irving Kristol; the new undersecretary of defense for intelligence, Stephen Cambone, a number of senior fellows at the American Enterprise Institute (AEI) (home to former Defense Policy Board chairman Richard Perle and Lynne Cheney), and Gary Schmitt, the director of the influential Project for the New American Century (PNAC), which is chaired by Kristol the Younger.

Strauss' philosophy is hardly incidental to the strategy and mindset adopted by these men—as is obvious in Shulsky's 1999 essay titled "Leo Strauss and the World of Intelligence (By Which We Do Not Mean Nous)" (in Greek philosophy the term *nous* denotes the highest form of rationality). As Hersh notes in his article, Shulsky and his coauthor Schmitt "criticize America's intelligence community for its failure to appreciate the duplicitous nature of the regimes it deals with, its susceptibility to social-science notions of proof, and its inability to cope with deliberate concealment." They argued that Strauss's idea of hidden meaning, "alerts one to the possibility that political life may be closely linked to deception. Indeed, it suggests that deception is the norm in political life, and the hope, to say nothing of the expectation, of establishing a politics that can dispense with it is the exception."

RULE ONE: DECEPTION

It's hardly surprising then why Strauss is so popular in an administration obsessed with secrecy, especially when it comes to matters of foreign policy. Not only did Strauss have few qualms about using deception in politics, he saw it as a necessity. While professing deep respect for American democracy, Strauss believed that societies should be hierarchical—divided between an elite who should lead, and the masses who should follow. But unlike fellow elitists like Plato, he was less concerned with the moral character of these leaders. According to Shadia Drury, who teaches politics at the University of Calgary, Strauss believed that "those who are fit to rule are those who realize there is no morality and that there is only one natural right—the right of the superior to rule over the inferior."

This dichotomy requires "perpetual deception" between the rulers and the ruled, according to Drury. Robert Locke, another Strauss analyst says, "The people are told what they need to know and no more." While the elite few are capable of absorbing the absence of any moral truth, Strauss thought, the masses could not cope. If exposed to the absence of absolute truth, they would quickly fall into nihilism or anarchy, according to Drury, author of *Leo Strauss and the American Right* (St. Martin's 1999).

SECOND PRINCIPLE: POWER OF RELIGION

According to Drury, Strauss had a "huge contempt" for secular democracy. Nazism, he believed, was a nihilistic reaction to the irreligious and liberal nature of the Weimar Republic. Among other neoconservatives, Irving Kristol has long argued for a much greater role for religion in the public sphere, even suggesting that the Founding Fathers of the American Republic made a major mistake by insisting on the separation of church and state. And why? Because Strauss viewed religion as absolutely essential in order to impose moral law on the masses who otherwise would be out of control.

At the same time, he stressed that religion was for the masses alone; the rulers need not be bound by it. Indeed, it would be absurd if they were, since the truths proclaimed by religion were "a pious fraud." As Ronald Bailey, science correspondent for *Reason* magazine points out, "Neoconservatives are pro-religion even though they themselves may not be believers."

"Secular society in their view is the worst possible thing," Drury says, because it leads to individualism, liberalism, and relativism, precisely those traits that may promote dissent that in turn could dangerously weaken society's ability to cope with external threats. Bailey argues that it is this firm belief in the political utility of religion as an "opiate of the masses" that helps explain why secular Jews like Kristol in *Commentary* magazine and other neoconservative journals have allied themselves with the Christian Right and even taken on Darwin's theory of evolution.

THIRD PRINCIPLE: AGGRESSIVE NATIONALISM

Like Thomas Hobbes, Strauss believed that the inherently aggressive nature of human beings could only be restrained by a powerful nationalistic state. "Because mankind is intrinsically wicked, he has to be governed," he once wrote. "Such governance can only be established, however, when men are united—and they can only be united against other people."

Not surprisingly, Strauss' attitude toward foreign policy was distinctly Machiavellian. "Strauss thinks that a political order can be stable only if it is united by an external threat," Drury wrote in her book. "Following Machiavelli, he maintained that if no external threat exists then *one has to be manufactured* (emphasis added)."

"Perpetual war, not perpetual peace, is what Straussians believe in," says Drury. The idea easily translates into, in her words, an "aggressive, belligerent foreign policy," of the kind that has been advocated by neocon groups like PNAC and AEI scholars—not to mention Wolfowitz and other administration hawks who have called for a world order dominated by U.S. military power. Strauss' neoconservative students see foreign policy as a means to fulfill a "national destiny"—as Irving Kristol defined it already in 1983—that goes far beyond the narrow confines of a "myopic national security."

As to what a Straussian world order might look like, the analogy was best captured by the philosopher himself in one of his—and student Allen Bloom's—many allusions to *Gulliver's Travels*. In Drury's words, "When Lilliput was on fire, Gulliver urinated over the city, including the palace. In so doing, he saved all of Lilliput from catastrophe, but the Lilliputians were outraged and appalled by such a show of disrespect."

The image encapsulates the neoconservative vision of the United States' relationship with the rest of the world—as well as the relationship between their relationship as a ruling elite with the masses. "They really have no use for liberalism and democracy, but they're conquering the world in the name of liberalism and democracy," Drury says.

JESUS IS NOT AFRAID OF THE FACTS

with quotations from Jesus

Fundamentalism, like the violence it often unleashes, is an unskillful response to fear. Fundamentalists—whether Christian, Jewish, Muslim or Hindu—cling to certain teachings (including the myths that grow up around any religion). They use those teachings to defend against personal, political, cultural and economic shifts that threaten their identity or well-being. Jesus understood that clinging to any position or identity would cause suffering. He was willing to learn what the world had to teach him, and to evolve with those teachings. He did not hide behind stories; he used them to show himself and to see the world with clarity.

"When the spirit of truth comes, he will guide you into all the truth."
—John 16: 12-15

The God Racket, from DeMille to DeLay

from *The New York Times* (3/27/05)

Frank Rich

As Congress and the president scurried to play God in the lives of Terri Schiavo and her family last weekend, ABC kicked off Holy Week with its perennial ritual: a rebroadcast of the 1956 Hollywood blockbuster, *The Ten Commandments*.

Cecil B. DeMille's epic is known for the parting of its Technicolor Red Sea, for the religiosity of its dialogue (Anne Baxter's Nefretiri to Charlton Heston's Moses: "You can worship any God you like as long as I can worship you.") and for a Golden Calf scene that DeMille himself described as "an orgy Sunday-school children can watch." But this year the lovable old war horse has a relevance that transcends camp. At a time when government, culture, science, medicine and the rule of law are all under threat from an emboldened religious minority out to remake America according to its dogma, the half-forgotten show business history of *The Ten Commandments* provides a telling back story.

As DeMille readied his costly Paramount production for release a half-century ago, he seized on an ingenious publicity scheme. In partnership with the Fraternal Order of Eagles, a nationwide association of civic-minded clubs founded by theater owners, he sponsored the construction of several thousand Ten Commandments monuments throughout the country to hype his product. The Pharaoh himself—that would be Yul Brynner—participated in the gala unveiling of the Milwaukee slab. Heston did the same in North Dakota. Bizarrely enough, all these years later, it is another of these DeMille-inspired granite monuments, on the grounds of the Texas Capitol in Austin, that is a focus of the Ten Commandments case that the United States Supreme Court heard this month.

We must wait for the court's ruling on whether the relics of a Hollywood relic breach the separation of church and state. Either way, it's clear that one principle, so firmly upheld by DeMille, has remained inviolate no matter what the courts have to say: American moguls, snake-oil salesmen and politicians looking to score riches or power will stop at little if they feel it is in their interests to exploit God to achieve those ends. While sometimes God racketeers are guilty of the relatively minor sin of bad taste—witness the crucifixion-nail jewelry licensed by Mel Gibson—sometimes we get the demagoguery of Father Coughlin or the big-time cons of Jimmy Swaggart and Jim Bakker.

The religio-hucksterism surrounding the Schiavo case makes DeMille's Hollywood crusades look like amateur night. This circus is the latest and most egregious in a series of cultural shocks that have followed Election Day 2004, when a fateful exit poll question on "moral values" ignited a take-no-prisoners political grab by moral zealots. During the commercial interruptions on *The Ten Commandments* last weekend, viewers could surf over to the cable news networks and find a Bible-thumping show as only Washington could conceive it. Congress was floating such scenarios as staging a meeting in Ms. Schiavo's hospital room or, alternatively, subpoenaing her, her husband and her doctors to a hearing in Washington. All in the name of faith.

Like many Americans, I suspect, I tried to picture how I would have reacted if a bunch of smarmy, camera-seeking politicians came anywhere near a hospital room where my own relative was hooked up to life support. I imagined summoning the Clint Eastwood of *Dirty Harry*, not *Million Dollar Baby*. But before my fantasy could get very far, star politicians with the most to gain from playing the God card started hatching stunts whose extravagant shamelessness could upstage any humble reverie of my own.

Senator Bill Frist, the Harvard-educated heart surgeon with presidential aspirations, announced that watching videos of Ms. Schiavo had persuaded him that her doctors in Florida were mistaken about her vegetative state— a remarkable diagnosis given that he had not only failed to examine the patient ostensibly under his care but has no expertise in the medical specialty, neurology, relevant to her case. No less audacious was Tom DeLay, last seen on *60 Minutes* a few weeks ago deflecting Lesley Stahl's questions about his proximity to allegedly criminal fund-raising by saying he would talk only about children stranded by the tsunami. Those kids were quickly forgotten as he hitched his own political rehabilitation to a brain-damaged patient's feeding tube. Adopting a prayerful tone, the former exterminator from Sugar Land, Texas, took it upon himself to instruct "millions of people praying around the world this Palm Sunday weekend" to "not be afraid."

The president was not about to be outpreached by these saps. The same Mr. Bush who couldn't be bothered to interrupt his vacation during the darkening summer of 2001, not even when he received a briefing titled "Bin Laden Determined to Strike in U.S.," flew from his Crawford ranch to Washington to sign Congress's Schiavo bill into law. The bill could have been flown to him in Texas, but his ceremonial arrival and departure by helicopter on the White House lawn allowed him to showboat as if he had just landed on the deck of an aircraft carrier. Within hours he turned Ms. Schiavo into a slick applause line at a Social Security rally. "It is wise to always err on the side of life," he said, wisdom that apparently had not occurred to him in 1999, when he mocked the failed pleas for clemency of Karla Faye Tucker, the born-again Texas death-row inmate, in a magazine interview with Tucker Carlson.

These theatrics were foretold. Culture is often a more reliable prophecy than religion of where the country is going, and our culture has been screaming its theocratic inclinations for months now. The anti-indecency campaign, already a roaring success, has just yielded a new chairman of the Federal Communications Commission, Kevin J. Martin, who had been endorsed by the Parents Television Council and other avatars of the religious right. The push for the sanctity of marriage (or all marriages except Terri and Michael Schiavo's) has led to the banishment of lesbian moms on public television. The Armageddon-fueled worldview of the Left Behind books extends its spell by the day, soon to surface in a new NBC prime-time mini-series, *Revelations*, being sold with the slogan "The End is Near."

All this is happening while polls consistently show that at most a fifth of the country subscribes to the religious views of those in the Republican base whom even George Will, speaking last Sunday on ABC's *This Week*, acknowledged may be considered "extremists." In that famous Election Day exit poll, "moral values" voters amounted to only 22 percent. Similarly, an ABC News survey last weekend found that only 27 percent of Americans thought it was "appropriate" for Congress to "get involved" in the Schiavo case and only 16 percent said it would want to be kept alive in her condition. But a majority of American colonists didn't believe in witches during the Salem trials either—any more than the Taliban reflected the views of a majority of Afghans. At a certain point—and we seem to be at that point—fear takes over, allowing a mob to bully the majority over the short term. (Of course, if you believe the end is near, there is no long term.)

That bullying, stoked by politicians in power, has become omnipresent, leading television stations to practice self-censorship and high school teachers to avoid mentioning "the E word," evolution, in their classrooms, lest they arouse fundamentalist rancor. The president is on record as saying that the jury is still out on evolution, so perhaps it's no surprise that the *Los Angeles Times* has uncovered a three-year-old "religious rights" unit in the Justice Department that investigated a biology professor at Texas Tech because he refused to write letters of recommendation for students who do not accept evolution as "the central, unifying principle of biology." Cornelia

Dean of the *New York Times* broke the story last weekend that some Imax theaters, even those in science centers, are now refusing to show documentaries like *Galápagos* or *Volcanoes of the Deep Sea* because their references to Darwin and the Big Bang theory might antagonize some audiences. Soon such films will disappear along with biology textbooks that don't give equal time to creationism.

James Cameron, producer of *Volcanoes* (and, more famously, the director of *Titanic*), called this development "obviously symptomatic of our shift away from empiricism in science to faith-based science." Faith-based science has in turn begat faith-based medicine that impedes stem-cell research, not to mention faith-based abstinence-only health policy that impedes the prevention of unwanted pregnancies and diseases like AIDS.

Faith-based news is not far behind. Ashley Smith, the twenty-six-year-old woman who was held hostage by Brian Nichols, the accused Atlanta courthouse killer, has been canonized by virtually every American news organization as God's messenger because she inspired Mr. Nichols to surrender by talking about her faith and reading him a chapter from Rick Warren's best seller, *The Purpose-Driven Life*. But if she's speaking for God, what does that make Dennis Rader, the church council president arrested in Wichita's B.T.K. serial killer case? Was God instructing Terry Ratzmann, the devoted member of the Living Church of God who this month murdered his pastor, an elderly man, two teenagers and two others before killing himself at a weekly church service in Wisconsin? The religious elements of these stories, including the role played by the end-of-times fatalism of Mr. Ratzmann's church, are left largely unexamined by the same news outlets that serve up Ashley Smith's tale as an inspirational parable for profit.

Next to what's happening now, official displays of DeMille's old Ten Commandments monuments seem an innocuous encroachment of religion into public life. It is a full-scale jihad that our government signed onto last weekend, and what's most scary about it is how little was heard from the political opposition. The Harvard Law School constitutional scholar Laurence Tribe pointed out this week that even Joe McCarthy did not go so far as this Congress and president did in conspiring to "try to undo the processes of a state court." But faced with McCarthyism in God's name, most Democratic leaders went into hiding and stayed silent. Prayers are no more likely to revive their spines than poor Terri Schiavo's brain.

Why are some Christians so frightened of death?

This Has Nothing to Do with the Sanctity of Life

from Salon.com (3/22/05)

Andrew Leonard

The Reverend John Paris, professor of bioethics, says Terri Schiavo has the moral and legal right to die, and only the Christian right is keeping her alive.

The decision on whether to allow Terri Schiavo to die has sparked endless controversy over what is legal and ethical when patients are unable to make their own wishes.

One observer who brings both legal and moral authority to the debate is the Reverend John Paris, the Walsh Professor of Bioethics at Boston College.

Paris has served as an expert witness on numerous cases involving patients who were being kept alive by artificial means. He is equally capable of discussing the legal details of the Schiavo case and the Catholic Church's view of it. According to Paris, every relevant legal issue has already been decided; the only thing keeping the case alive is the fact that the Christian right has made Schiavo a cause célèbre.

Paris did not serve as an expert witness in the Schiavo case. However, when the case was reviewed by the Florida Supreme Court, he signed an amicus brief on behalf of Michael Schiavo, who wants to take his wife off life support. *Salon* spoke to Paris by phone on Monday morning. "This case," he says, "is bizarre."

WHY IS THE CASE BIZARRE?

In most cases, the court has a theory, you have an appellate review, and that's the end. But this case, the parents keep coming back with new issues—every time that they lose, they come in with a new issue. *We want to reexamine the case. We believe she's competent. We need new medical tests being done. We think she's been abused. We want child protective services to intervene.* Finally, Judge George Greer denied them all. He said. "Look, we have had court-appointed neutral physicians examine this patient. You don't believe the findings of the doctors but the finding of the doctors have been accepted by the court as factual." There have been six reviews by the appellate court.

WHAT DID THE APPELLATE COURT FIND?

The Florida Court of Appeals found four very interesting things. And it found them by the highest legal standard you can have—clear and convincing evidence. The appellate court said that Judge Greer found clear and convincing evidence that Schiavo is in a well-diagnosed, persistent vegetative state, that there is no hope of her ever recovering consciousness, and that she had stated she would not ever want to be maintained this way. The court said we have heard the parents saying she didn't [say that], and we heard the husband say she did, and we believe the husband's statement is a correct statement of her position. The court also found that the husband was a caring, loving spouse whose actions were in Terri's best interests. The court said, "Remove the feeding tube," and the family protested. Of course, the family has the radical, antiabortion, right-to-life Christian right, with its apparently unlimited resources and political muscle, behind them.

SO WHAT DO YOU THINK THIS CASE IS REALLY ABOUT?

The power of the Christian right. This case has nothing to do with the legal issues involving a feeding tube. The feeding tube issue was definitively resolved by the U.S. Supreme Court in 1990 in *Cruzan v. Director*. The United States Supreme Court ruled that competent patients have the right to decline any and all unwanted treatment, and unconscious patients have the same right, depending upon the evidentiary standard established by the state. And Florida law says that Terri Schiavo has more than met the standard in this state. So there is no legal issue.

JESUS IS NOT AFRAID OF THE FACTS

ARE THERE ANY EXTENUATING CIRCUMSTANCES?

The law is clear, the medicine is clear, the ethics are clear. A presidential commission in 1983, appointed by Ronald Reagan, issued a very famous document called "Deciding to Forgo Life-Sustaining Treatment." It talked about the appropriate treatment for patients who are permanently unconscious. The commission said the only justification for continuing any treatment—and they specifically talked about feeding tubes—is either the slight hope that the patient might recover or the family's hope that the patient might recover. Terri Schiavo's legitimate family— the guardian, the spouse—has persuaded the court that she wouldn't want [intervention] and therefore it shouldn't happen. Now you have the brother and sister, the mother and father, saying that's all wrong. But they had their day in court, they had their weeks in court, they had their years in court!

ISN'T THE UNDERLYING SOCIAL ISSUE HERE ONE THAT SAYS THE LAW DOESN'T HAVE AUTHORITY OVER THIS KIND OF LIFE-OR-DEATH MATTER?

Let me give you a test that I've done a hundred times to audiences. And I guarantee you can do the same thing. Go and find the first twelve people you meet and say to them, "If you were to suffer a cerebral aneurysm, and we were able to diagnose that with a PET-scan immediately, would you want to be put on a feeding tube, knowing that you can be sustained in this existence?" I have asked that question in medical audiences, legal audiences and audiences of judges. I'll bet I have put that question before several thousand people. How many people do you think have said they wanted to be maintained that way? Zero. Not one person. Now that tells you about where the moral sentiment of our community is.

WHERE DO YOU THINK THIS CASE IS HEADED?
It's headed to federal court today. I cannot imagine what
the federal question is. Congress said, "All we are doing is
asking to have a federal court examine this." I don't know
what they thought the courts were doing in the last eight
years. They are saying, "We're asking a court to review this,
to be certain that due process has not been violated." I
don't think there is a case in the history of the United
States that has been reviewed six times by an appellate
court. Remember, the United States Supreme Court
refused to review this.

**AS A PRIEST, HOW DO YOU RESOLVE QUESTIONS IN WHICH THE "SANC-
TITY OF LIFE" IS INVOLVED?**
The sanctity of life? This has nothing to do with the sanctity of life. The Roman Catholic Church has a consistent
four-hundred-year-old tradition that I'm sure you are
familiar with. It says nobody is obliged to undergo
extraordinary means to preserve life.

This is Holy Week, this is when the Catholic community
is saying, "We understand that life is not an absolute good
and death is not an absolute defeat." The whole story of
Easter is about the triumph of eternal life over death.
Catholics have never believed that biological life is an end
in and of itself. We've been created as a gift from God and
are ultimately destined to go back to God. And we've been
destined in this life to be involved in relationships. And
when the capacity for that life is exhausted, there is no obligation to make officious efforts to sustain it.

This is not new doctrine. Back in 1950, Gerald Kelly, the
leading Catholic moral theologian at the time, wrote a
marvelous article on the obligation to use artificial means

to sustain life. He published it in Theological Studies, the leading Catholic journal. He wrote, "I'm often asked whether you have to use IV feeding to sustain somebody who is in a terminal coma." And he said, "Not only do I believe there is no obligation to do it, I believe that imposing those treatments on that class of patients is wrong. There is no benefit to the patient, there is great expense to the community, and there is enormous tension on the family."

HOW DO YOU SQUARE THAT WITH THE POPE'S COMMENTS LAST YEAR, WHICH SEEMED TO INDICATE THAT PEOPLE IN SCHIAVO'S SITUATION SHOULD BE KEPT ALIVE?
The bishops of Florida did it very nicely when they said, "There is a presumption to use nutritional fluid, unless the continued use of it would be burdensome to the patient." So it's not an absolute. That statement is a recognition that the Vatican is inhabited by the same cross section of people that inhabit the United States.

WHAT DO YOU MEAN?
I mean there are some radical right-to-lifers there, and they got that statement out. But it has to be seen in the context of the pope's 1980 declaration on euthanasia, and the pope's encyclical on death and dying, in which he repeats the long-standing tradition that I just gave you. His comment last year wasn't doctrinal statement, it wasn't encyclical, it wasn't a papal pronouncement. It was a speech at a meeting of right-to-lifers.

Again, this issue is not new. Every court, every jurisdiction that has heard it, agrees. So you'd think this issue would have ended. I thought it ended when we took it to the Supreme Court in 1990. But I hadn't anticipated the power of the Christian right. They elected him [George Bush]. And now he dances.

When the Christian Right doesn't like a fact, they ignore it— or they call it a theory.

Taking the Hospital
from *The Nation* (11/29/04)
Patricia J. Williams

I n the postelection world, holding evangelical Protestantism up to the light has become all the rage, which does seem somewhat like shutting the barn door after the horse has left the barn. I guess when George Bush kicked off his first campaign at Bob Jones University a lot of people didn't take it seriously. When he cozied up to Focus on the Family, some thought it was just politics. And when Ralph Reed became one of Bush's top advisers, there were a lot of people still saying there was no difference between Democrats and Republicans. Anyway, now we have lots of time to consider why all this might be really, really bad news, not just for liberals but for moderates of any stripe. These days we can take our morning coffee to James Dobson of Focus on the Family explaining to NPR precisely why secular humanists don't understand the power of moral values.

For me the big divide is as a basic as a battle about dinosaurs. As I write, the ACLU is in court challenging a sticker placed on all science textbooks by the Cobb

County, Georgia, school board. "The text of it is very, very simple and innocuous," says attorney Seth Cooper. "It says students should study evolution with an open mind." Jamie Self, director of the Georgia Family Council, explains, "If we really want to pursue intellectual honesty, when we're teaching our kids, it really is the only way to go. It is a theory; no one has ever come out and said 'evolution is a fact.' And so, if we're going to be teaching it, kids need to understand that it is a 'theory.'"

Of course, it comes down to what you mean by "theory." Scientists use the word to describe a set of governing principles that explain physical phenomena. It doesn't mean theoretical in the lay sense of hypothetical. A scientific theory is a schema of analysis. To say that evolution is not grounded in fact is to say that carbon-dating is wrong, that chemistry is fiction, that paleontological data are the artful conjuration of an intelligent God. It's fine to believe this if you want to, but it's no way to run a nation. I turned to Dobson's website for a sense of what's at stake in this debate. There you can purchase books like Phillip Johnson's *Reason in the Balance: The Case Against Naturalism in Science, Law and Education* to help you "know where you stand and why in this present cultural war against God!" *The Evolution Set* is a documentary collection "presenting solid evidence—even at the cellular level—for intelligent, purposeful design in living beings." *It Couldn't Just Happen: Fascinating Facts About God's World*, by Lawrence Richards, supposedly "delivers solid proof of God's existence and the evidence that He created and sustains the universe." *Dry Bones and Other Fossils*, by Gary and Mary Parker, invites young readers to join the Parker family on "their annual fossil hunt" and to learn how fossils "provide evidence for creation, rather than evolution. . . . Includes tips on fossil collection and preservation and a Gospel presentation." Another site, Contender Ministries, devoted to end-time theology and fears of the Satan-loving UN taking over the world, advises that "the evolutionist believes in evolution— not because it is scientific, but because he considers himself too wise to believe in God. . . . This humanist worldview, which denies God and instead chooses a scientifically unprovable theory, is the religious doctrine of the American educational system."

If a large majority of Democrats are arguing with a significant percentage of red-staters who believe that evolution is only an opinion, then we are not on the same page as to much of anything else about the planet. We do not share the same constructs of proof, evidence or the scientific method. If every sentence in the Bible is literally true, then what I call fact and what you call truth are separate genres, galaxies apart. And if, as an evangelical friend who is praying for my soul asserts, God made George Bush president, one might just as well concede that a large chunk of planetary history doesn't exist, that the future is preordained and that the battle in the Middle East is leading us to a great Armageddon among all God's tribes. Therefore, the debate about moral values has less to do with abortion rights than it does, as I said, with whether the dinosaurs existed as one link in life's eons-long chain of development. Because if they did not, then nothing in the material world remains "true"—indeed, the entire intellectual grounding of Western thought must be called into question, as must a moral schema grounded in material consequence.

As I write, American troops are pursuing an estimated two thousand insurgents, blasting away at Falluja, a city of approximately three hundred thousand residents. Some civilians have fled, but certainly not hundreds of thousands. It is interesting: The first thing our soldiers did when they entered the city was to take over the hospital, reportedly because our leaders worry that doctors there are really operating propaganda mills and milking sympathy for untoward ends. They believe that the number of civilian deaths reported by hospitals, in international mortality reports and by the Red Cross has been inflated. All those pictures of weeping families and bloody sheets are merely the heresy of freedom's nonbelievers, we are left to suppose. And so the Red Cross is no longer in the city. Médecins Sans Frontières was forced to pull out of Iraq weeks ago. A report from the British medical journal the *Lancet*, putting the Iraqi death toll at one hundred thousand since the U.S. invasion began, has been denounced as methodologically flawed, flat-out false and no more than a theory.

I waited for the non-propaganda figures to come out of this assault on Falluja, the truthful toll, some data to assure us that numbers of civilian deaths distinguish us from Saddam Hussein. At the end of three days of heavy fighting, the news was "good." Coalition casualties were reported to be light. But nowhere could I find any mention of numbers of residents killed. The silence has been light as a feather, warm as a blanket, gentle as faith. Perhaps they never existed, maybe it was all in our heads. But as American forces level this city in our name, let us stop acting stricken about what Jesus is supposedly whispering in the ears of our nation's home-grown fundamentalists. In the name of sanity, we must demand that this administration, not God, start talking some talk about our evolution to this dreadful point.

The New Monkey Trial

from Salon.com (1/10/05)

Michelle Goldberg

It was an ordinary springtime school board meeting in the bedroom community of Dover, Pennsylvania. The high school needed new biology textbooks, and the science department had recommended Kenneth Miller and Joseph Levine's *Biology*. "It was a fantastic text," said Carol "Casey" Brown, 57, a self-described Goldwater Republican and the board's senior member. "It just followed our curriculum so beautifully."

But Bill Buckingham, a new board member who'd recently become chair of the curriculum committee, had an objection. *Biology*, he said, was "laced with Darwinism." He wanted a book that balanced theories of evolution with Christian creationism, and he was willing to turn his town into a cultural battlefield to get it.

"This country wasn't founded on Muslim beliefs or evolution," Buckingham, a stocky, gray-haired man who wears a red, white and blue crucifix pin on his lapel, said at the meeting. "This country was founded on Christianity, and our students should be taught as such."

Casey Brown and her husband, fellow board member Jeff Brown, were stunned. "I was picturing the headlines," Jeff said months later.

"And we got them," Casey added.

Indeed, by the end of 2004, journalists from across the country and from overseas had come to Dover to report on the latest outbreak of America's perennial war over evolution. By then, Buckingham had succeeded in making

Dover the first school district in the country to mandate the teaching of "intelligent design"—an updated version of creationism couched in modern biological terms. In doing so, he ushered in a legal challenge from outraged parents and the ACLU that could turn into a twenty-first century version of the infamous "Scopes Monkey Trial."

The Dover case is part of a renewed revolt against evolutionary science that's been gathering force in America for the past four years, a symptom of the same renascent fundamentalism that helped propel George Bush to victory. Since 2001, the National Center for Science Education, a group formed to defend the teaching of evolution, has tallied battles over evolution in forty-three states, noting they're growing more frequent.

After 1987, when the Supreme Court declared the teaching of creationism in public school unconstitutional in *Edwards v. Aguillard*, the doctrine seemed to be shut out of public schools once and for all. In the last few years, though, intelligent design has given evolution's opponents new hope. Now, emboldened by their growing political power, religious conservatives are once again storming the barricades of science education.

The same month Bush was reelected, the rural Grantsburg, Wisconsin, school district revised its curriculum to allow the teaching of creationism and intelligent design. After a community outcry—including a letter of protest from two hundred Wisconsin clergy—the district revised the policy but continued to mandate that students be taught "the scientific strengths and weaknesses of evolutionary theory," a common creationist tactic that fosters the illusion that evolution is a controversial theory among scientists.

Other anti-evolution initiatives have affected entire states. In the November election, creationists took over the Kansas Board of Education. The last time the board had a majority, in 1999, it voted to erase any mention of evolution from the state curriculum. Kansas became a laughing-stock and the anti-evolutionists were defeated in the next Republican primary, leading to the policy's reversal. Now, newly victorious, the anti-evolutionists plan to introduce the teaching of intelligent design next year.

Similarly, this past December, the *New York Times* reported that Missouri legislators plan to introduce a bill that would require state biology textbooks to include at least one chapter dealing with "alternative theories to evolution." Speaking to the *Times*, state representative Cynthia Davis seemed to compare opponents of intelligent design to al Qaeda. "It's like when the hijackers took over those four planes on September 11 and took people to a place where they didn't want to go," she said. "I think a lot of people feel that liberals have taken our country somewhere we don't want to go. I think a lot more people realize this is our country and we're going to take it back."

Right-wingers in Congress, on talk radio and on cable TV, are stoking the anti-evolution rebellion, insisting that academic freedom means the freedom to teach creationism. Having shown their strength in the election, cultural conservatives aren't in the mood to compromise. America is a democracy and they have the numbers. They see no reason why the principles of science shouldn't be up for popular vote.

On December 14, the ACLU announced that it was representing eleven Dover parents in a lawsuit against the town. The school board's intelligent-design policy, their

complaint said, had violated the First Amendment's Establishment Clause, "which prohibits the teaching or presentation of religious ideas in public school science classes."

That day, a few of the parents joined their attorneys for a
press conference in the rotunda of Pennsylvania's capitol in
Harrisburg. Reporters and cameramen crowded around the
microphone as a succession of lawyers, liberal clergymen
and scientists spoke. The Reverend Barry Lynn, executive
director of Americans United for Separation of Church and
State, came from D.C. for the event. "We've been battling
this from Hawaii to California to New Hampshire to Cobb
County," he said, referring to the suburban Atlanta school
district that had recently put warning stickers on its biology
textbooks calling evolution "a theory, not a fact."

As the cameras rolled, a few protesters tried to edge
their way into the frame. A man named Carl Jarboe, in a
purple sport coat and a fur hat, stood near the parents
holding a fluorescent green sign saying, "ACLU Censors
Truth." His wife, wearing a kerchief on her head and small
round glasses, held a similar sign saying "Evolution:
Unscientific and Untrue. Why Does the ACLU Oppose
Schools Giving All the Evidence?"

The parents ignored them. Most were hesitant in front
of all the cameras. They weren't culture warriors and they
didn't speak in ideological terms. Instead, they talked
about what Buckingham and the other creationists were
doing to their school and their community.

"We don't believe that intelligent design is science, and
we have faith in ourselves as parents that we can do a good
job teaching our children about religion," Christy Rehm, a
thirty-one-year-old mother of four, said after the conference. "We have faith in our pastor, we have faith in our

community that our children are going to be raised to be decent people. So we don't feel that it's the school board's job to make that decision for our children."

Jarboe, who introduced himself as a former assistant professor of chemistry at Messiah College, a nearby Christian school, was convinced that the parents were being used by the ACLU to further its sinister agenda. Like a great many members of the Christian right, he sees the ACLU as a subversive, possibly demonic institution. Quoting James Kennedy, an influential Fort Lauderdale televangelist, he called the ACLU the "American Communist United League." "I maintain it's a communist front," he said.

He then pressed a flier into my hand from a two-day creation seminar he'd attended at the Faith Baptist Church in Lebanon, Pennsylvania. It was run by Dr. Kent Hovind, a young-Earth creationist who argues that, as the flier said, "it has been proven that man lived at the same time as dinosaurs." To underline this point, Hovind runs Dinosaur Adventure Land, a theme park in Pensacola, Florida, with rides and exhibits about the not-so-long-ago days when humans and dinosaurs roamed the planet together.

A few feet from Jarboe stood Robert Eckhardt, a professor of developmental genetics and evolutionary morphology at Penn State. Eckhardt had spoken at the press conference about the central role of evolution in biology. "The idea that intelligent design is a powerful upwelling of controversy within the scientific community is absolute nonsense," he said. Jarboe was unfazed by Eckhardt's expertise; he called him a "screaming leftist unbiblical liberal."

A wry man with a lined face, tweed jacket and owlish

glasses, Eckhardt, like most other experts in his field, has been dealing with creationists throughout his career and finds it tiresome to try to reason with them. He divided his opponents into several categories. "There are people who just feel that the world is changing very rapidly around them. Their children are coming home from school with ideas that are taught to them in biology class, the parents find this to be challenging and upsetting, and by God they're going to do something about it," he said. "They don't understand the world and they're trying to get the world to slow down and accommodate their thinking."

The second group, he said, are people "who are formerly associated with the creationist movement, who purposely misrepresent issues of science when in fact they are issues of religion." He didn't want to name names but it seemed he was speaking of the fellows at the Discovery Institute's Center for Science and Culture, headquarters of the intelligent-design movement. The third, he said, rolling his eyes a tiny bit toward Jarboe, who was listening to our conversation, "are people who are mentally unbalanced and who are so threatened by this that they perceive things going on around them that never happened."

As Eckhardt spoke, Jim Grove, the pastor of Heritage Baptist Church, a small congregation near Dover, stepped forward to challenge him to a debate. Eckhardt refused with a derisive laugh, saying, "I value my time." Grove interpreted this as a sign of evolution's weakness. "If he has facts, what about a forum to present them in public?" he asked. "It would be a perfect opportunity. If he has the facts."

Of Eckhardt's three categories of anti-evolutionists, the second—the proponents of intelligent design—are currently the most influential. They've created the terms that now dominate the debate from the halls of Congress to local school boards like Dover. They're the reason that, after a decade when the consensus on evolution in education seemed secure, Darwin's enemies are on the move.

Although Buckingham first argued for teaching creationism in Dover biology classes, he soon started using the phrase "intelligent design" instead. The change in language was significant because intelligent design was created in part to circumvent the Supreme Court ruling that made it illegal for public schools to teach creationism. Masquerading as a science, it aims to convince the public that evolution is a theory under fire within the scientific community and doesn't deserve its preeminent place in the biology curriculum.

At Dover's June 14 school board meeting, Buckingham said he wanted the board to consider the intelligent-design textbook, *Of Pandas and People: The Central Question of Biological Origin*. According to Nick Matzke, a spokesman for the National Center for Science Education, the original version of *Of Pandas and People*, published in 1989, contained one of the first uses of the phrase "intelligent design." Later, in the 1990s, the intelligent-design cause was taken up by the Center for Science and Culture.

Yet *Of Pandas and People* was never meant to be scientific. It was a strategic response to the Supreme Court's 1987 ruling in *Edwards v. Aguillard*, which overturned a Louisiana law mandating that "creation science" be taught alongside evolution. Because the court ruled that "creation science" is a religious doctrine, savvy opponents of evolution sought to recast the central tenets of creationism in a way that hid their religious inspiration. Thus intelligent design was born.

Percival Davis, one of the coauthors of *Of Pandas and People*, also co-wrote the old-school creationist text, *A Case for Creation*. An online ad for *Pandas* on the Web site of the creationist group Answers in Genesis describes the text as a "superbly written" book for public schools that "has no Biblical content, yet contains creationists' interpretations and refutations for evidences [sic] usually found in standard textbooks supporting evolution!"

The core idea in *Pandas*—and in the intelligent-design movement generally—is that of "irreducible complexity," the theory that the structure of proteins and amino acids in cells—the building blocks of life—is so complex that only a supernatural force could have choreographed it. "Because of the high level of improbability that cells could be generated by the random mixing of chemicals, some scientists believe that the first cells were created from the design of some outside, intelligent force," the book says.

Indeed, some "scientists" do believe this—the ones who work at the Discovery Institute's Center for Science and Culture. Outside the precincts of the religious right, though, the scientific consensus about evolution is very close to unanimous. For decades, biologists at the world's major universities, and in esteemed peer-reviewed journals, have proven that cellular processes have indeed evolved in sync with Darwin's theories. In November 2004, *National Geographic* ran a cover story asking, "Was Darwin Wrong?" Its subhead provided the answer: "No. The Evidence for Evolution Is Overwhelming."

"Evolution by natural selection, the central concept of the life's work of Charles Darwin, is a theory," wrote award-winning science author David Quammen in

National Geographic. "It's a theory about the origin of adaptation, complexity, and diversity among Earth's living creatures. If you are skeptical by nature, unfamiliar with the terminology of science, and unaware of the over-whelming evidence, you might even be tempted to say that it's 'just' a theory. In the same sense, relativity as described by Albert Einstein is 'just' a theory. The notion that Earth orbits around the sun rather than vice versa, offered by Copernicus in 1543, is a theory . . . Each of these theories is an explanation that has been confirmed to such a degree, by observation and experiment, that knowledgeable experts accept it as fact."

A statuesque woman with a strawberry blond bob and crisply proper diction, Casey Brown isn't a scientist, but she prides herself on being well read, and after ten years on the school board, she knows what a good biology textbook looks like. When she saw *Of Pandas and People,* she was appalled. "It's poor science and worse theology," she said.

Brown said that by the school board's August meeting, Buckingham had given up on the idea of using *Pandas* as the main text, but he insisted that the board buy it as a supplement. Otherwise, he said, he wouldn't approve the purchase of *Biology.*

One of Buckingham's supporters on the board was out sick that night, and without her, the vote deadlocked, 4–4. Finally, worried that the school would have to start the year without textbooks, one member switched her vote and *Biology* was approved. The town's little drama seemed to be at an end.

In fact, it was just beginning.

Shortly after the motion to have the school board buy *Of Pandas and People* was defeated, the Dover

School District received an anonymous donation of fifty copies of the book, and Buckingham and his allies set about figuring out how to integrate them into the curriculum.

On October 18, the board voted on a resolution written by Buckingham and his supporters on the board. It said, "Students will be made aware of gaps/problems in Darwin's theory and of other theories of evolution including, but not limited to, intelligent design. Note: *Origins of Life* is not taught." The *Pandas* books were to be kept in the science classroom, and teachers were instructed to read a statement referring students to them.

Casey and Jeff Brown argued against it. "We kept maintaining this is going to get us into legal trouble," Casey said. "It was a clear violation." As an alternative, she proposed offering a comparative world religions elective, which would teach the creation myths of various faiths.

But Buckingham was determined. "Two thousand years ago, someone died on a cross," he said at the meeting. "Can't someone take a stand for him?"

Jeff Brown spoke up in response, saying it was the wrong time and the wrong place for a religious debate. Buckingham called him a coward and said it was a good thing that he wasn't fighting the revolutionary war "because we would still have a queen."

Finally, they voted. The mandate to teach intelligent design passed 6–3. Casey and Jeff Brown quit the board in protest. The other dissenter, Noel Wenrich, turned to Buckingham and said, "We lost two good people because of you."

"And Mr. Buckingham said, with profanity, 'Good

riddance to bad rubbish,'" Casey recalled. "And he called Mr. Wenrich every name in the book."

Buckingham may have started the Dover crusade himself, but the Center for Science and Culture laid the groundwork years before. The group provides the "scientific" and philosophical arguments to bolster the opponents of evolution in local political struggles.

CSC operates out of the Discovery Institute, a Seattle think tank that's funded in part by savings and loan heir Howard Ahmanson. As Max Blumenthal reported in a 2004 *Salon* article, Ahmanson spent twenty years on the board of R. J. Rushdoony's Chalcedon Foundation, a theocratic outfit that advocates the replacement of American civil law with biblical law.

The Center for Science and Culture also aims, in a far more elliptical way, to put God at the center of civic life. Originally called the Center for the Renewal of Science and Culture, CSC usually purports to be motivated by science, not religion. At times, though, it's refreshingly candid about its true goal—a grandiose scheme to undermine the secular legacy of the Enlightenment and rebuild society on religious foundations. As it said in a 1999 fundraising proposal that was later leaked online, "Discovery Institute's Center for the Renewal of Science and Culture seeks nothing less than the overthrow of materialism and its cultural legacies."

The proposal was titled "The Wedge Strategy." It began: "The proposition that human beings are created in the image of God is one of the bedrock principles on which Western civilization was built . . . Yet a little over a century ago, this cardinal idea came under wholesale attack by intellectuals drawing on the discoveries of modern science.

Debunking the traditional conceptions of both God and man, thinkers such as Charles Darwin, Karl Marx, and Sigmund Freud portrayed humans not as moral and spiritual beings, but as animals or machines who inhabited a universe ruled by purely impersonal forces and whose behavior and very thoughts were dictated by the unbending forces of biology, chemistry, and environment. This materialistic conception of reality eventually infected virtually every area of our culture, from politics and economics to literature and art."

As "The Wedge Strategy" suggests, many CSC fellows are troubled more by the philosophical consequences of evolutionary theory than by the fact that it contradicts a literal reading of the Bible's book of Genesis. Most of them—though not all—are too scientifically sophisticated to hew to a young-Earth creationist line like Hovind's. In mainstream forums, they eschew sectarian religious language. As seekers of mainstream credibility, they don't want to be associated with the medieval persecutors of Copernicus and Galileo. Instead, they try to present themselves as heirs to those very visionaries, insisting that dogmatic secularists desperate to deny God are thwarting their open-minded quest for truth.

Most CSC fellows even accept that evolution occurs within individual species. What they dispute is the idea that random mutation and natural selection led to the evolution of higher species from lower ones—of man from ape-like ancestors. Such a process seems to them incompatible with the belief that man was created in the image of God and that God takes a special interest in him.

Several CSC fellows come with impressive credentials from prestigious universities, and they know how to argue in mainstream forums. Philip Johnson, one of the fathers of the movement, is a law professor at UC-Berkeley. Jonathan Wells, author of the influential intelligent-design book, *Icons of Evolution*, has a Ph.D. in molecular and cell biology from Berkeley and another in religious studies from Yale. A member of the Unification Church whose education was bankrolled by the Reverend Sun Myung Moon, he's written that he sought his degrees specifically to fight the teaching of evolution. As he put it in an article on the Moonie Web site True Parents, "Father's words, my studies, and my prayers convinced me that I should devote my life to destroying Darwinism, just as many of my fellow Unificationists had already devoted their lives to destroying Marxism. When Father [Sun Myung Moon] chose me (along with about a dozen other seminary graduates) to enter a Ph.D. program in 1978, I welcomed the opportunity to prepare myself for battle."

Armed with advanced degrees, CSC fellows have secured invitations to testify before state boards of education. They've published opinion pieces in mainstream newspapers and are regularly consulted for "balance" in stories about evolution controversies.

They've also found important allies within the Republican Party, especially Senator Rick Santorum of Pennsylvania. Santorum tried to attach an amendment to the No Child Left Behind Act that would encourage the teaching of intelligent design. It said, "[W]here topics are taught that may generate controversy (such as biological evolution), the curriculum should help students to understand the full range of scientific views that exist, why such topics may generate controversy, and how scientific discoveries can profoundly affect society." The statement was eventually adopted as part of a Conference Report on the law, which means it has advisory power only.

The language sounds innocuous, but Santorum's intent was clear. In 2002, Ohio debated adding intelligent design to its statewide science standards. In a *Washington Times* Op-Ed supporting the change, Santorum quoted his amendment and then wrote, "If the Education Board of Ohio does not include intelligent design in the new teaching standards, many students will be denied a first-rate science education. Many will be left behind."

Santorum has also come out in favor of Dover's policy. The school board, in turn, distributed copies of one of Santorum's pro-intelligent design Op-Eds along with the agenda at its January 3 meeting.

Oddly enough, although Santorum is supporting the Dover school board's policy, the Center for Science and Culture isn't. On December 14, CSC put out a statement calling Dover's policy "misguided" and saying it should be "withdrawn and rewritten." The statement quoted CSC's associate director John West as saying that discussion of intelligent design shouldn't be prohibited but it also shouldn't be required. "What should be required is full disclosure of the scientific evidence for and against Darwin's theory," said West, "which is the approach supported by the overwhelming majority of the public."

This, of course, is a departure from the position laid out in "The Wedge Strategy," which specifically calls for the integration of intelligent design into school curriculum.

Why the change? Matzke, from the National Center for Science Education, is convinced that the CSC wanted to wait for a better test case and a friendly Supreme Court, which they'll get if Bush is able to nominate a few new justices. The Dover policy, Matzke said, probably won't survive a court challenge right now, and if it's overturned, the precedent will be a setback for the missionaries of intelligent design.

"Their current strategy is not to have an intelligent-design policy passed," Matzke said. "They just want a policy that says students should analyze the strengths and weakness of evolution." CSC did not return calls for comment.

It's not hard for creationists to convince the public that the evidence for evolution is weak. Scientists accept evolution as something very close to fact, but Americans never have. In a November 2004 CBS News/*New York Times* poll, about evolution, 55 percent of the respondents said that God created humans in their present form. Twenty-seven percent believed in the evolution of man guided by God, and 13 percent believed in evolution without God.

So it should come as no surprise that the majority of Americans—65 percent, according to the poll cited above—favor teaching creationism alongside evolution in public schools. Creationism is the perfect culture-war issue because it inevitably pits majorities in local communities against interloping lawyers and scientists. In a country gripped by right-wing populism, it's not hard to stoke resentment against scientists who have the gall to think that they know more than everybody else.

In fact, some historians date the start of our culture wars to 1925, the year of the "Scopes Monkey Trial" in Dayton, Tennessee.

At the time, the battle over evolution had been raging throughout the country. It came to a head when twenty-four-year-old teacher John Scopes challenged Tennessee's Butler Act, which prohibited the teaching of evolution in the state's public schools and universities. His persecution set the stage for a legendary courtroom showdown that pit celebrated Chicago defense attorney Clarence Darrow against Williams Jennings Bryan, the crusading populist, fundamentalist and three-time presidential candidate.

Bryan, the nation's leading anti-evolutionist, made his case in populist terms. In his 1993 book *The Creationists*, historian Ronald Numbers wrote, "Throughout his political career, Bryan had placed his faith in the common people, and he resented the attempt of a few thousand elitist scientists 'to establish an oligarchy over the forty million American Christians' to dictate what should be taught in the schools."

Bryan and his fellow Scopes prosecutors won their trial, but the national mockery that followed it did much to alienate conservative Christians from secular society, setting the stage for the culture wars of later decades. In his Pulitzer Prize–winning history of the Scopes trial, *Summer for the Gods*, Edward Larson wrote about the birth of the right-wing religious counterculture in the wake of the Pyrrhic victory in Tennessee:

"Indeed, fundamentalism became a byword in American culture as a result of the Scopes trial, and fundamentalists responded by withdrawing. They did not abandon their faith, however, but set about constructing a separate subculture with independent religious, educational and social institutions."

Eventually, of course, the religious right emerged from its subculture to renew its attack on secularism. Today, cultural conservatives are mustering almost exactly the same arguments that Bryan made in Dayton eighty years ago.

This past December, Republican strategist Jack Burkman

appeared on MSNBC's *Scarborough Country* to back creationism in terms of populist democracy. "Why should the state and the federal government have a monopoly on defining what constitutes science?" he asked. "I see no problem with presenting a creationist view in the schools, given that 70 percent of Americans want that. The law should reflect democratic desires. It should reflect public desires."

Of course, public desires don't determine the physical facts of the world. "The best argument that the creationists have got is that it's only fair to teach both sides," Matzke said. "The problem with that argument is that science is not a democracy and a lot of times there aren't two correct sides. There are people who believe that the sun goes around the earth. They're called geocentrists. That doesn't mean we should teach that."

In Dover, though, people tend to interpret positions like Matzke's as elitism. Much of the public seems to desire schools that teach creationism, although many balk at the cost of a lawsuit. For defenders of Darwin, the most troubling thing isn't that the Dover school board is dominated by extremists—it's that the board is, in a local context, fairly mainstream. Supporters of evolution are the ones who stand out. Resentment of the ACLU runs high even among some who opposed the school board's intelligent-design policy. Most opposition to the policy comes from worry over the cost of the lawsuit.

Most people in Dover say that the town is split fairly evenly over the school board's intelligent-design policy. The division isn't one of principle, though. People know that the ACLU's lawsuit is going to be expensive and are worried that defending the policy in court will drain the school budget and force a tax increase.

"I would say that people who are against what the school board is doing in principle are a minority, a great minority," former school board member Noel Wenrich told me. "However, when it comes to spending money on it, it's a whole other issue. When you ask people, Do you support the board's decision on this? they say yes." Ask them if they're willing to pay more taxes to finance a court case, though, and they'll give you a resounding no, he said. "It's a money issue."

The school board doesn't need to worry about most of its legal fees, however. It's being represented pro bono by the Thomas More Law Center, a right-wing Catholic firm that describes itself as "the sword and shield for people of faith." Wenrich told me that Thomas More lawyers had been advising Buckingham for months.

Despite the law firm's help, though, the lawsuit will likely be financially devastating to the district, the second poorest in the county. Dover would have to pay for lost wages of people called to testify, and it would have to provide outside counsel for some witnesses, like the Browns, who don't want Thomas More representing them. Jeff Brown guessed that depositions alone would cost the district $30,000. Then, if Dover loses, federal civil rights law would make it liable for the ACLU's legal fees. "It won't be cheap," said Witold Walczak, the ACLU's Pennsylvania legal director.

"It will kill us," said Casey Brown. In fact, Dover is already broke. The board had just been forced to cut its library budget almost in half, from $68,000 to $38,000, and to eliminate all field trips.

Wenrich himself, a thirty-six-year-old Army veteran and father of two, doesn't believe in evolution. But he felt honor-bound to put his duty to the school above his personal politics. "If it were my money, I'd have no problem," he said. "I'd go out and fight it. But to use the public's money that's supposed to be educating our kids is absolutely irresponsible. They're already looking at putting off buying textbooks, not buying library books, not updating computer equipment. When we're looking at those budget cuts, it's irresponsible to go out and pick a fight with the Supreme Court."

If Wenrich is angry with Buckingham, though, he's even angrier at the outside forces that are challenging the school district. "It is going full circle now from the religious community ruling what can be thought—that's what they tried to do in the Middle Ages," he said. "We've come down to the scientific community trying to tell us what we can think. Basically what the scientific community currently is doing is saying, 'You'll have no god before mine. Mine happens to be Darwin.' Any other thought will not be tolerated."

Evolution's allies might win the battle for Dover's biology classes, but they're losing America.

"The truth shall make you free."
—John 8:32

The Christian Right is confused about sex.

You're Nothing but Dirty, Dirty Sinners, Boys and Girls!

from gadflyer.com (12/3/04)

Paul Waldman

Congressman Henry Waxman has released a study of the abstinence-only sex "education" programs that your tax dollars are currently paying for. For those who haven't followed this issue, the federal government provides sex education funding to public schools, but the funding comes with the requirement that teachers are *not allowed* to discuss any means of birth control other than abstinence, and when students ask about contraception, the teachers can only discuss various methods by mentioning that they sometimes fail. So maybe we have to lie to kids—it's all for the cause of keeping them from sin!

Since this funding has been available, a few privately produced curricula have become popular in public schools. As the Waxman report shows, these curricula are filled with misinformation, distortions, religious indoctrination masquerading as science, and outright lies. The abstinence-only programs reflect a neo-Puritan agenda, based on the propositions that sex is dirty and sinful, abortion is wrong, contraception doesn't work, and, in the unforgettable words of Nancy Reagan, "Sex is death."

One program actually tells kids that touching another person's genitals "can result in pregnancy." Oddly, there is no mention of hair growing on palms. Kids are told that you can get HIV from someone's sweat, and that if you have an abortion you will become mentally ill and your future children will have birth defects. The programs also reflect a nineteenth-century view of sex roles:

> The father gives the bride to the groom because he is the one man who has had the responsibility of protecting her throughout her life. He is now giving his daughter to the only other man who will take over this protective role.

One book in the Choosing the Best series presents a story about a knight who saves a princess from a dragon. The next time the dragon arrives, the princess advises the knight to kill the dragon with a noose, and the following time with poison, both of which work but leave the knight feeling "ashamed." The knight eventually decides to marry a village maiden, but did so "only after making sure she knew nothing about nooses or poison." The curriculum concludes: "Moral of the story: Occasional suggestions and assistance may be alright, but too much of it will lessen a man's confidence or even turn him away from his princess."

So girls, don't go putting lots of ideas and thoughts into that pretty little head of yours, or you'll never get a man! Boys don't make passes at girls who wear glasses!

So we see more evidence of the hold the non-reality-based community has over our government and our tax dollars. So what if teaching kids to keep their dirty parts covered and lying to them is going to keep them ignorant and at risk? To worry about whether the programs *work* would be giving in to the march of modernity, that dangerous rational thinking that finds its sinful end in things like scientific inquiry and tolerance of other views.

JESUS IS NOT A FUNDAMENTALIST

with quotations from Jesus and Jerry Falwell

Fundamentalists aim to live by the essential and original teachings of a church. Trouble is, someone has to decide which teachings are essential and original, and which are not. Fundamentalists often pick the teachings that make them feel most comfortable (or powerful), regardless of other consequences. They turn away from their own deepest wisdom, which is impossible to find in any text.

American Wahabbis and the Ten Commandments

from *Mother Jones* (3/8/2005)

William Thatcher Dowell

For anyone who actually reads the Bible, there is a certain irony in the current debate over installing the Ten Commandments in public buildings. As everyone knows, the second commandment in the King James edition of the Bible states quite clearly: "Thou shalt not make unto thee any graven image, or any likeness of anything that is in heaven above, or that is in the earth below, or that is in the water under the earth." It is doubtful that the prohibition on "graven images" was really concerned with images like the engraving of George Washington on the dollar bill. Rather it cautions against endowing a physical object, be it a "golden calf" or a two-ton slab of granite, with spiritual power.

In short, it is the spirit of the commandments, not their physical representation in stone or even on a parchment behind a glass frame, which is important. In trying to publicize the commandments, the self-styled Christian Right has essentially forgotten what they are really about. It has also overlooked the fact that there are several different versions of them. The King James Bible lists three: Exodus 20:2–17, Exodus 34: 12–26, and Deuteronomy 5:6–21. Catholic Bibles and the Jewish Torah also offer variants.

If the commandants are indeed to be green-lighted for our official landscape, however, let's at least remember that Christianity did not exist when the commandments were given. It might then seem more consistent to go with the Hebrew version rather than any modified Christian version adopted thousands of years after Moses lived. Since the Catholic Church predates the Protestant Reformation, it would again make more sense to go with the Catholic version than later revisions.

It is just this kind of theological debate which has been responsible for massacres carried out in the name of religion over thousands of years. It was, in fact, the mindless slaughter resulting from King Charles' efforts to impose the Church of England's prayer book on Calvinist Scots in the seventeenth century which played an important role in convincing the founding fathers to choose a secular form of government clearly separating church and state. They were not the first to recognize the wisdom in that approach. Jesus Christ, after all, advised his followers to render unto Caesar what was Caesar's due and unto God that which was due God.

The current debate, of course, has little to do with genuine religion. What it is really about is an effort to assert a cultural point of view. It is part of a reaction against social change, an American counter-reformation of sorts against the way our society has been evolving, and ultimately against the negative fallout that is inevitable when change comes too rapidly. The people pushing to blur the boundaries between church and state are many of the same who so fervently back the National Rifle Association and want to crack down on immigration. They feel that they are the ones losing out, much as, in the Middle East, Islamic fundamentalists fear they are losing out—and their reactions are remarkably similar. In the Arab Middle East and Iran, the response is an insistence on the establishment of Islamic Law as the basis for political life; while in Israel, an increasingly reactionary interpretation of Jewish law which, taken to orthodox extremes, rejects marriages by reform Jewish rabbis in America, has settled over public life.

In a strange way, George Bush may now find himself in the same kind of trap that ensnared Saudi Arabia's founder, King Abdul Aziz ibn Saud. To gain political support, Saud mobilized the fanatical, ultra-religious Wahabbi movement—the same movement which is spiritually at the core of al Qaeda. Once the bargain was done, the Saudi Royal Family repeatedly found itself held political hostage to an extremist, barely controllable movement populated by radical ideologues. Israel's Prime Minister Ariel Sharon has found himself in a similar situation, drawing political power from the swing votes of the ultra-orthodox right-wing religious and fanatical settler's movement, and then finding his options limited by their obstinacy to change. President Bush has spent the last several months cajoling evangelicals and trying to pay off the political bill for their support.

In Saudi Arabia, the Wahabbis consider themselves ultra-religious, but what really drives their passions is a deep sense of grievance and an underlying conviction that a return to spiritual purity will restore the lost power they believe once belonged to their forefathers. The extremism that delights in stoning a woman to death for adultery or severing the hand of a vagrant accused of stealing depends on extreme interpretations of texts that are at best ambiguous. What is at stake is not so much service to God, as convincing oneself that it is still possible to enforce draconian discipline in a world that seems increasingly chaotic.

We joke about a hassled husband kicking his dog to show he still has power. In the Middle East, it is often women who bear the brunt of the impotence of men. Nothing in the Koran calls for the mistreatment of women or even asks that a woman wear a veil. What is at stake here is not religion, but power, and who has a right to it.

The Christian Right, the evangelical movement that provided the added push needed to nudge President Bush past a tight election, is equally prone to selective interpretations of scripture. The Ten Commandments are used as a wedge to put across what is essentially a cultural protest against social change, but in the bitter disputes that have followed these seemingly ridiculous arguments the message of the commandments is usually lost. The Christian Right pretends to be concerned about the life of an unborn fetus, but expresses little interest for the fate of the living child who emerges from an unwanted pregnancy, and is even ready to kill or at least destroy the careers of those who do not agree with them. Although the commandments prohibit killing, and Christ advised his followers to leave vengeance to God, the fundamentalists seem to delight in the death penalty, and in reducing welfare support to unwed mothers who are struggling to deal with the results of pregnancies that they could not control and never wanted to have.

In the United States as in the Middle East, the core of this Puritanism stems from a nostalgia for an imaginary past—in our case, a belief that the U.S. was a wonderful place when it was peopled mostly by pioneers who came from good northern European stock, who knew right from wrong, and weren't afraid to back up their beliefs with a gun, or by going to war, if they needed to.

The founding fathers, of course, had a very different vision. They had seen the damage caused by the arcane disputes which triggered the religious wars of the seventeenth century. They preferred the ideas of the secular enlightenment, which instead of forcing men to accept the religious interpretations of other men, provided the space and security for each man to seek God in his own way.

The idea that religious values should affect, and indeed control politics, is something that you hear quite often in the Islamic world. But perhaps the strongest rationale for separating these two dimensions of our daily lives is that politics inevitably involves compromise, while religion involves a spiritual ideal in which compromise can be fatal. The conflict is easy to see in contemporary Iran. Iran's rulers have had to choose whether they consider politics or religion to be most important. Ayatollah Khomeini himself once stated that if forced to choose between Islamic law and Islamic rule, he would choose Islamic rule. The effect of that decision was to betray Islamic law and ultimately God. Iran's genuine Islamic scholars have found themselves under continual pressure to change their understanding of God in order to conform to political realities.

The appointment of Ayatollah Sayyid al Khamenei to replace Khomeini as the supreme guide, is a case in point. Khamenei's credentials as a religious thinker are comparable to a number of other Iranian ayatollahs. But his real power stems from his political status. Because of that, he is in a position to affect and ultimately censor the religious writings of religious scholars who may be more thoughtful than he is, but whose thinking is considered threatening to Khamenei's vision of a theocratic state.

Politics inevitably trumps religion when the two domains are merged. Religion, when incorporated into a political structure, is almost invariably diluted and deformed, and ultimately loses its most essential power. Worse, as we have seen recently in the Islamic world (as in the Spanish Inquisition and the Salem witch trials in the Christian world), a fanatical passion for one's own interpretation of justice often leads to horror—as in the obsession of some practitioners of Sharia law to engage such punishments as amputations or stoning women to death.

The fact is that, as Saint Paul so eloquently put it, "Now we see through a glass darkly." We have a great deal of religious experience behind us, but only God can understand to the full extent what it really means. Men have their interpretations, but they are only human and, by their nature, they are flawed. We see a part of what is there—but only a part. In that context, isn't it best to keep our minds open, the Ten Commandants in whatever version out of our public buildings or off our governmental lawns, and to lead by example rather than pressuring others to see life the way we do. As Christ once put it, "And why beholdest thou the mote that is in thy brother's eye, but considerest not the beam that is in thine own eye?"

"Be careful not to do your righteous acts in public, in order to be seen. When you give charity, don't blow a trumpet to announce it, as the hypocrites do in the synagogues and in the streets, so that people will praise them . . .
"And when you pray, don't be like the hypocrites, who love to stand and pray in the synagogues and the street corners, so that people will see them. But when you pray, go into your inner room and shut the door and pray in secret to your Father; and your Father, who sees what is secret, will reward you."
—from *The Gospel According to Jesus Christ,* edited and translated by Stephen Mitchell

Between Religion and Morality

from Salon.com (5/27/02)

Robert Scheer

For a long time now, we secular humanists and other skeptics have been denigrated as the apostles of decadence and social decay. A rowdy parade of right-wing pundits has used those of us who refuse to wear our religion on our sleeves as scapegoats for all that ails the United States and the world.

What apparently defines us "nonbelievers" in the minds of right-wing talk show hosts, the Christian right, pompous czars of virtue such as Bill Bennett and the arts censors of the Catholic Church is that we have abandoned religious certainty—the rights and wrongs that ensure passage to heaven or hell—for a grayer area of moral relativism in which we have to decide for ourselves what is proper behavior. The assumption is that our decisions, as opposed to those of true believers, inevitably will be hedonistic and most likely perverse.

Let me confess that I do not conduct my life with a constant eye on the literal truths of scripture because they seem often contradictory and at times downright immoral. For example, the proper procedure for branding one's slaves discussed in the Old Testament and the equally forceful condemnation of eating crustaceans and lying with the same sex all seem provincial when not primitively cruel.

And the notion related each year at Passover of God's killing the firstborn of Egyptians smacks of primitive animal revenge. Sorry, but the Talmudic explanations and harsh rules of the rabbis in my mother's family tree work only as interesting tribal lore.

As to my father's Lutheran relatives, most of whom still live in Germany, they would be the first to tell you that during World War II their fascist pastor appearing in his Nazi uniform was hardly a stalwart in the battle against genocide. As the child of European immigrants, I spent the first ten years of my life confronting the horror that my father's relatives were drafted to massacre my mother's people because of their religion.

Growing up in such moral ambiguity, I came to be attracted to the sermons on a New York radio station broadcast by something called the Society for Ethical Culture. The message, similar to that of Unitarians, deists and some of the New Age and Eastern religions, was that life's creation remains a mystery and therefore morality, in any mechanically simple way, cannot be derived from ancient texts or assumptions about the rewards and fears associated with an afterlife.

Instead, we are left—as in the writings of such deists as Thomas Jefferson, Benjamin Franklin and Thomas Paine—to sort out decent moral principles from the welter of human experience, including that of all religions.

Never a fully satisfying exercise, I know, compared with the moral certainties expounded by those who claim a direct link with an almighty power.

In my section of the Bronx, the Catholic Church, with its magnificent structures and frightening crypts, expressed that authority in its most intimidating form. There were many times when I envied the moral clarity of those priests as they tended their flocks of young believers, incessantly preaching the demands of sexual purity.

Even nonbelievers in my crowd would shun sex, auto-erotic or otherwise, before taking a major academic test for fear of weakening the brain, such was the ancillary influence of the church in matters sexual.

How then to explain that for a significant number of priests, the fear not merely of failing a college midterm but rather of spending an eternity in hell did not still their sexual impulses?

What we have learned from recent headlines and from the exposure of similar transgressions by fundamentalist Protestant and Jewish leaders is that "traditional values" are not necessarily best upheld by traditional institutions.

Repetition of divine commandments is an insufficient guarantee of exemplary behavior, and blind allegiance to the leadership cadre and moral cant of any church can be quite dangerous.

The imperative to question the words and actions of religious figures of authority should, of course, be applied to all associations—whether political, academic, social or cultural—including those populated by secular humanists. The record of the Catholic Church is likely no more hypocritical than that of other institutions claiming to inspire behavior that rises far above that demanded by the animalist dictates of survival of the fittest.

In the end, it is up to us as individuals to figure out what makes us human and then to act accordingly.

"Don't judge, and you will not be judged. For in the same way that you judge people, you yourself will be judged.
"Why do you see the splinter that is in your brother's eye, but don't notice the log that is in your own eye? First take the log out of your own eye, and then you will see clearly enough to take the splinter out of your brother's eye."
—from *The Gospel According to Jesus Christ*, edited and translated by Stephen Mitchell

The most dangerous rulers include those who claim to know the will of God.

Just Another Word for Everything Left to Lose

from therevealer.org (1/21/05)

David Domke

In his second-term inaugural address on Thursday, George W. Bush used the words freedom or liberty, in some form, forty-nine times. Say this for the president: He can hammer home a message.

Among these instances was this declaration: "We have

confidence because freedom is the permanent hope of mankind, the hunger in dark places, the longing of the soul. When our Founders declared a new order of the ages; when soldiers died in wave upon wave for a union based on liberty; when citizens marched in peaceful outrage under the banner 'Freedom Now'—they were acting on an ancient hope that is meant to be fulfilled. History has an ebb and flow of justice, but history also has a visible direction, set by liberty and the Author of Liberty."

Freedom. Liberty. God. Bush's emphasis on these, so consistently highlighted in his public communications over the past four years, both lay bare and obscure underlying truths about the administration. Regarding the former, the president's linkage of freedom and liberty with divine wishes is indicative of how central an evangelical worldview is to his conception of the United States' role in the world, particularly in the struggle against terrorism. At the same time, emphasis on these values masks the reality that the administration is determined to define what counts as freedom and liberty and who will have the privilege to experience it. Let's consider each of these points.

An omnipresent consideration for evangelicals is the "Great Commission" biblical mandate, in the book of Matthew, to "go therefore and make disciples of all the nations." The felt responsibility to live out this command, both locally and globally, has become intertwined in the eyes of many Christian conservatives with support for the principles of political freedom and liberty. In particular, the individualized religious liberty present in the United States (particularly available historically for European-American Protestants) is something that religious conservatives long to extend to other cultures and nations.

In the 1980s, fundamentalist preacher and leader Jerry Falwell argued that the dissemination of Christianity could not be carried out if other nations were communist —a perspective which provided a good reason to support Ronald Reagan's combination of a strong U.S. military, conservative foreign policy, and the spreading of individual freedoms. In that era, Falwell famously told his flock that they could "vote for the Reagan of their choice."

Falwell's perspective on the 2004 presidential matchup was similarly unequivocal: In the July 1 issue of his email newsletter and on his website, Falwell declared, "For conservative people of faith, voting for principle this year means voting for the re-election of George W. Bush. The alternative, in my mind, is simply unthinkable." He added, "I believe it is the responsibility of every political conservative, every evangelical Christian, every pro-life Catholic, every traditional Jew, every Reagan Democrat, and everyone in between to get serious about re-electing President Bush."

The certitude present in Bush's rhetoric and in the support for Bush by Falwell (and by other Religious Right leaders such as James Dobson, Pat Robertson, and Gary Bauer) is emblematic of fundamentalists' confidence that their understanding of the world provides what religion scholar Bruce Lawrence terms "mandated universalist norms" to be spread across cultural and historical contexts. For Bush and the Religious Right, those norms first and foremost are U.S. conceptions of freedom and liberty. Since September 11, 2001, these values have gained a special resonance among Americans—and the administration, both because of genuine ideological as well as strategic reasons, has capitalized. Since the attacks, Bush has consistently claimed that the freedom and liberty he seeks to spread is God's will for the world. Consider a few examples.

• In his address before Congress and a national television audience nine days after the terrorist attacks, Bush declared, "The course of this conflict is not known, yet its outcome is certain. Freedom and fear, justice and cruelty have always been at war, and we know that God is not neutral between them."

• In the 2003 State of the Union address, with the conflict in Iraq imminent, Bush declared, "Americans are a free people, who know that freedom is the right of every person and the future of every nation. The liberty we prize is not America's gift to the world, it is God's gift to humanity."

• And in his address at the Republican Party Convention in September 2004, Bush made this claim: "I believe that America is called to lead the cause of freedom in a new century. I believe that millions in the Middle East plead in silence for their liberty. I believe that given the chance, they will embrace the most honorable form of government ever devised by man. I believe all these things because freedom is not America's gift to the world, it is the Almighty God's gift to every man and woman in this world."

Bush's words Thursday offered a variation on this theme, with God now the "Author of Liberty." Some might wonder if all of these words should be attributed to

Michael Gerson, a graduate of evangelical Wheaton College who served as Bush's primary speechwriter in his first term. The words are Bush's. Bob Woodward, in his book about the administration's push toward Iraq, *Plan of Attack*, includes this quote from Bush: "I say that freedom is not America's gift to the world. Freedom is God's gift to everybody in the world. I believe that. As a matter of fact, I was the person that wrote the line, or said it. I didn't write it, I just said it in a speech. And it became part of the jargon. And I believe that. And I believe we have a duty to free people. I would hope we wouldn't have to do it militarily, but we have a duty."

The claim that the U.S. government is doing God's work may appeal to many Americans, but it frightens those who might run afoul of administration wishes-cum-demands. This is particularly so when one considers how declarations of God's will have been used by European-Americans in past eras as rationale for subjugating those who are racially and religiously different, most notably Native Americans, Africans, Chinese, and African Americans.

Indeed, scholar R. Scott Appleby in 2003 declared that the administration's omnipresent emphasis on freedom and liberty functions as the centerpiece for "a theological version of Manifest Destiny." Unfortunately, this twenty-first century adaptation of Manifest Destiny differs little from earlier American versions: The goal remains to vanquish any who do not willingly adopt the supposedly universal norms and values of Protestant conservatives. The result, by implication in the president's rhetoric, is that the administration has transformed Bush's "Either you are with us, or you are with the terrorists" policy to "Either you are with us, or you are against God."

To the great misfortune of American democracy and the global public, such a view is indistinguishable from that of the terrorists it is fighting. One is hard pressed to see how the perspective of Osama bin Laden, that he and his followers are delivering God's wishes for the United States, is much different from Bush's perspective that the United States is delivering God's wishes to the Taliban or Iraq.

Clearly, flying airplanes into buildings in order to kill innocent people is an indefensible immoral activity. So too, some charge, is an unprovoked pre-emptive invasion of another nation, the cost in casualties of which has been paid by U.S. military personnel sent to fight on the basis of erroneous intelligence, and by Iraqi civilians—1,382 (with 10,372 wounded) and 15,365 (with no reliable estimate of Iraqi civilian wounded), respectively, according to conservative estimates at this writing.

In both instances, the aggression manifested in a form that was available to the leaders. Fundamentalism in the White House is different in degree, not kind, from fundamentalism exercised in dark, damp caves. Democracy is always the loser.

"If you're not a born-again Christian, you're a failure as a human being."
—Jerry Falwell

JESUS IS NOT AN END-TIMER

with quotations from Jesus

Jesus offered a generous vision of life that has helped many people to find their own potential for love and connection. Many conservative Christians are drawn to an apocalyptic vision that mirrors their alienation from life. They dream of a God who will lift them up, away from their suffering—and inflict hellish pain on the rest of us. They get to watch. Jesus did not approve this message.

Bill Moyers gave this speech in 2004 upon receiving the Global Environmental Citizen Award from Harvard's Center for Health and the Global Environment.

Battlefield Earth

from AlterNet.org (12/8/04)

Bill Moyers

Writing in *Mother Jones* recently, Bill McKibben described how the problems we journalists routinely cover—conventional, manageable programs like budget shortfalls and pollution—may be about to convert to chaotic, unpredictable, unmanageable situations. The most unmanageable of all, he writes, could be the accelerating deterioration of the environment, creating perils with huge momentum like the greenhouse effect that is causing the melting of the Arctic to release so much freshwater into the North Atlantic that even the Pentagon is growing alarmed that a weakening gulf stream could yield abrupt and overwhelming changes, the kind of changes that could radically alter civilizations.

That's one challenge we journalists face—how to tell such a story without coming across as Cassandras, without turning off the people we most want to understand what's happening, who must act on what they read and hear.

As difficult as it is, however, for journalists to fashion a readable narrative for complex issues without depressing our readers and viewers, there is an even harder challenge—to pierce the ideology that governs official policy today. One of the biggest changes in politics in my lifetime is that the delusional is no longer marginal. It has come in from the fringe, to sit in the seat of power in the Oval Office and in Congress. For the first time in our history, ideology and theology hold a monopoly of power in Washington. Theology asserts propositions that cannot be proven true; ideologues hold stoutly to a world view despite being contradicted by what is generally accepted as reality. When ideology and theology couple, their offspring are not always bad but they are always blind. And there is the danger: voters and politicians alike, oblivious to the facts.

One-third of the American electorate believes the bible is literally true, if a recent Gallup poll is accurate. In this past election several million good and decent citizens went to the polls believing in the rapture index. That's right—the rapture index. Google it and you will find that the best-selling books in America today are the twelve volumes of the Left Behind series written by the Christian fundamentalist and religious right warrior, Timothy LaHaye. These true believers subscribe to a fantastical theology concocted in the nineteenth century by a couple of immigrant preachers who took disparate passages from the Bible and wove them into a narrative that has captivated the imagination of millions of Americans.

Its outline is rather simple, if bizarre (the British writer George Monbiot recently did a brilliant dissection of it and I am indebted to him for adding to my own understanding): once Israel has occupied the rest of its "biblical lands," legions of the anti-Christ will attack it, triggering a final showdown in the valley of Armageddon. As the Jews who have not been converted are burned, the Messiah will return for the rapture. True believers will be lifted out of their clothes and transported to heaven, where, seated next to the right hand of God, they will watch their political and religious opponents suffer plagues of boils, sores, locusts, and frogs during the several years of tribulation that follow.

I'm not making this up. Like Monbiot, I've read the literature. I've reported on these people, following some of them from Texas to the West Bank. They are sincere, serious and polite as they tell you they feel called to help bring the rapture on as fulfillment of biblical prophecy. That's why they have declared solidarity with Israel and the Jewish settlements and backed up their support with money and volunteers. It's why the invasion of Iraq for them was a warm-up act, predicted in the Book of Revelation where four angels "which are bound in the great river Euphrates will be released to slay the third part of man." A war with Islam in the Middle East is not something to be feared but welcomed—an essential conflagration on the road to redemption. The last time I Googled it, the rapture index stood at 144—just one point below the critical threshold when the whole thing will blow, the son of god will return, the righteous will enter heaven and sinners will be condemned to eternal hellfire.

So what does this mean for public policy and the environment? Go to *Grist* to read a remarkable work of reporting by the journalist, Glenn Scherer—"The Road to Environmental Apocalypse." Read it and you will see how millions of Christian fundamentalists may believe that environmental destruction is not only to be disregarded but actually welcomed—even hastened—as a sign of the coming apocalypse.

As *Grist* makes clear, we're not talking about a handful of fringe lawmakers who hold or are beholden to these beliefs. Nearly half the U.S. Congress before the recent

election—231 legislators in total—more since the election
—are backed by the religious right. Forty-five senators and
186 members of the 108th congress earned 80 to 100 percent approval ratings from the three most influential
Christian right advocacy groups. They include Senate
Majority Leader Bill Frist, Assistant Majority Leader Mitch
McConnell, Conference Chair Rick Santorum of Pennsylvania, Policy Chair Jon Kyl of Arizona, House Speaker
Dennis Hastert, and Majority Whip Roy Blunt. The only
Democrat to score 100 percent with the Christian coalition was Senator Zell Miller of Georgia, who recently
quoted from the biblical book of Amos on the senate
floor: "the days will come, sayeth the Lord God, that I will
send a famine in the land." he seemed to be relishing the
thought.

And why not? There's a constituency for it. A 2002
TIME/CNN poll found that 59 percent of Americans
believe that the prophecies found in the book of Revelations are going to come true. Nearly one-quarter think
the Bible predicted the 9/11 attacks. Drive across the
country with your radio tuned to the more than 1,600
Christian radio stations or in the motel turn some of
the 250 Christian TV stations and you can hear some
of this end-time gospel. And you will come to understand why people under the spell of such potent
prophecies cannot be expected, as Grist puts it, "to
worry about the environment. Why care about the earth
when the droughts, floods, famine and pestilence
brought by ecological collapse are signs of the apocalypse foretold in the bible? Why care about global climate change when you and yours will be rescued in the
rapture? And why care about converting from oil to

solar when the same god who performed the miracle of the loaves and fishes can whip up a few billion barrels of light crude with a word?"

Because these people believe that until Christ does return, the lord will provide. One of their texts is a high school history book, *America's Providential History.* You'll find there these words: "the secular or socialist has a limited resource mentality and views the world as a pie . . . that needs to be cut up so everyone can get a piece." However, "[t]he Christian knows that the potential in god is unlimited and that there is no shortage of resources in god's earth . . . while many secularists view the world as overpopulated, Christians know that god has made the earth sufficiently large with plenty of resources to accommodate all of the people." No wonder Karl Rove goes around the White House whistling that militant hymn, "Onward Christian Soldiers." He turned out millions of the foot soldiers on November 2, including many who have made the apocalypse a powerful driving force in modern American politics.

I can see in the look on your faces just how hard it is for the journalist to report a story like this with any credibility. So let me put it on a personal level. I myself don't know how to be in this world without expecting a confident future and getting up every morning to do what I can to bring it about. So I have always been an optimist. Now, however, I think of my friend on Wall Street whom I once asked: "What do you think of the market?" "I'm optimistic," he answered. "Then why do you look so worried?" And he answered: "Because I am not sure my optimism is justified."

I'm not, either. Once upon a time I agreed with Eric

Chivian and the Center for Health and the Global Environment that people will protect the natural environment when they realize its importance to their health and to the health and lives of their children. Now I am not so sure. It's not that I don't want to believe that—it's just that I read the news and connect the dots:

I read that the administrator of the U.S. Environmental Protection Agency has declared the election a mandate for President Bush on the environment. This for an administration that wants to rewrite the Clean Air Act, the Clean Water Act and the Endangered Species Act protecting rare plant and animal species and their habitats, as well as the National Environmental Policy Act that requires the government to judge beforehand if actions might damage natural resources.

That wants to relax pollution limits for ozone; eliminate vehicle tailpipe inspections; and ease pollution standards for cars, sports utility vehicles and diesel-powered big trucks and heavy equipment.

That wants a new international audit law to allow corporations to keep certain information about environmental problems secret from the public.

That wants to drop all its new-source review suits against polluting coal-fired power plans and weaken consent decrees reached earlier with coal companies.

That wants to open the Arctic [National] Wildlife Refuge to drilling and increase drilling in Padre Island National Seashore, the longest stretch of undeveloped barrier island in the world and the last great coastal wild land in America.

I read the news just this week and learned how the Environmental Protection Agency had planned to spend

9 million dollars—2 million of it from the administration's friends at the American Chemistry Council—to pay poor families to continue to use pesticides in their homes. These pesticides have been linked to neurological damage in children, but instead of ordering an end to their use, the government and the industry were going to offer the families $970 each, as well as a camcorder and children's clothing, to serve as guinea pigs for the study.

I read all this in the news.

I read the news just last night and learned that the administration's friends at the international policy network, which is supported by ExxonMobil and others of like mind, have issued a new report that climate change is "a myth, sea levels are not rising," [and] scientists who believe catastrophe is possible are "an embarrassment."

I not only read the news but the fine print of the recent appropriations bill passed by Congress, with the obscure (and obscene) riders attached to it: a clause removing all endangered species protections from pesticides; language prohibiting judicial review for a forest in Oregon; a waiver of environmental review for grazing permits on public lands; a rider pressed by developers to weaken protection for crucial habitats in California.

I read all this and look up at the pictures on my desk, next to the computer—pictures of my grandchildren: of Henry, age 12; of Thomas, age 10; of Nancy, 7; Jassie, 3; Sara Jane, 9 months. I see the future looking back at me from those photographs and I say, "Father, forgive us, for we know not what we do." And then I am stopped short by the thought: "That's not right. We do know what we are doing. We are stealing their future. Betraying their trust. Despoiling their world."

And I ask myself: Why? Is it because we don't care? Because we are greedy? Because we have lost our capacity for outrage, our ability to sustain indignation at injustice?

What has happened to our moral imagination?

On the heath Lear asks Gloucester: "How do you see the world?" And Gloucester, who is blind, answers: "I see it feelingly."

I see it feelingly.

The news is not good these days. I can tell you, though, that as a journalist I know the news is never the end of the story. The news can be the truth that sets us free—not only to feel but to fight for the future we want. And the will to fight is the antidote to despair, the cure for cynicism, and the answer to those faces looking back at me from those photographs on my desk. What we need to match the science of human health is what the ancient Israelites called "hochma"—the science of the heart . . . the capacity to see . . . to feel . . . and then to act . . . as if the future depended on you.

Believe me, it does.

"And someone asked him, 'When will the kingdom of God come?' And he said, 'The kingdom of God will not come if you watch for it. Nor will anyone be able to say, 'It is here' or 'It is there.' For the kingdom of God is within you."
—from *The Gospel According to Jesus Christ*, edited and translated by Stephen Mitchell

Religious fundamentalists help to guide our foreign policy. God help us.

Apocalypse Please
from *The Guardian* (4/20/04)
George Monbiot

To understand what is happening in the Middle East, you must first understand what is happening in Texas. To understand what is happening there, you should read the resolutions passed at the state's Republican party conventions last month. Take a look, for example, at the decisions made in Harris County, which covers much of Houston.

The delegates began by nodding through a few uncontroversial matters: homosexuality is contrary to the truths ordained by God; "any mechanism to process, license, record, register or monitor the ownership of guns" should be repealed; income tax, inheritance tax, capital gains tax and corporation tax should be abolished; and immigrants should be deterred by electric fences. Thus fortified, they turned to the real issue: the affairs of a small state seven thousand miles away. It was then, according to a partici-pant, that the "screaming and near fistfights" began.

I don't know what the original motion said, but appar-ently it was "watered down significantly" as a result of the shouting match. The motion they adopted stated that Israel has an undivided claim to Jerusalem and the West Bank, that Arab states should be pressured to absorb refugees from Palestine, and that Israel should do what-ever it wishes in seeking to eliminate terrorism. Good to see that the extremists didn't prevail then.

But why should all this be of such pressing interest to the people of a state which is seldom celebrated for its fas-cination with foreign affairs? The explanation is slowly becoming familiar to us, but we still have some difficulty in taking it seriously.

In the United States, several million people have suc-cumbed to an extraordinary delusion. In the nineteenth century, two immigrant preachers cobbled together a series of unrelated passages from the Bible to create what appears to be a consistent narrative: Jesus will return to earth when certain preconditions have been met. The first of these was the establishment of a state of Israel. The next involves Israel's occupation of the rest of its "Biblical lands" (most of the Middle East), and the rebuilding of the Third Temple on the site now occupied by the Dome of the Rock and al Aqsa mosques. The legions of the Antichrist will then be deployed against Israel, and their war will lead to a final showdown in the valley of

Armageddon. The Jews will either burn or convert to Christianity, and the Messiah will return to earth.

What makes the story so appealing to Christian fundamentalists is that before the big battle begins, all "true believers" (i.e. those who believe what THEY believe) will be lifted out of their clothes and wafted up to heaven during an event called the Rapture. Not only do the worthy get to sit at the right hand of God, but they will be able to watch, from the best seats, their political and religious opponents being devoured by boils, sores, locusts and frogs, during the seven years of Tribulation which follow.

The true believers are now seeking to bring all this about. This means staging confrontations at the old temple site (in 2000 three U.S. Christians were deported for trying to blow up the mosques there), sponsoring Jewish settlements in the occupied territories, demanding ever more U.S. support for Israel, and seeking to provoke a final battle with the Muslim world/Axis of Evil/United Nations/European Union/France or whoever the legions of the Antichrist turn out to be.

The believers are convinced that they will soon be rewarded for their efforts. The Antichrist is apparently walking among us, in the guise of Kofi Annan, Javier Solana, Yasser Arafat or, more plausibly, Silvio Berlusconi. The Walmart corporation is also a candidate (in my view a very good one), because it wants to radio-tag its stock, thereby exposing humankind to the Mark of the Beast. By clicking on www.raptureready.com, you can discover how close you might be to flying out of your pyjamas. The infidels among us should take note that the Rapture Index currently stands at 144, just one point below the critical threshold, beyond which the sky will be filled with floating nudists. Beast Government, Wild Weather and Israel are all trading at the maximum five points (the EU is debating its constitution, there was a freak hurricane in the South Atlantic, Hamas has sworn to avenge the killing of its leaders), but the second coming is currently being delayed by an unfortunate decline in drug abuse among teenagers and a weak showing by the Antichrist (both of which score only two).

We can laugh at these people, but we should not dismiss them. That their beliefs are bonkers does not mean they are marginal. American pollsters believe that between 15 and 18 percent of U.S. voters belong to churches or movements which subscribe to these teachings. A survey in 1999 suggested that this figure included 33 percent of Republicans. The best-selling contemporary books in the United States are the twelve volumes of the Left Behind series, which provide what is usually described as a "fictionalized" account of the Rapture (this, apparently, distinguishes it from the other one), with plenty of dripping details about what will happen to the rest of us. The people who believe all this don't believe it just a little; for them it is a matter of life eternal and death.

And among them are some of the most powerful men in America. John Ashcroft, the attorney general, is a true believer, so are several prominent senators and the House majority leader, Tom DeLay. Mr. DeLay (who is also the co-author of the marvelously-named DeLay-Doolittle Amendment, postponing campaign finance reforms) traveled to Israel last year to tell the Knesset that "there is no middle ground, no moderate position worth taking."

So here we have a major political constituency—

representing much of the current president's core vote—
in the most powerful nation on earth, which is actively
seeking to provoke a new world war. Its members see
the invasion of Iraq as a warm-up act, as Revelations
(9:14–15) maintains that four angels "which are bound
in the great river Euphrates" will be released "to slay the
third part of men." They batter down the doors of the
White House as soon as its support for Israel wavers:
when Bush asked Ariel Sharon to pull his tanks out of
Jenin in 2002, he received one hundred thousand angry
emails from Christian fundamentalists, and never mentioned the matter again.

The electoral calculation, crazy as it appears, works like
this. Governments stand or fall on domestic issues. For 85
percent of the U.S. electorate, the Middle East is a foreign
issue, and therefore of secondary interest when they enter
the polling booth. For 15 percent of the electorate, the
Middle East is not just a domestic matter, it's a personal
one: if the president fails to start a conflagration there, his
core voters don't get to sit at the right hand of God. Bush,
in other words, stands to lose fewer votes by encouraging
Israeli aggression than he stands to lose by restraining it.
He would be mad to listen to these people. He would also
be mad not to.

JESUS IS NOT AN END-TIMER

In the introduction to his recent book, James Carroll compares the original Crusades to our recent wars in the Middle East.

from *Crusade* (2004)
James Carroll

At the turn of the millennium, the world was braced for terrible things. Most "rational" worries were tied to an anticipated computer glitch, the Y2K problem, and even the most scientifically oriented of people seemed temporarily at the mercy of powerful mythic forces. Imagined hobgoblins leaped from hard drives directly into nightmares. Airlines canceled flights scheduled for the first day of the new year, citing fears that the computers for the traffic control system would not work. The calendar as such had not previously been a source of dread, but all at once, time itself held a new danger. As the year 2000 approached, I bought bottled water and extra cans of tuna fish. I even withdrew a large amount of cash from the bank. Friends mocked me, then admitted to having done similar things. There were no dances-of-death or outbreaks of flagellant cults, but a millennial fever worthy of medieval superstition infected the most secular of cultures. Of course, the mystical date came and went, the computers did fine, airplanes flew, and the world went back to normal.

Then came September 11, 2001, the millennial catastrophe —just a little late. Airplanes fell from the sky, thousands died, and an entirely new kind of horror gripped the human imagination. Time, too, played its role, but time as warped by television, which created a global simultaneity, turning the whole human race into a witness, as the awful events were endlessly replayed, as if those bodies leaping from the Twin Towers would never hit the ground. Nightmare in broad daylight. New York's World Trade Center collapsed not just onto the surrounding streets but into the hearts of every person with access to CNN. Hundreds of millions of people instinctively reached out to those they loved, grateful to be alive. Death had shown itself in a new way. But if a vast throng experienced the terrible events of 9/11 as one, only one man, the president of the United States, bore a unique responsibility for finding a way to respond to them.

George W. Bush plumbed the deepest place in himself, looking for a simple expression of what the assaults of September 11 required. It was his role to lead the nation, and the very world. The president, at a moment of crisis, defines the communal response. A few days after the assault, George W. Bush did this. Speaking spontaneously, without the aid of advisers or speechwriters, he put a word on the new American purpose that both shaped it and gave it meaning. "This crusade," he said, "this war on terrorism."

Crusade. I remember a momentary feeling of vertigo at the president's use of that word, the outrageous ineptitude of it. The vertigo lifted, and what I felt then was fear, sensing not ineptitude but exactitude. My thoughts went to the elusive Osama bin Laden, how pleased he must have been, Bush already reading from his script. I am a Roman Catholic with a feeling for history, and strong regrets, therefore, over what went wrong in my own tradition once the Crusades were launched. Contrary to schoolboy romances, Hollywood fantasies, and the nostalgia of royalty, the Crusades were a set of world-historic crimes. I hear the word with a third ear, alert to its dangers. Bush's use of *crusade*, as it were, conscripted my complete attention, and from that instant on I found myself an unwilling witness to the slow-motion wreck of American values that has occurred over the past three years. I had long been a writer of slice-of-life essays. My subject had been the passing scene, but once George Bush launched his crusade, it became my only subject. Week after week, despite myself, I wrote, in my column in the *Boston Globe*, of almost nothing else. This is the record of what I witnessed, and I offer it here to mark the most extraordinary shift in American meaning and purpose of which I am aware.

Memory fades, and the past gets forever twisted up in arguments of the present. But a close reading of what actually happened as Bush and his circle used the moment of postmillennial crisis in an attempt to transform politics and culture can make plain why that transformation must not be brought to completion. How Bush used a crime to justify a war. How he deflected one failure—to capture bin Laden—into another—bringing "order" to Afghanistan. How he declared victory in Iraq, as a slow, grinding defeat was just beginning. How the airy ambitions of a neoconservative clique were thwarted by a combination of primitive fervor, tribal factionalism, and the simple stubbornness of human beings who refuse to be told what to think and feel. How the expectation that other nations, including once firm allies, would have no choice but to obey an imperial Washington proved to be illusion. How the wars of the Middle East went from bad to worse. How George W. Bush proved to be the ultimate proliferator. How he lied to us. How he betrayed, above all, the young men and women whom he so carelessly sent into harm's way. On September 11, 1990, as it happened, George W. Bush's father had declared a "new world order." Eleven years to the day later, the son set out on his crusade to make that order his. Destruction followed upon destruction, and this is its chronicle.

For George W. Bush, *crusade* was an offhand reference. But all the more powerfully for that, it was an accidental probing of unintended but nevertheless real meaning. That the president used the word inadvertently suggests how it expressed his exact truth, an unmasking of his most deeply felt purpose. *Crusade,* he said. Later, his embarrassed aides suggested that he had meant to use the word only as a synonym for *struggle,* but Bush's own syntax belied that. He defined *crusade* as *war.* Even offhandedly, he had said exactly what he meant.

Osama bin Laden was already understood to be trying to spark a "clash of civilizations" that would set the West against the whole House of Islam. After 9/11, agitated voices on all sides insisted that no such clash was inevitable. But *crusade* was a match for *jihad,* and such words threatened nothing less than apocalyptic conflict between irreconcilable cultures. Indeed, the president's reference flashed through the Arab news media. Its resonance went deeper, even, than the embarrassed aides expected—and not only among Muslims. After all, the word refers to a long series of military campaigns, which, taken together, were the defining event in the shaping of what we call Western civilization. A coherent set of political, economic, social, and even mythological traditions of the Eurasian continent, from the British Isles to the far side of Arabia, grew out of the transformations wrought by the Crusades. And it is far from incidental still, both that those campaigns were conducted by Christians against Muslims, and that they, too, were attached to the irrationalities of millennial fever.

If the American president was the person carrying the main burden of shaping a response to the catastrophe of September 11, his predecessor in such a grave role, nearly a thousand years earlier, was the Catholic pope. Seeking to overcome the century-long dislocations of a post-millennial Christendom, he rallied both its leaders and commoners with a rousing call to holy war. Muslims were the infidel people who had taken the Holy Land hundreds of years before. Now, that occupation was defined as an intolerable blasphemy. The Holy Land must be redeemed. Within months of the pope's call, a hundred thousand people had "taken the cross" to reclaim the Holy Land for Christ. As a proportion of population of Europe, a comparable movement today would involve more than a million people, dropping everything to go to war.

In the name of Jesus, and certain of God's blessing, crusaders launched what might be called "shock and awe" attacks—laying siege, first, to the Asia Minor city of Nicaea, where they used catapults to hurl the severed heads of Muslim defenders over fortified walls. In Jerusalem they savagely slaughtered Muslims and Jews alike—practically the whole city. Eventually, Latin crusaders would turn on Eastern Christians, and then on Christian heretics, as blood-lust outran the initial "holy" impulse. That trail of violence scars the earth and human memory even to this day—especially in the places where the crusaders wreaked their havoc. And the mental map of the Crusades, with Jerusalem at the center of the earth, still defines world politics. But the main point, in relation to Bush's instinctive response to 9/11, is that those religious invasions and wars of long ago established a cohesive Western identity precisely in opposition to Islam, an opposition that survives to this day.

With the Crusades, the violent theology of the killer God came into its own. To save the world, in this understanding, God willed the violent death of God's only beloved son. Here is the relevance of that mental map, for the crusaders were going to war to rescue the site of the salvific death of Jesus, and they displayed their devotion to the cross on which Jesus died by wearing it on their breasts. When Bush's remark was translated into Arabic for broadcast throughout the Middle East, the word *crusade* was rendered as *war of the cross*.

Before the Crusades, Christian theology had given central emphasis to the resurrection of Jesus, and to the idea of incarnation itself, but with the war of the cross, the bloody crucifixion began to dominate the Latin Christian imagination. A theology narrowly focused on the brutal death of Jesus reinforced the primitive notion that violence can be a sacred act. The cult of martyrdom, even to the point of suicidal valor, was institutionalized in the Crusades, and it is not incidental to the events of 9/11 that a culture of sacred self-destruction took equally firm hold among Muslims. The suicide-murderers of the World Trade Center, like the suicide-bombers from the West Bank and Gaza, exploit a perverse link between the willingness to die for a cause and the willingness to kill for it. Crusaders, thinking of heaven, honored that link, too.

Here is the deeper significance of Bush's inadvertent

reference to the Crusades: instead of being a last recourse or a necessary evil, violence was established then as the perfectly appropriate, even chivalrous, first response to what is wrong in the world. George W. Bush is a Christian for whom this particular theology lives. While he identified Jesus as his "favorite political philosopher" when running for president in 2000, the Jesus of this evangelical president is not the "turn-the-other-cheek" one. Bush's savior is the Jesus whose cross is wielded as a sword. George W. Bush, having cheerfully accepted responsibility for the executions of 152 death-row inmates in Texas, had already shown himself to be entirely at home with divinely sanctioned violence. After 9/11, no wonder it defined his deepest urge.

But sacred violence, once unleashed in 1096, as in 2001, had a momentum of its own. The urgent purpose of war against the "enemy outside"—what some today call the "clash of civilizations"—led quickly to the discovery of an "enemy inside." The crusaders, en route from northwestern Europe to attack the infidel far away, first fell upon, as they said, "the infidel near at hand." Jews. For the first time in Europe, large numbers of Jews were murdered for being Jews. A crucifixion-obsessed theology saw God as willing the death of Jesus, but in the bifurcated evangelical imagination, Jews could be blamed for it, and the offense the crusaders took was mortal.

The same dynamic—war against an enemy outside leading to war against an enemy inside—can be seen at work today. It is a more complex dynamic now, with immigrant Muslims, and people of Arabic descent, coming under heavy pressure in the West. In Europe, Muslims are routinely demonized. In America, they are "profiled," even to the point of being deprived of basic rights. But at the same time, once again, Jews are targeted. The broad resurgence of anti-Semitism, and the tendency to scapegoat Israel as the primary source of the new discord, reflect an old tidal pull. This is true notwithstanding the harsh fact that Ariel Sharon's government took up the Bush "dead-or-alive" credo with enthusiasm and used the "war on terrorism" to fuel self-defeating overreactions to Palestinian provocations. But some of Israel's critics fall into the old pattern of measuring Jews against standards to which no one else is held, not even our president. That the war on terrorism is the context within which violence in Israel and Jerusalem has intensified should be no surprise. It wasn't "Israel" then, but conflict over Jerusalem played exactly such a flashpoint role a thousand years ago.

The Crusades proved to have other destructive dynamics as well. The medieval war against Islam, having also targeted Europe's Jews, soon enough became a war against all forms of cultural and religious dissent, a war against heresy. As it hadn't been in hundreds of years, doctrine now became rigidly defined in the Latin West, and those who did not affirm dominant interpretations— Cathars, Albigensians, Eastern Orthodox—were attacked. Doctrinal uniformity, too, could be enforced with sacred violence. When the U.S. attorney general defines criticism of the administration in wartime as treason, or when Congress enacts legislation that justifies the erosion of civil liberties with appeals to patriotism, they are enacting a Crusades script.

All of this is implicit in the word that President Bush first used, that came to him as naturally as a baseball reference, to define the war on terrorism. That such a dark, seething religious history of sacred violence remains largely unspoken in our world does not defuse it as an explosive force in the human unconscious. In the world of Islam, of course, its meaning could not be more explicit, or closer to consciousness. The full historical and cultural significance of *crusade* is instantly obvious, which is why a howl of protest from the Middle East drove Bush into instant verbal retreat. Yet the very inadvertence of his use of *crusade* is the revelation: Americans do not know what fire they are playing with. Osama bin Laden, however, knows all too well, and in his periodic pronouncements, he uses the word *crusade* to this day, as a flamethrower.

Religious war is the danger here, and it is a graver one than Americans think. Despite our much vaunted separation of church and state, America has always had a quasi-religious understanding of itself, reflected in the messianism of Puritan founder John Winthrop, the Deist optimism of Thomas Jefferson, the embrace of redemptive suffering that marked Abraham Lincoln, and, for that matter, the conviction of Eisenhower's secretary of state, John Foster Dulles, that communism had to be opposed on a global scale if only because of its atheism. But never before has America been brought deeper into a dynamite-wired holy of holies than in our president's war on terrorism. Despite the post-Iraq toning down of Washington's rhetoric of empire, and the rejection of further crusader references—although Secretary of State Colin Powell used the word in March 2004—Bush's war openly remains a cosmic battle between nothing less than the transcendent forces of good and evil. Such a battle is necessarily unlimited and open-ended, and so justifies radical actions—the abandonment, for example, of established notions of civic justice at home and of traditional alliances abroad.

A cosmic moral-religious battle justifies, equally, risks of world-historic proportioned disaster, since the ultimate outcome of such a conflict is to be measured not by actual consequences on this earth but by the earth-transcending will of God. Our war on terrorism, before it is anything else, is thus an *imagined* conflict, taking place primarily in a mythic realm beyond history.

In waging such a "war," the enemy is to be engaged everywhere and nowhere, not just because the actual nihilists who threaten the social order are faceless and deracinated, but because each fanatical suicide-bomber is only an instance of the transcendent enemy—and so the other face of us. Each terrorist is, in effect, a sacrament of the larger reality, which is "terrorism." Instead of perceiving unconnected centers of inhuman violence—tribal warlords, mafia chieftains, nationalist fighters, xenophobic Luddites—President Bush projects the grandest and most interlocking strategies of conspiracy, belief, and organization. By the canonization of the war on terrorism, petty nihilists are elevated to the status of world-historic warriors, exactly the fate they might have wished for. This is why the conflict readily bleeds from one locus to another—Afghanistan now, Iraq then, Iran or some other land of evil soon—and why, for that matter, the targeted enemies are entirely interchangeable—here Osama bin Laden, there Saddam Hussein, here the leader of Iran, there of North Korea. They are all essentially one enemy—one "axis"—despite their differences from each other, or even hatred of each other.

George W. Bush has taken on, as he pridefully declares,

Evil itself. (In 2004, shapers of the "Bush Doctrine" David Frum and Richard Perle published a book titled *An End to Evil.*) Bush does this with no awareness of the association between his project and larger, mythic forces, but future historians may well look back on America's panic-stricken global campaign in the context of millennial fever. It happened a thousand years ago, and it is happening now. The idea of the millennium seems to stimulate an apocalyptic imagination, a sense that end-time is dawning, an epoch when some final battle between good and evil is destined to be undertaken. (And one sign of that end-time in the evangelical imagination is the elimination—through conversion or sacred violence—of the infidel, an expectation that unconsciously plays its part in the hatred of Muslims, in fresh hostility toward Jews, and even in the Christian right's anxious support of Israel, as a prelude to Jewish conversion.) One needn't attribute the kooky extremes of this intuition to Bush to recognize in his rhetoric signs of a cosmic concern that transcends geopolitics and national security.

The Crusades, too, were a manifestation of end-time millennialism. When crusaders slaughtered the infidel, and forced conversion on Jews, they thought they were ushering in the new age. Robert Jay Lifton shows how this phenomenon manifests itself now, with Islamist and American apocalyptic visions in fierce competition, both aimed at "purification and renewal." In his book *Superpower Syndrome*, Lifton observes, "We are experiencing what could be called an apocalyptic face-off between Islamist forces, overtly visionary in their willingness to kill and die for their religion, and American forces claiming to be restrained and reasonable but no less visionary in their projection of a cleansing war-making and military power."

Hard-boiled men and women who may not share Bush's fervent spirituality can nonetheless support his purpose because, undergirding the new ideology, there is an authentic global crisis that requires an urgent response. New technologies are now making it possible for small groups of nihilists, or even single individuals, to wreak havoc on a scale unprecedented in history. This is the ultimate "asymmetric threat." The attacks of 9/11, amplified by the murderous echo of the anthrax mailer, the as yet unapprehended psychopath who sent deadly letters to journalists and government officials in the weeks after 9/11, put that new condition on display for all the world to see. Innovations in physics, biology, chemistry, and information technology—and soon, possibly, in nanotechnology and genetic engineering—have had the unforeseen effect of threatening to put in a few hands the destructive power that, in former times, could be exercised only by sizable armies. The millennialist Adolf Hitler was a crackpot nonentity until he had the German nation behind him, and promises of a thousand-year Reich helped him do it. Today's Hitler needs no nation, no party, no army. A pound of anthrax will do. A suitcase nuke. Even a cleverly manipulated computer virus. Such power in the hands of any one person amounts to a new sphere of existence on the earth, to a "new metaphysics," as the journalist Lance Morrow put it in his book *Evil*, that "transforms both the political and personal dynamics of evil."

This is the *real* condition to which the Bush administration is responding. The problem is actual, if not yet fully present. The danger *is* transcendent—after all, the 9/11 attackers, using far more modest means, created a televised version of a mini-apocalypse—but the Bush administration is taking steps that, instead of meeting the danger, make it far worse. The impulse that has driven this administration's global policies is defined, at its simplest, by the determination that no hostile power will be allowed to have so-called weapons of mass destruction. Leaders of "rogue regimes," so the Bush reading goes, by definition lust after such weapons, and so "regime change" has become the dominant purpose of American power, whether by means of "preventive war," as in Afghanistan and Iraq, or by other forms of coercion. Even as the difficulties of Iraq have undercut glib American assertions of imperial sway, it remains likely that Washington will permit neither Iran nor even North Korea, which evidently has a head start on the process, nor any number of other unfriendly states to develop active and usable nuclear arsenals. It is nukes, above all, that roil the sleep of the White House, with the recurrent dream of 9/11 as the mildest hint of what would come if such an act went nuclear.

So, to put the best face on the Bush agenda (leaving aside questions of oil, global market control, and economic or military hegemony), a humane project of antiproliferation can be seen at its core. Yet a nation that was trying to *promote* the proliferation of weapons of mass destruction, especially nuclear weapons, would behave precisely as the Bush administration has behaved over the past three years. The Pentagon's chest-thumping concept of "full spectrum dominance" itself motivates other nations to seek sources of countervailing power, and when the United States actually goes to war to impose its widely disputed notion of order on some states, but not others, nations—friendly as well as unfriendly—find themselves with an urgent reason to acquire some means of deterring such intervention.

On December 19, 2003, the Bush administration claimed a victory for its "counterproliferation" belligerency in announcing that Libya had agreed to dismantle its weapons of mass destruction, but Libyan leader Moammar Khadafy's decision actually put the lie to the Bush approach. Following revelations of its complicity in the terror bombing of Pan Am Flight 103 in 1988, Libya had been subject to years of coercive diplomacy, sanctions, and isolation. These U.N.-centered pressures, firmly advanced by the Clinton administration, finally worked. Preventive war and regime change were simply not necessary to stem Khadafy's aggression. And not incidentally, with Libya's new cooperation, it was confirmed that a steady supporter of its abandoned nuclear project had been Pakistan, which the Bush administration counts as an ally, proving that proliferators do not fall into the good-versus-evil categories favored in Washington. And in counterpoint to the December announcement of Libya's compliance, it was announced on the same day that Japan would spend billions of dollars on a U.S.-sponsored ballistic missile shield. Another "victory" for the Bush administration. But this first major exporting of "Stars Wars" abroad amounted to an unprecedented escalation both of Japanese military expenditures and of the arms race in Asia. It will inevitably prompt countermeasures from North Korea, China, and Russia. Those will, in turn, spark the further militarization of Japan, as defense leads to offense, an upward spiraling that is likely to increase the dangers of nuclear war. Here on earth and in the heavens could be found the real meaning of the Bush approach to the problem of proliferation.

The odd and tragic thing is that the world before Bush was actually nearing consensus on how to manage the problem of the proliferation of weapons of mass destruction, and had begun to put in place promising structures designed to prevent such spread. Centrally embodied in the Nuclear Nonproliferation Treaty of 1968, which had successfully and amazingly kept the number of nuclear powers, actual as well as admitted, relatively low, that consensus gave primacy to treaty obligations, international cooperation, and a serious commitment by existing nuclear powers to move toward ultimate nuclear abolition. All of that has been trashed by Bush. "International law?" he smirked in December 2003. "I better call my lawyer."

Now indications are that nations all over the globe— Japan, Saudi Arabia, Argentina, Brazil, Australia—have begun reevaluating their rejections of nukes, and some are positively rushing to acquire them. Iran and North Korea are likely to be only the tip of this radioactive iceberg. Nuclear-armed Pakistan and India are a grim forecast of the future on every continent. And the Bush administration —by declaring its own nuclear arsenal permanent, by threatening nuclear first strikes against other nations, by "warehousing" treaty-defused warheads instead of destroying them, by developing a new line of "usable" nukes, by moving to weaponize the "high frontier" of outer space, by doing little to help Russia get rid of its rotting nuclear stockpile, by embracing "preventive war"—is enabling this trend instead of discouraging it. How can this be?

The problem has its roots in a long-term American

forgetfulness, going back to the acid fog in which the United States ended World War II. There was never a complete moral reckoning with the harsh momentum of that conflict's denouement—how American leaders embraced a strategy of terror bombing, slaughtering whole urban populations, and how, finally, they ushered in the atomic age with the attacks on Hiroshima and Nagasaki. Scholars have debated those questions, but politicians have avoided them, and most citizens have pretended they aren't really questions at all. America's enduring assumptions about its own moral supremacy, its own altruism, its own exceptionalism, have hardly been punctured by consideration of the possibility that we, too, are capable of grave mistakes, terrible crimes. Such awareness, drawn from a fuller reckoning with days gone by—with August 6 and 9, 1945, above all—would inhibit America's present claim to moral grandeur, which is simultaneously a claim, of course, to economic and political grandiosity. The indispensable nation must dispense with what went before.

"The past is never dead," William Faulkner said. "It isn't even past." How Americans remember their country's use of terror bombing affects how they think of terrorism; how they remember the first use of nuclear weapons has profound relevance for how the United States behaves in relation to nuclear weapons today. If the long American embrace of nuclear "mutual assured destruction" is unexamined; if the Pentagon's treaty-violating rejection of the ideal of eventual nuclear abolition is unquestioned—then the Bush administration's embrace of nukes as normal, usable weapons will not seem offensive.

Memory is a political act. Forgetfulness is the handmaiden

of tyranny. The Bush administration is fully committed to maintaining what the historian Marc Trachtenberg calls our "nuclear amnesia" even as the administration seeks to impose a unilateral structure of control on the world. As it pursues a world-threatening campaign against *other* peoples' weapons of mass destruction, that is, the Bush administration refuses to confront the moral meaning of America's own weapons of mass destruction, not to mention their viral character, as other nations seek smaller versions of the American arsenal, if only to deter Bush's next "preventive" war. The United States' own arsenal, in other words, remains the primordial cause of the WMD plague.

"Memory," the novelist Paul Auster has written, "is the space in which a thing happens for the second time." No one wants the terrible events that came after the rising of the sun on September 11, 2001, to happen for a second time *except* in the realm of remembrance, leading to understanding and commitment. All the ways George Bush exploited those events, betraying the memory of those who died in them, must be lifted up and examined again, so that the outrageousness of his political purpose can be felt in its fullness. Exactly how the war on terrorism unfolded; how it bled into the wars against Afghanistan, then Iraq; how American fears were exacerbated by administration alarms; how civil rights were undermined, treaties broken, alliances abandoned, coarseness embraced—none of this should be forgotten.

Given how they have been so dramatically unfulfilled, Washington's initial hubristic impulses toward a new imperial dominance should not be forgotten. That the first purpose of the war—Osama "dead or alive"—

changed when al Qaeda proved elusive should not be forgotten. That the early justification for the war against Iraq—Saddam's weapons of mass destruction—changed when they proved nonexistent should not be forgotten. That in former times the U.S. government behaved as if facts mattered, as if evidence informed policy, should not be forgotten. That Afghanistan and Iraq are in shambles, with thousands dead and hundreds of thousands at risk from disease, disorder, and despair, should not be forgotten. That a now disdainful world gave itself in unbridled love to America on 9/11 should not be forgotten.

We remember the past, even the recent past, to motivate resistance in the present. We remember the past so that the future can be different.

JESUS IS NOT BUSH'S BRAIN

with quotations from David Kuo, John Diulio and Jesus;
and an anagram

George W. Bush calls himself a "born-again" Christian, and claims to take his cues from Jesus—but he takes them from Karl Rove. Jesus wouldn't advise the president to cut taxes on the rich and cut benefits for the poor. Jesus wouldn't advise the president to lie to justify an unjustifiable war. Jesus wouldn't advise the president to let corporations lay waste to the environment and exploit workers and consumers in the name of profit.

How Bush's God-Talk Is Different

from Beliefnet.com (2004)

David Domke and Kevin Coe

In his address on Thursday at the inauguration of his second term, George W. Bush will invoke God. We guarantee it—presidents always do so at inaugurations. That he believes in or refers to a supreme power is not what distinguishes Bush from other modern American presidents. What makes Bush notable is how much he talks about God and what he says when he does so.

Bush referenced a higher power ten times in his first inaugural four years ago, including this claim: "I will work to build a single nation of justice and opportunity. I know this is in our reach because we are guided by a power larger than ourselves, who creates us equal, in His image." In his three State of the Union addresses since, Bush invoked God another fourteen times.

No other president since Franklin Roosevelt took office in 1933 has mentioned God so often in his inaugurations or State of the Unions. The closest to Bush's average of 6 references per each of these addresses is Ronald Reagan, who averaged 4.75 in his comparable speeches. Jimmy Carter, considered as pious as they come among U.S. presidents, only had 2 God mentions in 4 addresses. Other also-rans in total God talk were Franklin Roosevelt at 1.69 and Lyndon Johnson at 1.50 references per inaugurals and State of the Unions.

God-talk in these addresses is important because in these ritualized occasions any religious language becomes fused with American identity. This is particularly so since the advent of radio and television, which have facilitated presidents' ability to connect with the U.S. public writ large; indeed, inaugurals and State of the Unions commonly draw large media audiences.

Bush also talks about God differently than most other modern presidents. Presidents since Roosevelt have commonly spoken as petitioners of God, seeking blessing, favor, and guidance. This president positions himself as a prophet, issuing declarations of divine desires for the nation and world. Among modern presidents, only Reagan has spoken in a similar manner—and he did so far less frequently than has Bush.

This striking change in White House rhetoric is apparent in how presidents have spoken about God and the values of freedom and liberty, two ideas central to American identity. Consider a few examples.

Roosevelt in 1941, in a famous address delineating four essential freedoms threatened by fascism, said: "This nation has placed its destiny in the hands and heads and hearts of its millions of free men and women; and its faith in freedom under the guidance of God."

Similarly, Dwight Eisenhower in 1954, during the height of the Cold War, said: "Happily, our people, though blessed with more material goods than any people in history, have always reserved their first allegiance to the kingdom of the spirit, which is the true source of that freedom we value above all material things. . . . So long as action and aspiration humbly and earnestly seek favor in the sight of the Almighty, there is no end to America's forward road; there is no obstacle on it she will not surmount in her march toward a lasting peace in a free and prosperous world."

Contrast these statements, in which presidents spoke as petitioners humbly asking for divine guidance, with Bush's claim in 2003 that "Americans are a free people, who know that freedom is the right of every person and the future of every nation. The liberty we prize is not America's gift to the world, it is God's gift to humanity." This is not a request for divine favor; it is a declaration of divine wishes.

Such rhetoric positions the president as a prophetic spokesman for God rather than as a petitioning supplicant. Such certitude is dangerous—even for those who share such views—because U.S. presidents have the unique ability to act upon their beliefs in ways that affect billions of people worldwide. Indeed, it has become clear that a good number of Americans—including many of religious faith—and billions of global citizens are leery of this president's fusion of politics and religion. To cite just one example, more than two hundred U.S. church and seminary leaders in October signed a petition that criticizes the administration's convergence of God and nation as constructing a "theology of war."

All of this prompts the hope that, in these challenging times, a president who spoke after his re-election about his newly earned "political capital" not only speaks about God but also is one who listens.

ANAGRAM

George Bush and Christianity:
Unheroic, shaggiest banditry

"Sadly, four years later [Bush's] promises remain unfulfilled in spirit and in fact. In June 2001, the promised tax incentives for charitable giving were stripped at the last minute from the $1.6 trillion tax cut legislation to make room for the estate-tax repeal that overwhelmingly benefited the wealthy. The Compassion Capital Fund has received a cumulative total of $100 million during the past four years. And new programs including those for children of prisoners, at-risk youth, and prisoners reentering society have received a little more than $500 million over four years— or approximately $6.3 billion less than the promised $6.8 billion."

—Former Bush aide David Kuo, about funding for faith-based initiatives during Bush's first term

"There is a virtual absence as yet of any policy accomplishments that might, to a fair-minded nonpartisan, count as the flesh on the bones of so-called compassionate

conservatism . . . What you've got is every-thing, and I mean everything, being run by the political arm. It's the reign of the May-berry Machiavellis."

—John Diulio, former director of Bush's faith-based initiative, quoted by the *New York Times*, 12/2/02

Leading Like Jesus
from gadflyer.com (12/3/04)
Sarah Posner

Why did YUM! Brands, the oxymoronically named corporate conglomerate that owns Taco Bell, Pizza Hut, Kentucky Fried Chicken, Long John Silver, and A&W Restaurants, stop advertising on *Desperate Housewives* in the face of a boycott threat by a fringe right-wing Christian group, the American Decency Association?

Maybe it has something to do with Jesus.

YUM!'s CEO, David Novak, is a member of the evangel-ical Southeast Christian Church in Louisville. With eighteen thousand members, Southeast is one of the largest churches in the country and the largest in Kentucky. In March, the church sent busloads of people to lobby the Kentucky legislature to pass an anti-gay marriage amend-ment and later spent $150,000 on advertising to support the anti-gay marriage referendum on the Kentucky ballot. Southeast has hosted former Alabama Supreme Court Justice Roy "Ten Commandments" Moore at its church. Its head pastor, Bob Russell, said during the 2004 presidential campaign that "we [evangelicals] have more reasons to start a revolution than they did in 1776. . . . I don't see how you can be a dedicated Christian and remain neutral."

Novak and Russell are also speakers for Lead Like Jesus, a group that stages motivational seminars across the country to teach people how to, well, you get the idea.

So how, exactly, does Novak lead like Jesus? Let's take a look.

Novak, as YUM!'s CEO, made $8.8 million last year in salary, bonuses, and stock gains (not including unexercised stock options), according to *Forbes*. By contrast, Pizza Hut drivers make about $6 an hour, and franchisees have actively discouraged their efforts to organize a union. Someone making $6 an hour (the equivalent of about $12,000 a year if the person worked a forty-hour week every week of the year) would have to work for about 730 years to equal Novak's 2003 compensation. And Pizza Hut drivers aren't reimbursed for gas or mileage, either.

At Pizza Hut in China, a pizza, at $8, costs almost three times an average Chinese person's daily $3 wage.

It took YUM! just a few weeks to relent to the pressure from the American Decency Association to withdraw its advertising from *Desperate Housewives*. Yet for the last three and a half years, YUM! and its subsidiary Taco Bell have ignored the boycott of the Coalition of Immokalee Workers (CIW), a group representing farmworkers who pick the tomatoes supplied to YUM! restaurants. The CIW boycott is supported by the Presbyterian Church USA, the United

Methodist Church, the United Church of Christ, the Christian Church (Disciples of Christ), the American Friends Service Committee (Quakers), the National Council of Churches, and the Unitarian Universalist Service Committee. Yet YUM! has refused to give into CIW's demand in order to end the boycott. And what is the CIW's demand? That farmworkers who pick the tomatoes that are supplied to Taco Bell and other YUM! subsidiaries be paid an additional penny—yes, that's one additional penny—per pound of tomatoes they pick. [YUM! Brands relented and granted the workers' demands in early 2005.] To give you some perspective on that, these farmworkers are paid forty to fifty cents per thirty-two-pound bucket of tomatoes they pick. That amounts to about $7,500 a year, well below the poverty level. Even John Ashcroft's Justice Department has prosecuted cases against bosses who held these tomato pickers in slavery conditions. What has YUM's response been? To send the CIW a check for $110,000 to end the boycott (which CIW returned). Meanwhile, conditions haven't changed for the farmworkers.

YUM! actually has some control over the price it pays for the tomatoes. In the same way that Wal-Mart forces its suppliers to charge it rock-bottom prices for merchandise because of the sheer size of its market share, the market-dominating Unified Foodservice Purchasing Co-Op (UFPC) leverages the supply chain for all of YUM!'s subsidiaries. But instead of paying more for tomatoes so the farmworkers can have a higher wage, both YUM! and UFPC match employee donations to the radical right-wing Christian group, James Dobson's Focus on the Family.

YUM! tries to portray itself as a model corporate citizen with its Supplier Code of Conduct, through which it claims that its suppliers "are required to abide by all applicable laws, codes or regulations including, but not limited to, any local, state or federal laws regarding wages and benefits, workmen's compensation, working hours, equal opportunity, worker and product safety." But it's an empty promise with respect to the farmworkers, who are not covered by the National Labor Relations Act, any state unionizing law in Florida, or the overtime provisions of the Fair Labor Standards Act. But they do have to pay payroll taxes on their sub-poverty wages. So if you're wondering where Jesus stands on whether it's fair that these farmworkers still have to pay a payroll tax while CEOs like Novak get hefty tax cuts, YUM!'s PAC, according to the Center for Responsive Politics, donated to Republican rather than Democratic candidates by about an 80 percent to 20 percent margin, which is in line with the rest of the restaurant industry.

Other outside pressure YUM! has ignored was the protest of the AFL-CIO over the YUM! board membership of corporate executive Kenneth Langone. Langone, who has a net worth of $820 million, is under scrutiny for his closeness with former NYSE Chairman Dick Grasso, and for his role as chair of NYSE's compensation committee when Grasso was given his excessive compensation package. That leadership must be A-OK with Jesus, though, just like involuntary servitude is good for the company's bottom line. But fictional depictions of sex, murder, and dysfunctional families? Unacceptable.

It's obvious that all of this has a lot more to do with money than it does with Jesus. But, according to a recent "American Decency Update" from the American Decency Association, money was Jesus's favorite topic. The newsletter quotes Richard Halverson, the former chaplain of the United States Senate, at length on the topic: "Jesus Christ said more about money than about any other single thing because, when it comes to a man's real nature, money is of first importance. Money is an exact index to a man's true character. All through Scripture there is an intimate correlation between the development of a man's character and how he handles his money."

So if "money is an exact index to a man's true character," I think we now all know a bit more about David Novak's true character.

"Children, how hard it is for the rich to enter the kingdom of God. It is easier for a camel to go through the eye of a needle than for a rich man to enter the kingdom of God."

—from *The Gospel According to Jesus Christ*, edited and translated by Stephen Mitchell

JESUS WASN'T BORN ON CHRISTMAS

Every winter, conservatives argue that secular liberals and their Jewish friends want to abolish Christmas. Granted, Christmas is deeply tainted by commerce these days, but most of us liberals (and even many Jews!) enjoy a Christmas tree and carols. Some of us even go to church and pray, and we hand out presents to our kids and each other. Why the annual fuss, then? Conservative Christians like to think of themselves as an embattled minority, even as they tighten their stranglehold on our laws, our economy and our culture.

The Grinch Who Saved Christmas

from Salon.com (12/16/04)

Eric Boehlert

F or most people, Christmas may be a time of peace and joy, but for Bill O'Reilly it's another chance to wage an us-versus-them cultural war. O'Reilly and Fox News, along with a cadre of hard-charging right-wing talkers, have declared war on the anti-Christmas crowd, that dangerous mix of radical secularists and school board do-gooders determined to "bring about their own Godless version of this nation," as Reverend Jerry Falwell wrote in a column published Monday on the conservative Web site WorldNetDaily.com.

The thorny issue of striking the proper balance between America's predominant Christian population and the country's historic separation of church and state returns every holiday season like unwanted fruitcake. But as ABC News recently noted, "This year, people in red, or Republican America—particularly Christian conservatives—are in an unprecedented uproar."

Fresh off Republican wins in November, O'Reilly and company have ratcheted up the rhetoric. Mixing a kernel of truth with a grab bag of unconfirmed anecdotes, as well as some outright falsehoods, and then repeating the dire warnings, they've helped manufacture the impression that a tidal wave of anti-Christian activity, fueled by Democrats, is threatening to drive Christmas underground in America.

"All over the country, Christmas is taking flak," O'Reilly

recently announced, as he complained about "the anti-Christmas jihad" that's gripping the nation. "If they could, secularists would cancel Christmas as a holiday. That's how much they fear the exposition of the philosophy of Jesus." During his syndicated radio show O'Reilly intoned darkly, "The small minority that is trying to impose its will on the majority is so vicious, so dishonest—and has to be dealt with."

Fox News pundit Morton Kondracke recently argued, "The logical extension of what [secularists are] saying is [to] ban Christmas." Meanwhile, his colleague Tony Snow concocted stories about how "you're not allowed to say 'Merry Christmas' in a lot of department stores" and then complained it was part of an elaborate "attack on Christianity." (Snow was apparently referring to a decision by Macy's to change its official store greeting to "Happy Holidays." Obviously people are still allowed to say "Merry Christmas"—or whatever else they want to—inside the stores.)

Throughout December, O'Reilly has positioned himself as the lone ranger, willing to step up and defend the baby Jesus. "Nobody sticks up for Christmas except me. Did Peter Jennings stick up for Christmas last night? I don't believe he did. How about Brian Williams, did he? Did Rather stick up for Christmas? No."

Since O'Reilly began chronicling how Christmas was "under siege," the host has been using a slew of vague catchphrases—"those people," "these creeps," "secular progressives," "the secular bunch," "extremists"—to describe the lurking, godless forces who want to take Christ out of Christmas.

But during his December 3 radio show, O'Reilly got more specific. When a caller identified himself as Jewish and began to complain about "the secularization of Jews and about Christmas going into schools," O'Reilly shot back that "overwhelmingly, America is Christian. And the holiday is a federal holiday honoring the philosopher Jesus. So, you don't wanna hear about it? Impossible. And that is an affront to the majority. You know, the majority can be insulted, too. And that's what this anti-Christmas thing is all about."

At one point, O'Reilly told the caller, "Come on, if you are really offended, you gotta go to Israel then." (Media Matters for America, a liberal media monitoring organization, quickly posted transcripts from the radio show.) "It was offensive and over the top," says Steven Freeman, associate director of the civil liberties division at the Anti-Defamation League, a leading Jewish civil rights organization.

Representative Nita Lowey, D-N.Y., is circulating a letter among colleagues on the Hill that urges O'Reilly to apologize for his remarks. "By suggesting that Jews do not have a place in American society unless they accept without comment its 'predominantly Christian' nature, you are brushing aside the basic freedoms guaranteed to all by our Constitution," she writes. Lowey tells Salon, "Bill O'Reilly's comments were the tip of the iceberg from some conservative news outlets that are suggesting minorities should keep quiet or leave the country. It's really dangerous and I'd hope wiser heads would understand this and cease and desist."

"O'Reilly crossed the line to overt anti-Semitism," adds Michael Lerner, head of the progressive Jewish organization Tikkun. "He's trying to tell his audience that Jews have no legitimate role in public life except as second-class citizens."

O'Reilly is not alone in singling out Jews this Christmas season. In a column for the conservative Web site *FrontPage*, former *Boston Herald* writer Don Feder mocked the notion that "Myron may fear the onset of another Crusade if he hears the strains of 'O Little Town of Bethlehem' drifting through the hallways." He added, "The brave men who fought and died for America in every war from the Revolution to Iraq, overwhelmingly were Christians. Count the number of crosses in Arlington National Cemetery (on federal property, no less). Add the Stars of David."

Things got even uglier during a segment on MSNBC December 8, when William Donahue of the arch-conservative Catholic League insisted, "Hollywood is controlled by secular Jews who hate Christianity in general and Catholicism in particular. It's not a secret, OK? Hollywood likes anal sex. They like to see the public square without nativity scenes."

O'Reilly, who in a pique of anger on December 9 called Media Matters' transcribers "the worst non-criminal element in the country," seems to wear the accusations of anti-Semitism as a badge of honor—proof that he's upsetting the media elite and standing up for traditional American values. "If you think that's anti-Semitic, I wanna know. Do you think that's anti-Semitic?" O'Reilly asked listeners after replaying a tape of his December 3 caller.

Early this year, O'Reilly's blanket defense of Mel Gibson's *The Passion of the Christ* against charges that its portrayal of Jews was anti-Semitic initially raised some suspicions among some Jews. When O'Reilly asked one guest on his Fox News show if the *Passion* controversy was being driven by the fact that "the major media in Hollywood and a lot of the secular press is controlled by Jewish people," many considered their suspicions confirmed.

O'Reilly has insisted he's a friend to Jews. During a March 10 appearance on the Don Imus radio show, responding to *New York Times* columnist Frank Rich, who ridiculed O'Reilly's question about Jews controlling the secular press, O'Reilly said, "I did a benefit in L.A. four weeks ago where we raised millions of dollars for Israel. OK, pal? Get off it." Following O'Reilly's lead, *Business Week* reported that the host had "chaired a benefit for Israel that raised $40 million."

But as noted by the *Forward*, the New York Jewish weekly, O'Reilly was simply the paid speaker for the fundraising event, not a volunteer chair who helped raise money. (His going rate is $60,000 per speech.) The event, sponsored by the Jewish Federation of Greater Los Angeles, raised $3 million, not $40 million, and most of that $3 million was spent on local causes, not given to support Israel.

Aside from baiting Jews, who continued to vote over-whelmingly Democratic in November, despite elaborate efforts by Republicans to sway their votes this year, the larger target in the Christmas crusade is the progressive movement and the Democratic Party. "There's no question that some sections of the political right think it's time to finish off liberal and progressive forces forever," says Lerner. "And they're not restrained by any sense of fairness. They're sore winners. They won and now they want to beat up on the people they've already defeated."

Who are the defeated? O'Reilly laid out his conspiracy theory for Fox News guest Newt Gingrich on December 10: "It's like the MoveOn people [saying], 'We're never going to get gay marriage, euthanasia, partial birth if we have a Christian nation. We've got to get rid of that Christian nation designation like Canada has, and then we can get our agenda through.' And what's the biggest display of Christian? It's Christmas."

"These guys are nuts, simply nuts," answers Ira Foreman, executive director of the National Jewish Democratic Council. "Either they're woefully ignorant or it's the worst kind of demagoguery. If Jews or progressives or Democrats are supposed to be behind this plot to ruin Christmas, somehow they left me out."

Nonetheless, the crusaders seem to have no shortage of dire anecdotes about the absurd lengths that secularists will go to to destroy Christmas in America.

For instance, conservative pundits blame Target for no longer allowing the Salvation Army to collect money outside its stores. But the retail chain made the move simply because it was getting requests to solicit donations in front of stores from so many nonprofit groups—presumably several faith-based ones—that executives didn't feel that it was right to make a lone exception for the Salvation Army.

Right-wingers chastise organizers of Denver's downtown holiday Parade of Lights for rejecting the nearby Faith Bible Church's religious float. But organizers of the event, fearful of being put in the position of having to choose one faith's float over another for its small parade, have never allowed religious floats of any kind in the procession. So how does that fit into a specifically anti-Christian "jihad" gripping America? (P.S. The Faith Bible Church was notified more than six months ago that its float would not be in the parade, so the incident hardly qualifies as news.)

And take the example of a school principal in Kirkland, Washington, who allegedly canceled a performance of Charles Dickens's *A Christmas Carol* out of fear that it violated the district's holiday policy of keeping church and state separate. The story has become a touchstone in the anti-Christmas crusade movement. O'Reilly cited the play's being "banned" as a prime example of "anti-Christmas madness," while conservative *Washington Times* columnist Deborah Simmons wrote matter-of-factly that the principal "lowered the curtain on a production of the classic *A Christmas Carol* because feeble Tiny Tim says, 'God bless us everyone.'" That assertion is pure fiction.

Reading the very first news account of the manufactured controversy, from a December 5 article in the *King County Journal*, it's plain the school's principal, Mark Robertson, "canceled the December 17 matinee by the Attic Theatre cast because students would have been charged to see the performance." Robertson himself told the paper: "We don't allow any private organizations to come and sell products in the schools, or we'd have everybody down here." The principal mentioned in passing that even if the play were free it would have prompted "a secondary discussion about public school and religion," such as whether the play was tied to any particular curriculum and whether attendance was mandatory.

Yet on December 8, *Seattle Times* columnist Danny Westneat, reaching a much wider audience than the *Kings County Journal*, wrote that Kirkland "students were to see a staging of Dickens's story on December 17, but the principal has canceled it, in part because it raised the issue of religion in the public schools."

Two days later, Westneat conceded he "went too far" in

his original column, admitting the play was canceled because it was improperly booked. "The principal's comments about the play raising issues of religion in school were misunderstood," he wrote. By then, however, the tale of the canceled Christmas play had ricocheted around the talk-radio echo chamber and become permanently lodged inside Fox News.

In an interesting footnote, Westneat wrote, "Few things I've written have generated as loud and disparate a response as Wednesday's column. I'm surprised at how many rallied to the secular cause. Nearly half of more than 200 readers who weighed in said schools should avoid the [Christmas] issue." Which hardly supports O'Reilly's claim that fed-up Americans are rising up against anti-Christmas forces.

That said, Lerner suggests liberals would be making a serious mistake if they failed to acknowledge the real sense that the spiritual side of Christmas is being undermined in American culture. He says Jews, progressives and secularists aren't the real Grinches, but rather the material-obsessed marketplace. "It's turning the symbolic values of Christmas into an excuse to convince people to buy and buy and buy," he says. "Christians are right to feel spiritual values are under assault; they are responding to a very real problem. But secularists are not to blame."

JESUS IS NOT A SADIST

Jesus would feel compassion for Americans who sanction torture in this country and elsewhere—but he would not stand with them.

Reverend Fleming Rutledge of the Princeton Theological Seminary delivered this sermon.

Unfair Treatment
from CFBA.info (6/28/04)
Fleming Rutledge

While we were still weak, at the right time Christ died for the ungodly . . . God shows his love for us in that while we were yet sinners Christ died for us. Since, therefore, we are now justified by his blood, much more shall we be saved by him from the wrath of God. For if while we were enemies we were reconciled to God by the death of his Son, much more, now that we are reconciled, shall we be saved by his life . . . . (Romans 5:6, 8–10)

A few days ago, I heard something on the radio about the young Korean Christian who was working in Iraq as a foreign contractor when he was captured and held hostage. As I'm sure you know, he was filmed pleading for his life in the most heartbreaking fashion. Finally he was beheaded in the hideous ritual that has become all too familiar. His funeral was held yesterday in South Korea. According to the broadcast I heard, the terrorist who announced the gruesome and barbarous deed said, "The infidel got his fair treatment."

That got me thinking about what fair treatment is.

A few days ago a news report described the scene of chaos just after one of the many recent bombings in Iraq. American, British and French contractors were killed. Near the carnage, a young Iraqi man stood at his watermelon stand. The reporter wrote that, like many Iraqis, he seemed to have mixed feelings. He watched as a gathering mob looted and pounded the destroyed vehicles. He said, "That is wrong, that is disrespectful." But a moment later, he said, speaking of the butchered victims, "They deserved this."[1]

A third episode: The army recently released a number of internal documents reporting that five former Iraqi generals, handcuffed and blindfolded, were beaten until bloody by American soldiers. (Indeed, one of them died later.) A military analyst who witnessed this reported it to his sergeant, but the sergeant took no action. He said that the prisoners "probably deserved it."[2]

Who deserves what? And who decides? Isn't it obvious to any thinking person that the whole matter of "deserving" depends upon your point of view, your allegiances, your priorities, your cultural conditioning? Whole histories are constructed around who deserves what. The Nazis fabricated a narrative about the Jews. The Serbs constructed a narrative about the Kosovo Albanians to justify the "ethnic cleansing," and now that the Albanian Kosovars have returned home, they are retaliating against the Serbs, because "they deserve it."[3] One of the American hostages presently being held in Iraq is a young Marine, a Muslim born in Lebanon. Being an Arabic speaker, he joined the Marines to serve as a translator. He was displayed on video, blindfolded with a sword held menacingly above his head. As far as we know he is still alive. The latest news about him is that he had become emotionally distraught, deserted the Marines and then got picked up by the insurgents.[4] This means that if he is killed, both sides will have reason to think that he got fair treatment— the Marines will think so because he was a weakling and a deserter, and the insurgents will think so because he was enlisted with the infidels.

Who deserves what? And who decides? That phrasing comes from one of my favorite stories about a reunion I attended. It was the fiftieth reunion of some of the men who had served in World War II with the fabled Tenth Mountain Division. One of the men there, whom I knew, was a very bookish person, very unprepossessing physically, a lover of poetry and other quiet pursuits. He was the least military, least bellicose person you could imagine. Very few people in the community knew that he had won the Silver Star until this reunion when he was called up front for special mention. He gently but firmly brushed aside the homage with these deeply wise words: "Nobody knows who deserves what." I think I know just what he meant. Many people are quiet heroes—the person who learns to live with cerebral palsy, or struggles to overcome an addiction, or fights against despair in prison, or speaks out against injustice even though it costs him his job— these are often known to God alone.

Who deserves what? I have often quoted a line from the Clint Eastwood movie *Unforgiven*. Clint's young sidekick has shot a man. They watch him dying slowly and in pain. The young man is uneasy about this spectacle. Seeking to justify what he has done, he says to the Clint Eastwood character, "He had it coming." Clint says, "We all got it coming." A more recent movie is called, aptly enough, *The Road to Perdition*. It features a terrific performance by Paul Newman, playing against type in the role of a mobster. Here's the scenario. Tom Hanks plays a young man who pretends to have a legitimate occupation but in fact works for Newman. On Newman's orders, Hanks carries out a gangland-style execution of several men. Unfortunately, Tom Hanks's young son accidentally witnesses this event.

A hit man is therefore dispatched to rub out Tom Hanks's wife and son in cold blood.[5] Hanks therefore goes to Newman to ask for justice. The two of them sit together in a room facing each other. Tom Hanks says to Paul Newman: "He murdered my wife and son." Paul Newman leans across and says to Tom Hanks: "There are only murderers in this room." With this memorable stroke the story Hanks has constructed for himself is unmasked.

When it comes to deciding who deserves what, the universal human tendency is to declare oneself innocent. Then this is followed by a sense of personal injury and a wish to strike back. If there is a conflict we see only our own wounded innocence, or the wounded innocence of our own family, friends and countrymen. We feel the pain only of those who are like ourselves. I most certainly include myself here. I am disappointed in myself when I catch myself in an involuntary reaction against some of the people I see in the subways in New York City. Everyone has these kinds of thoughts sometimes. We have great difficulty understanding the lives of those from cultures that are strange to us, so we don't have empathy for them. We have recently learned from news reports about the numerous innocent people who have been held in our federal detention centers for months on end. They have suffered because of their cultural strangeness; simply being short, or dark, or speaking no English opens the door to a degree of abuse and mistreatment that seems antithetical to everything that our country is supposed to stand for.[6] Someone in power, sometimes a very petty and small kind of power, decides that these people do not deserve the same sort of treatment that more privileged Americans take for granted.

Is something happening to our American values?

Where is the Christian Church in all this? I have recently
collected testimony from three witnesses, not one of them
a practicing Christian. The first is a prominent writer,
Michael Ignatieff of Harvard, who gave a long interview
on C-SPAN two weeks ago. He had been a strong supporter of the invasion of Iraq, but now that we are talking
about torture and quite probably engaging in it, Ignatieff
is having second thoughts. He has written a new book and
is on the circuit talking about torture. He states his belief
that it can never be justified. The second witness is Ron
Reagan, the son of the late president. He is emphatically
not a Christian and says so, but he has some challenges for
us. In an interview last week he said, "If you are going to
call yourself a Christian . . . then you have to ask yourself
a fundamental question, and that is, whom would Jesus
torture? Whom would Jesus drag around on a dog leash?
How can Christians tolerate it? It is unconscionable." The
third witness is Dr. Allen Keller, director of the
Bellevue/NYU Program for Survivors of Torture. In an
interview he recounted the ghastly histories of some of his
patients who survived torture, and then he said, "How
could people do such things? I'm scared that it's easier
than we think." Since that interview his words have
proven distressingly prophetic. He opposes torture to
extract information from terrorists. "We mustn't go there,"
he said; "It cheapens who we are."[7]

Who is competent to decide whether to torture another
person? Rowan Williams, in his little book called *Christ
on Trial*, recounts an experience of Jean Vanier, the man
who founded and directed the L'Arche communities for
people who are developmentally disabled. He had made
the choice to step down from his position as leader and live

alongside one particular disturbed young adult (Henri Nouwen did this also). The young man screamed and ranted in a very aggressive way. Jean Vanier testified that the young man's behavior was deeply disturbing to him. He discovered that he had within himself deep deposits of anger that he had not known were there. He wrote, "If I had been alone with him, not in community, I could have been tempted to hit him." Notice two things here: one is the subterranean potential for punitive violence that lies within each of us, and the other is the need for communities committed to the mind of Christ, communities of mutual accountability where the darker urges of its individual members find no place to grow.

The mind of Christ. What does that mean? Here is some of what Paul writes in one of his key passages:

> While we were still helpless, at the right time Christ died for the ungodly . . . God shows his love for us in that while we were still sinners Christ died for us. Since, therefore, we are now justified by his blood, much more shall we be saved by him from the wrath of God. For if while we were enemies we were reconciled to God by the death of his Son, much more, now that we are reconciled, shall we be saved by his life. . . .

While we were helpless, while we were weak, while we were sinners, while we lay in bonds under the sentence of the wrath of God, *while we were God's enemies* and enemies of one another—those were our circumstances. Those were the circumstances in which Christ came into this world and offered himself up to death by torture. *While we*

were enemies we were reconciled to God by the death of his Son.
This is the mind of God, this is the mind of Christ. This is
what God did for his enemies. What did we deserve? The
passage is quite clear; we were deserving of God's wrath.
For reasons not entirely clear to me, people love to sing
the "Battle Hymn of the Republic," but we never seem to
entertain the idea that "the fateful lightning of [God's] terrible swift sword" might have been turned against us.
Instead, God deflected it, taking his own stroke himself.

I'm going to read something that Augustine of Hippo
wrote about this passage from Romans.

> . . . The fact that we were reconciled through
> Christ's death must not be understood as if his Son
> reconciled us to [God] so that he might now begin
> to love those whom he had hated. Rather . . . "God
> shows his love for us in that while we were still sin-
> ners Christ died for us" [Romans 5:8]. Therefore he
> loved us even when we practiced enmity toward
> him and committed wickedness. Thus in a mar-
> velous and divine way he loved us even when he
> hated us. For he hated us for what we were that he
> had not made; yet because our wickedness had not
> entirely consumed his handiwork, he knew how, at
> the same time, to hate in each one of us what we
> had made, and to love what he had made.[8]

That, I think, is one of the most wonderful things I have
ever read about any passage of Scripture.

Who deserves what? What is fair treatment? Who
decides? If only we can rise up and act according to our bap-
tismal identity! May it happen in us! May we be convicted

in this truth! We were saved from the Wrath of God. We who were God's enemies have become his friends by reconciliation through Christ. We have been saved by the intervention of the One who had the power and the right to obliterate us but instead pitied us in our enslavement to Sin and Death. We were saved "by his blood," that is, by his life-offering poured out in pain and abandonment as One who had no power and no standing in the world, One who took his place along with the least and last of us—no, even more than that, One who was numbered with the transgressors, with the perpetrators. And in this way we who were God's enemies were clothed with a new righteousness, the righteousness of the Son of God. None of this had anything whatsoever to do with our deserving. Who among us alone in the middle of the night with insomnia, or awakened by a sudden stab of physical pain, or suffering from a grief that won't heal—who among us is comforted with the thought of our *deserving*? Deserving has nothing to do with it. The gospel is not about who deserves what. The Kingdom of God is like a man who works one hour in the cool of the evening and then receives the same wage as those who worked all day in the heat.

Fair treatment? Who wants that? "While we were enemies we were reconciled to God by the death of his Son. How much more, now that we are reconciled, shall we be saved by his life . . ."

Let us pray.

Come, Almighty Word, we pray, and give voice to your Church in the crisis of our time. O Lord of all the nations, we pray for the soul of Western civilization that we may not fail in this hour of testing to embody the highest that you have called us to be. We, your people called by your name, beseech you to strengthen in us what is right and true, reform what is false and wrong, purge what is cruel and heartless, and give us the grace to grant us true repentance when we are in error. Give moral courage to all Christians serving in the armed forces, especially the commanders, granting them wisdom for their mission of forming young hearts and minds for what is humane and right even in the midst of war. Give courage to those who feel called to protest against injustice, and increase their numbers. Be merciful to all prisoners and give patience to those who must work as prison guards. Give us hearts of compassion toward all families who suffer from the horrors of war. Help us to look for your hidden presence among those who are presently our enemies, and turn the hearts of all those who plan evil. Grant wisdom and insight to our leaders and O Lord, do not let us fall away from our vocation to be a people willing to sacrifice for the freedom of all your creatures in every kindred and tongue. We pray in the power of the Holy Spirit, who together with you and our Lord Jesus Christ reigns, one God, for ever and ever.

Amen.

NOTES

1. Jeffrey Gettleman, "21 Killed in Iraq and Dozens Hurt in Bomb Attacks," *The New York Times*, 6/15/04.
2. Andrea Elliott, "Unit Says It Gave Earlier Warning of Abuse in Iraq," *The New York Times*, 6/24/04.
3. There is a story illustrating this in a sermon called "Adam and Christ" in my book *Help My Unbelief*.
4. Jeffrey Gettleman and Nick Madigan, "Abducted Marine Had Reportedly Deserted," *The New York Times*, 6/30/04.

5. I have left out some details of the plot (the hit man is the Newman character's biological son, for instance, and Tom Hanks has two sons, not one) because I wanted to concentrate on a single point.
6. See for instance the front-page article about a Nepalese man who spoke no English and was arrested, detained for months, kept naked and incommunicado in a tiny cell, and finally freed—the final humiliation—with no clothes except his orange prison jump suit.
7. Jan Hoffman, Treating Torture Victims, Body and Soul," 7/30/03.
8. Augustine, *John's Gospel*, cx.6. Quoted in Calvin's *Institutes*, II/xvi/5.

Here to Tell You
from *The New Yorker* (2/28/05)
Ian Frazier

There were times that Dad's pranks bordered on cruelty. One of his oil-company workers, a one-legged man he nicknamed "Crip" Smith, complained about everything. Dad and Crip's co-workers got tired of the old man's bellyaching and decided to take revenge. One morning Crip called in sick and Dad volunteered to send by lunch to his grateful but suspicious employee. Dad and his chums caught Crip's old black tomcat, killed it, skinned it, and cooked it in the kitchen of one of Dad's little restaurants. They called it squirrel meat and delivered it to Crip on a linen-covered tray. When Crip returned to work the next morning, Dad and his co-conspirators asked him how he liked his meal. They knew he would complain even about a free home-cooked lunch, and when Crip

*called it "the toughest squirrel meat" he had ever eaten, they were glad
to tell him why.*

—The Reverend Jerry Falwell, in *Strength for the Journey: An
Autobiography*

There were times that Dad's pranks bordered on what
your out-of-control activist judges might call
felonies. One of his employees was an effeminate fellow
he nicknamed "Sissybritches" Jones, who had a live-in
male homosexual companion for the purposes of
sodomy. Ol' Sissy mentioned one day that since he and
this guy he did sodomy with had been together for years,
they had decided to go ahead and get married. Well, that
did it, and so Dad and his friends decided to take
revenge. This sodomite couple had an old black golden
retriever, and because it was old it didn't matter if it died.
Dad and the other dads killed it, doused it with kerosene,
set it on fire, hung it up in automobile headlights for a
while, and then served it as dog meat on linen-covered
trays in their little restaurants. When Sissy and the other
one came around afterward and complained, Dad and
his squad were happy to let them in on the joke. Then
they shot and killed them both.

Of course, I'm exaggerating a little bit here. Every good
story gets exaggerated some in the retelling, and there's
nothing wrong with that. I seem to recall that the two men
were not actually shot and killed, or not at that time. But
I think the underlying point of the story remains the same,
and it is this: First, we sometimes forget how much humor
there is in the Bible. The Bible is full of wonderful, earthy
humor, if not on every page, at least on many pages, particularly in the Letters of Paul. And, second, we should

never lose sight of the fact that Jesus said—get out your Bibles, it's Matthew 10, verse 34—he said, "I have come not to bring peace, but a sword."

Note that Jesus does not say he came to bring a dagger, or a wooden club with pointed spikes in it. He specifies a sword. Why does he do that? Probably because the sword was the most advanced weapon of Jesus' day. And if we transpose this saying into our own era, if we wanted a weapon, none of us would be likely to reach for a sword. The verse could perhaps be better understood in our terms if it referred not to a sword but to an automatic rifle or shotgun sold out of the trunk of a person's car in a lumber-company parking lot in Dothan, Alabama. When we see it like that we have a better idea of what Jesus was trying to say.

Now, some of the so-called cultural elites in Hollywood and Washington and Raleigh-Durham want to tell us that our long-standing traditions have become somehow unfashionable in the modern world. And don't kid yourselves—when they say that, they're really telling us they're right and we're wrong. They'll say, for example, that you can't blow up a bag of kittens with a shotgun, just because they themselves never did it for a harmless prank when they were young. Then these folks want to turn around and put their values, or lack of values, on everybody else.

Once again, the answer I have for them is simple: Go back to your Bible. In the very first book, first chapter, twenty-sixth verse—read along with me—it says God gave man, quote, "dominion over the fish of the sea, and over the birds of the air, and over all living things on the earth," unquote. What does this mean? If you said that it means you can bury an old black chihuahua up to its neck in your yard and run over its head with a lawnmower, then you have been paying attention, because you are exactly correct. The key is that little word "dominion." When God uses that word he is saying, in essence, man can do to the beasts of the earth whatever he wants or feels like at any particular time.

This is especially true, by the way, regarding cats. I happen not to be fond of cats, and that includes secular-humanist catlike dogs such as chihuahuas and golden retrievers. This is just a personal preference that I and most of my fellow-pastors share. But when I or any other pastor am asked to perform a marriage of homosexual cats, or of homosexual cat-owning people—well, then I think the hour has come for a scourging of wickedness such as God used to do in the biblical lands. I know you all are familiar with the story of the old black tomcat and the one-legged newlywed lesbian couple from Massachusetts. If you'd be interested to study it further, there's a copy of it on the pink sheet in your bulletin insert. After you read it you will see several phone numbers at the bottom that you can call.

But that's not what I'm here to talk to you about today. No, it isn't. I am here to tell you that I have never in my life been happier than I am right now. This evening, I actually shed tears of joy at the recent success of our efforts. And as I wept I also danced a little bit, not lewdly like on MTV, but with a couple crossover steps and a godly kind of hop, I felt so blessed. What miracles have been achieved!

Then I strutted for a while, and gave myself high fives in the full-length mirror in my office in the rectory. My son heard me and he came in, and we did some complicated handshakes that I could share with you all if you would like to learn them. Oh, last November was glorious for those who care, as we do, about the traditional, non-homosexual, one-man-and-one-woman-with-children-whose-paternity-can-be-verified family! (And by that I mean, of course, a family in which both the man and the woman were born a man and a woman, and can prove it—that is, they are still exactly the same sex as they were when they were born, and haven't had any of those operations that are all the rage, I'm told.)

By now, it may be obvious to many of you that I'm on the verge of hysteria. I split the back of my jacket in my gyrations before I came out here—those of you behind me would be able to see it if I weren't wearing this beautiful robe. Friends, remember our constitutional Federal Marriage Amendment! We have got to make Congress pass that thing! I believe in my soul that we will. And, before we do, we better remember to put in a couple of sentences about the requirement that you be born a man or a woman, et cetera. I honestly thought of that only just now.

Oh, I feel an unusual presence of administering angels. Truly the spirit has descended upon us tonight. I want you all to bow your heads, and take out your Palm Pilots and BlackBerries and cell phones and laptops, and then work and work them with all your strength, until the kingdom of us begins to appear.

JESUS IS NOT AN AMERICAN

One of the formulas by which some people try to live goes something like this: God first, country second, family third, self last. Yet anyone who tries hard enough to place God first will find that boundaries between countries, families and individuals dissolve. It is then impossible to place anything—even God—above anything else.

Peter J. Gomes is a minister and professor at The Harvard School of Divinity.

Patriotism Is Not Enough

from *Sojourners* magazine (Jan./Feb. 2003)

Peter J. Gomes

This fall I was in a large suburban Presbyterian church in Kansas City. I found that almost everyone in that large congregation had our present war fever on his or her heart and mind. These were not by any means your garden-variety leftists or pacifists, who form the usual list of suspects, and these were not Cambridge crunchies, by any means. This was Kansas, for heaven's sake—Alf Landon and Bob Dole country—and these were Presbyterians. They love their country, and they love their God; and what do you do when your country is headed where you think your faith and your God don't want you to go?

How can we have an intelligent conversation on the most dangerous policy topic of the day without being branded traitors, self-loathing Americans, anti-patriotic, or soft on democracy? That's a good question, especially when even the president of the United States questions the patriotism of those few in the U.S. Senate who question his policy or challenge his authority to wage war at will. Must the first casualty of patriotism always be dissent, debate, and discussion?

This is a frightening time, and if one cannot speak out of Christian conscience and conviction now, come what may, then we are forever consigned to moral silence. We hear much talk of "moral clarity," but it sounds more to me like moral arrogance, and it must not be met with moral silence. Anthony Lewis, formerly of the *New York Times*, said recently that if the purpose of the terrorists of September 11, 2001, was to destroy our confidence in our own American values, then, he feared, they had succeeded. In the name of fighting terror both abroad and at home, our government—particularly through the attorney general, together with a culture of patriotic intimidation—has suspended our constitutional liberties, stifled dissent, and defined a good American as one who goes along with the powers-that-be, in a "my way or the highway" mentality. When patriotism is defined in this narrow, partisan, opportunistic, jingoistic way, then perhaps that old cynic Dr. Samuel Johnson was right when he defined patriotism as the "last refuge of a scoundrel."

Frankly, I prefer his contemporary, Edmund Burke, who said, "To make us love our country, our country ought to be lovely." Our country is lovely, which is why we love it and are willing to serve it and, if necessary, to die for it. It is because we love it that we dare to speak to affirm the goodness and righteousness in it, the virtue and the power of its core values, and to speak against the things that would do harm to it and to those core values. What is and has always been lovely about our country is our right and our duty to criticize those in power, to dissent from their policies if we think them to be wrong, and to hold our alternative vision to be as fully valid as theirs.

In 1952, Adlai Stevenson was running for president against the patriotic and heroic Dwight D. Eisenhower. Charges of egg-headism, of intellectualism, of being soft on communism and soft on patriotism had been leveled on the intelligent and eloquent Stevenson. In a speech to the American Legion convention called "Patriotism in America," Stevenson said, "What do we mean by patriotism in the context of our time? I venture to suggest that what we mean is a sense of national responsibility, a patriotism which is not short, frenzied outbursts of emotion, but the tranquil and steady dedication of a lifetime." How carefully, poignantly, and aptly chosen are those words in comparison with some of the language we hear flashed about in recent days.

How many of you have seen the white marble statue of a British nurse standing just above Trafalgar Square and beneath Leicester Square in London? It is the statue of Nurse Edith Cavell. One of her claims to fame is that in the early morning hours of October 12, 1915, she was tied to a stake in German-occupied Belgium and shot as a traitor for the "crime" of assisting soldiers in their flight to neutral Holland. Her last moments were described by an eyewitness: "After receiving the sacrament, and within minutes of being led out to her death, she said, 'Standing as I do in view of God and eternity, I realize that patriotism is not enough. I must have no hatred or bitterness toward anyone.'"

On the base of her London statue are carved the words, "Patriotism is not enough." This is an impressive message from one who lost her life in the name of somebody else's patriotism.

Edith Cavell, an English vicar's daughter, lived and died a Christian, but her last words are almost too enigmatic and too simple, and they compel us to ask now, in a time of war and of rumors of war, what ought to be the proper relationship between love of God and love of country. If mere patriotism is not enough, what is it that will help us to be both conscientious citizens and faithful Christians? Are the two mutually exclusive, or is it possible, somehow, to live responsibly in the tension between those two claims? That is always the business of any Christian who takes seriously his allegiance to Jesus Christ and his responsibility to his country and his society.

In the text from Jeremiah, wisdom, might, and riches are set in clear opposition to love, justice, and righteousness. That creates for us a self-conscious biblical tension not easily resolved or explained away. Jeremiah knows that we are inclined to boast of our wisdom, and that is what the Hebrew word that is translated as "glory" really means: boasting, and the thumping of our intellectual chests. We know how to boast about our might and our riches in this land of opportunity. Washington these days is full of rich, smart, and powerful people, many of them in the oil business: Jeremiah knows that it is our natural penchant to seize upon and celebrate our achievements, for they define who we are, what we have, and what we do. This is the way of the world, and when we are "number one" in the world, it is "our way or the highway."

The prophet does not deny the reality of these claims, but over and against them he sets God's claims of love, justice, and righteousness. That is not only intellectual symmetry; it is moral symmetry. He is unambiguously clear here. If we as God's people are to glory in anything, we must glory in the things that God values, that God loves, and that God blesses. Why should God bless America if America does not bless the things that God delights in? What are they? Here they are, right in front of us: "[B]ut let him who glories glory in this, that he understands and knows me, that I am the Lord who practices steadfast love, justice, and righteousness in the earth; for in these things I delight."

If we do not delight in the things that the Lord delights in, why should the Lord delight in us? Try that one on for size. This will not fit on a bumper sticker or on a T-shirt, but you might carry it around to ponder in your hearts and minds.

Listen to how J. B. Phillips translates Romans 12; it is meant to grab us by our vitals: "With eyes wide open to the mercies of God, I beg you, as an act of intelligent worship, to give him your bodies as a living sacrifice, consecrated to him and acceptable by him."

Note "With eyes wide open." Not in fake devotion or in pseudo-piety, but with eyes wide open as an act of intelligent, thoughtful worship. Your mind's engaged, and not on hold. That's what Paul says. He goes on: "Don't let the world around you squeeze you into its own mold, but let God remold your minds from within, so that you may prove in practice that the plan of God for you is good, meets all his demands, and moves toward the goal of true maturity" (Romans 12:1–3; Phillips).

Think about that call to nonconformity. Think about that call to transformation. Think of that in the context of a choice you have made and have to make. That tension simply will not go away; it will not easily be resolved, and we, like all faithful Christians and honest citizens throughout all time, will have to live with it and through it. If we are uncomfortable in this conflict of values, we are meant to be uncomfortable. The easy syllogism, that we go to war in order to keep the peace, ought not to comfort us or our Christian president. It is that same alleged "moral clarity" that led to the infamous Vietnam logic. Perhaps you will remember it, that we had to destroy the village in order to "save" it. If that is "moral clarity," then I am Peter Rabbit.

Yet, my beloved friends, we are not without guidance or hope. Many, and perhaps some of you, will argue: Who are we to challenge the moral clarity and vision of our government, of people who presumably know more than we do, and who have the awful duty not only to protect and to serve, but to anticipate and to initiate? Who are we to kibitz from the sidelines without access to secret briefings, intelligence, knowledge, and all of the apparatus of government? Well, who, indeed, are we?

We do not require degrees from the Kennedy School or the Wharton School to have an opinion about the moral future of our country. In fact, it has usually been the so-called experts who have managed to get us into wars in the first place. We have a duty to speak, to dissent, and to demand a better case for compromising our most fundamental principles as Christians and citizens than has thus far been made. As a citizen I demand a better excuse than revenge, or oil, for the prosecution of a war that is likely to do more harm than good, that will destabilize not only the region but the world for years to come, and that, worst of all, will confirm for all the world to see our country's reputation as an irrational and undisciplined bully who acts not because it ought, but because it can; we make up the rules, so it seems, as we please. I love my country too much to see it complicit in its own worst stereotype. Right after September 11 a year ago, we asked, in some agonizing perplexity, "Why do they hate us?" Remember that question? Well, if we persist in making war the first rather than the last option, we will soon find out. The answer will be all too terribly manifest.

I know that in the mighty roar of wisdom, might, and riches, the sounds of love, justice, and righteousness—those things in which God delights, and in which God's people are meant to delight—sound thin, feeble, and anemic. Yet my Christian conscience tells me that these "soft" values should prevail every time over the "hard," even though they often do not. If I am compelled to compromise those Christian values in the service of the state, I had better be as certain as is humanly possible that such a compromise is worth sacrificing the things I hold most precious; and I certainly won't know that, nor will you, unless there is a great deal more thoughtful discussion, debate, and dissent than there has been so far.

It pleases me to join with other religious leaders who are beginning to speak and be heard on behalf of a thoughtful case for peace and to engage in a rigorous debate. Religious opinion is by no means unanimous: those evangelicals who have found little fault with anything that this administration has done or proposes to do, and who seldom met a war they didn't like, lined up to be counted on the president's side.

Polls show that most Americans, frustrated, alas, by the ephemeral character of the "war on terrorism" and still angry and confused about September 11, 2001, want to do something. As we know, however, in angry, vengeful moments, the desire to do "something" is easily translated into the will to do "anything," and that "anything" may very well be the wrong thing. Bombing Iraq into oblivion as payback to those who have done us injury at this moment seems to me to be the wrong thing to do. Polls do not get at the truth. Thirty-five years ago, most polls showed significant majorities in favor of whatever it was we were doing in Vietnam, and eventually the majority in favor concluded that the minority opposed were, in fact, right. Polls simply tell us where we are, not where we ought to be.

The gospel, however, does tell us where we ought to be, tough, untenable, and difficult as that place may be. Love, justice, and righteousness are superior to wisdom, might, and riches. How often do we have to be told that? "And these are God's words," says Paul at the end of Romans 12: "If thine enemy hunger, feed him; if he thirst, give him drink; for in so doing thou shalt heap coals of fire upon his head." Don't allow yourself to be overpowered with evil: Take the offensive and overpower evil with good. That is what Paul is saying: Take the offensive: Overpower evil with good! Now that is a radical foreign policy. That would scare the bejesus out of a lot of people, to know that with all of our power we decided that we were going to overpower evil with good—and what a topsy-turvy world this would be! That should give all the hawks in Washington something to think about, that if they want us to be noticed, the world would notice us if we took seriously the idea of overpowering evil with good.

Nurse Cavell was right: "Patriotism is not enough." If we wish to be on God's side rather than making God into our own ally of American realpolitik, then we would do well to remember our text from Jeremiah. God's values are clear; so too ought ours to be. If you love the Lord, you will love the things the Lord loves. There is no other way around it.

JESUS IS NOT A BIGOT

*with quotations from Jesus, Pat Robertson, Jerry Falwell and
General William Boykin*

Bigotry is a symptom of fear and self-hatred. When we judge our fellows, we set ourselves apart from them—and we lose the opportunity for exploration, understanding and connection. Jesus was not afraid; his compassion encompassed all of us.

"And when the Sabbath came, he began to teach in the synagogue, and many people who heard him were bewildered, and said . . . 'What makes him so wise?' and 'How can he be a miracle-worker? Isn't this the carpenter, Mary's bastard, the brother of James and Joseph and Judas and Simon, and aren't his sisters here with us?' And they were prevented from believing in him."
—from *The Gospel According to Jesus Christ,* edited and translated by Stephen Mitchell

The following is satire. It is meant to be funny. Berger made it up.

Memo re: *The Passion of the Christ*
J. M. Berger

From: Harvey Weinstein
      Chairman
      Miramax Films

To: Mel Gibson
Re: *The Passion of the Christ*
Date: October 12, 2003

Mel, babe, I just finished screening the movie. Quite the

spectacle! Congratulations on bringing *The Greatest Story Ever Told* into the twenty-first century!

Now, I know you've been having trouble finding a distributor, and I have a few things to say about that. But I'm a producer at heart, so you knew I would have notes on the movie! Let me get them out of my system, and then we can talk about the distribution situation.

NOTES

00:05:52—Love the devil guy, very Robert Blake in *Lost Highway*. Not to quibble, but I don't seem to remember him from the actual Bible. But, hey, you're the Christian. I'm sure it's in there somewhere.

00:09:10—I sincerely hope no snakes were harmed in the making of this film. The last thing you need is trouble with PETA. Those guys are tough!

00:11:23—Great fight scene, very *Last Supper* meets *The Matrix*. But then, Jesus was the original Neo. Am I right?

00:15:00—I understand that civil rights were not a big issue during this historical period, but is there some storyline reason why the Jewish guards would beat a totally passive prisoner? Isn't that just more work for them?

00:23:10—Like I said, you're the expert on the whole Christian thing. But I know a thing or two about Judaism. So FYI, Pharisees and Sadducees are not the same thing. They're all Jews, but it's like Franciscans vs. Jesuits. The High Priest was a Sadducee, not a Pharisee. With all the historical research, I'm surprised you missed that.

00:29:20—I find it hard to believe that the authorities would open the floor for random citizens to beat on a prisoner. Even John Ashcroft doesn't do that.

00:36:23—I'm pretty sure the Bible didn't say anything about ugly children and dead camels hounding Judas to death.

00:50:34—Did Jesus speak Latin? They must have had great schools in Nazareth. I guess that's why Mary and Joseph moved to the suburbs.

00:55:58—This flogging scene sure is dragging on.

00:57:03—I see our PG-13 rating going out the window here.

01:00:00—The flogging scene has gone on for longer than the ballroom scene in *The Magnificent Ambersons*. Seriously, Mel. I love you, babe. But Orson Welles you are not.

01:01:53—OK, this scene with Robert Blake and the ugly baby. There's *no way* that was in the Bible. Was it?

01:03:49—I am beginning to understand the phrase "flogging a dead horse."

01:04:03—I see our R rating going out the window here.

01:05:46—*Pulp Fiction* meets *Spartacus*. I don't remember anything about Jesus being anally raped in the Bible.

01:13:30—Why is Jesus carrying an entire cross, while his fellow convicts are only carrying the crossbeams?

01:14:22—For that matter, this whole thing is supposedly the product of a spontaneous Jewish mob scene over Jesus. So why would there be any other convicts at all?

01:17:30—Jesus! I mean, ouch! Is there a rating past NC-17? Children under eighteen shouldn't be allowed to pass within twenty yards of a theater *playing* this movie.

01:19:23—Mel. Babe. Think about what you're doing here. Your audience isn't exactly the Dario Argento crowd. When you have people in a religious frame of mind who aren't accustomed to viewing splatter movies . . . Well, let's just say this movie could really freak people out.

01:25:11—Just a few minutes ago, the Romans realized that beating Jesus was counterproductive. Now they're beating him again! What gives? If the guards are just generally sadistic, wouldn't they beat the other prisoners, too? I understand you're going for the whole martyr thing here, but that doesn't mean we have to throw logic out the window. There's a fine line between Bruce Willis in *Die Hard* and Bruce Willis in *Die Hard II*. Know what I'm saying?

01:31:31—We get it. Jesus falls down a lot. Let's move on.

01:34:02—Oh. My. God. I just looked at my watch and realized there's still a half hour to go. We have a little thing in the movie business called "editing." Google it. You'll be glad you did.

01:38:40—It's hard to understand how conservative Christians could advocate capital punishment after watching all this nailing. But hey, I'm a member of the Jewish liberal media elite, so what do I know? (Mel, I could have sworn you were in *favor* of the death penalty. After watching this movie, I see that can't possibly be true.)

01:40:09—Tobe Hooper called. He wants to know how you got your blood packs to have that phlegmy consistency.

01:46:10—*The Birds* meets *Dead Man Walking*. Doesn't the attack of the angry crow undercut the whole Jesus message of "love thy enemy" and "turn the other cheek"?

01:55:12—Well, Robert Blake is not a happy man. Should I be offended that the Devil and the Jews are having the exact same reaction to the death of Jesus within twelve seconds of each other?

On that last point, Mel, I had to admit I was a little worried going into this movie. People are talking. I heard that this was a very anti-Semitic movie. After viewing the film, I realize it isn't just anti-Semitic, it's also anti-Italian. I mean, 95 percent of the hitting and virtually all of the bloodletting is done by Romans. If *The Sopranos* can take the heat, I guess you can, too.

Look, Mel, I'm going to be blunt. Here's my big problem with distributing your movie in the coming year: Too political. I'm already stuck in one political mess over a new documentary by Michael Moore, and I don't need another.

As you know, Disney owns Miramax. The Mouse House made me renege on Moore's distribution contract because they think his movie is too liberal to release during the 2004 election season.

They'll nix *The Passion* too, for the same reason. It's just too liberal!

You have created a devastating indictment of conservative policy and ideology. *The Passion* is a story about the devastating effects of institutional racism in the criminal justice system. And Jesus is denied the protections of due process because of his religion—just like Muslims in America after 9/11.

Furthermore, *The Passion* portrays imperialist occupiers as brutal and evil. I'm sure no one will miss the blatant parallels between the Roman occupation of Judea and the American occupation of Iraq.

If all that wasn't enough, *The Passion* is the most powerful statement against capital punishment since *I Want To Live!* with Susan Hayward way back in '58. I wept like a baby when I saw this innocent man cruelly executed for crimes he didn't commit!

Now some people might think *The Passion* is a right-wing movie, or that it will energize the religious right to vote in droves in November.

That's ridiculous, of course. Anyone with half a brain can see *The Passion* is the most liberal movie of 2004— possibly the most liberal movie of all time.

I can't imagine anyone coming out of *The Passion* energized about right-wing issues. They'd have to be idiots! And I didn't get to be the producer of such Hollywood blockbusters as *Spy Kids 3-D* and *Air Bud* by assuming moviegoers are idiots.

I'm sorry, Mel, but we're going to have to pass. It's obvious you're pushing a radical liberal agenda here, and Disney just won't allow it.

However, I want to personally wish you the best of luck. I know *The Passion of the Christ* will one day be remembered in the same breath as *The Song of Bernadette* and *The Bells of St. Mary's*. It's that good.

Regards,
Harvey

"Feminism encourages women to leave their husbands, kill their children, practice witchcraft, destroy capitalism and become lesbians."
—Pat Robertson

We're All Damned
from *The Guardian* (11/19/96)
George Monbiot

Leviticus is pretty clear about homosexuality. "Thou shalt not lie with mankind as with womankind: it is abomination." Like those who defile themselves with beasts, such sinners will be, the Bible tells us, vomited out by the land itself. If evidence of this hideous destiny were ever required, one need look no further than the eructations which greeted the twentieth anniversary of the Lesbian and Gay Christian Movement, celebrated on Saturday in Southwark Cathedral.

Never having lain with a man as with a woman, or with a beast to defile myself therewith, I was, until this weekend, fairly complacent about my chances of being vomited. Then, however, hoping to discover what the fuss was all about, I made the mistake of taking a look at Leviticus. It's odd that no one else seems to have noticed it, but the news is much worse than we thought: terrestrial regurgitation awaits those who commit any one of the "abominable customs" listed in the book. All of us habitually defile ourselves before the Lord, but, as if to prove that He is a just God, food manufacturers and estate agents would seem to have the most to fear, as they lead all the rest of us into temptation. If anyone should be looking out for a cosmic spew, it should surely be them.

Leviticus leaves little room for doubt. Thou shalt not eat animal fat, or the fruit of a tree you've owned for less than five years. Thou shalt not round the corners of your head, or mar the corners of your beard. Thou shalt not touch a woman, or anything she's sat on, until seven days after her menstruation begins. Thou shalt not put a stumbling block before the blind (which does for anyone parking on the pavement). Thou shalt not trade in freehold: after fifty years, all property must revert to the people it was bought from.

While God doubtless appreciates the fuss about gays being accepted into the priesthood, He surely can't be very pleased that the rest of His injunctions in this regard have been so manifestly flouted. Leviticus prohibits from officiating in church anyone that hath a blemish, be he lame, crookbacked, with a flat nose, "or any thing superfluous."

Quite what this means is anyone's guess, but it must certainly cover deaf aids, spectacles, dentures and toupees, thus barring the greater part of the priesthood from its duties.

Obviously, an awful lot of turtle doves are going to have to have their heads pulled off to atone for this lot. On the plus side, we have banned the import of ostrich meat from South Africa on the grounds of its uncleanliness, and incinerated plenty of oxen this year, which could be taken as a sort of expiatory sacrifice. We have been diligent in making bondmen of the heathen, and if we aren't smiting the enemies of the Lord ourselves, at least we are supplying the hardware. But God's land must surely be starting to gag.

In need of spiritual guidance, I telephoned the Reverend Philip Hacking, Chairman of Reform, the group which led the protests against the service on Saturday. Why have he and his fellow evangelicals, so quick to warn homosexuals of the perils they face, been so slow to warn the rest of us?

Homosexuality, he told me, unlike other Old Testament abominations, is also recognized as a sin in the New Testament. There is no comparison, for example, with the sin of Onan, which "the Bible doesn't take very seriously."

Conspicuously, however, homosexuality is condemned in the New Testament not in the four Gospels, but in Romans, Corinthians and Revelations, along with stacks of wonderful material about many-horned beasts and the ordination of all governments by God. These books, like Leviticus, relay the words not of God, but of men striving, just as they do today, to apply His teachings to everyday life. Philip Hacking has rightly rejected the prejudices of four thousand years ago, only to embrace those of two thousand years ago.

There is, however, one small anti-nausea drug of hope, which may yet delay the global barf. Among Free Presbyterians in Glasgow, a small group is beginning to take the Bible seriously. The "theonomists," like the Taliban, would replace the judiciary with religious courts. Homosexuals, adulterers and disobedient children would be stoned to death.

This honesty in sentencing may be as relevant to Britain in 1996 as the politics of Pol Pot would be, but at least the theonomists don't succumb to the "pick and mix morality" so often lamented by groups like Reform. By concentrating on homosexuality and choosing to reject as irrelevant the other teachings of the Bible, evangelical Christians are surely committing the very sin of which they accuse the homophiles. They are pandering to the whims of the moment, rather than listening to the God of their hearts.

"AIDS is the wrath of a just God against homosexuals. To oppose it would be like an Israelite jumping in the Red Sea to save one of Pharaoh's charioteers."

—Jerry Falwell

"Many of those people involved with Adolph Hitler were Satanists, many of them were homosexuals—the two things seem to go together."
—Pat Robertson

The Only King We Have Is Jesus
from *The Nation* (2/5/01)
Calvin Trillin

(A newly unearthed gospel song credited to John Ashcroft)

As I told the Bob Jones students,
Seated white and black apart,
This nation is unique, not like the rest.
As I faced those godly youngsters,
I told them from the heart
Just why this land will always be the best:

The only king we have is Jesus.
And I feel blessed to bring that news.
The only king we have is Jesus.
I can't explain why we've got Jews.

So because our king is Jesus,
I'm often heard to say,
Our kids should pray to Him each day in class.

JESUS IS NOT A BIGOT

If some kids just stay silent,
That's perfectly OK.
But they'll all be given Jesus tests to pass.

The only king we have is Jesus.
That's the truth we all perceive.
The only king we have is Jesus
So Hindus may just have to leave.

Now Jesus hates abortion,
'Cause Jesus loves all life.
They call it choice; it's murder all the same.
The killers must be punished—
The doctor, man and wife.
We'll execute them all in Jesus' name.

The only king we have is Jesus.
It's Jesus who can keep us pure.
The only king we have is Jesus.
And He's Republican for sure.

The homosexual lifestyle
Could make our Jesus weep.
He loathed their jokes about which cheek to turn.
Yes, Jesus came to teach us
With whom we're supposed to sleep.
Ignore that and you'll go to Hell to burn.

(Final chorus sung in tongues:)
Tron smleck gha dreednus hoke b'loofnok
Frak fag narst fag madoondah greeb.
Tron smleck gha dreednus hoke b'loofnok
Dar popish, flarge dyur darky, hebe.

"Well, you know what I knew, that my God was bigger than his. I knew that my God was a real God, and his was an idol." —General William Boykin, deputy undersecretary of defense, in January, 2004. Boykin was referring to a Somali Muslim fighter who claimed Allah would protect him from U.S. capture.

JESUS IS A PROGRESSIVE

with a quotation from William Sloane Coffin

There is no such thing as a truly Christian conservative. Conservatives by definition resist change. Jesus was executed as a revolutionary who threatened the belief system that upheld the powerful in his society. Today, he would urge us to revolt against a culture that values commerce over connection, that substitutes addiction for joy, that promotes cynicism over purpose and that protects the profits of rich men rather than the rights of children.

from *Jesus: A Revolutionary Biography* (1994)

John Dominic Crossan

He was an illiterate peasant, but with an oral brilliance that few of those trained in literate and scribal disciplines can ever attain. When today we read his words in fixed and frozen texts we must recognize that the oral memory of his first audiences could have retained, at best, only the striking image, the startling analogy, the forceful conjunction, and, for example, the plot summary of a parable that might have taken an hour or more to tell and perform. I give several examples of what the here-and-now Kingdom of God meant for Jesus, from each of the major genres in which that oral memory preserved, developed, but also created such traditions.

TEARING THE FAMILY APART

If the supreme value for the twentieth-century American imagination is *individualism*, based on economics and property, that for the first-century Mediterranean imagination can be called, to the contrary, *groupism*, based on kinship and gender. And there were really only two groups—the familial and the political, kinship and politics —to be considered. But we have, precisely against both those groups, biting aphorisms and dialogues from the historical Jesus. There is, first of all, an almost savage attack on family values, and it happens very, very often. Here are four quite different examples. Each has different versions available, but I give only one version for each example. The first one is from the *Gospel of Thomas* 55, the second from Mark 3:31–35, the third from the *Q Gospel* in Luke 11:27–28 but with no Matthean parallel, and the final one from the *Q Gospel* in Luke 12:51–53 rather than in Matthew 10:34–36.

> 1. Jesus said, "Whoever does not hate father and mother cannot be a follower of me, and whoever does not hate brothers and sisters . . . will not be worthy of me."

> 2. Then his mother and his brothers came; and standing outside, they sent to him and called him. . . . And he replied, "Who are my mother and my brothers?" And looking at those who sat around him, he said, "Here are my mother and my brothers! Whoever does the will of God is my brother and sister and mother."

> 3. A woman from the crowd spoke up and said to him, "How fortunate is the womb that bore you, and the breasts that you sucked!" But he said, "How fortunate, rather, are those who listen to God's teaching and observe it!"

> 4. "Do you think that I have come to bring peace to the earth? No, I tell you, but rather division! From now on five in one household will be divided, three against two and two against three; they will be divided: father against son and son against father, mother against daughter and daughter against mother, mother-in-law against her daughter-in-law and daughter-in-law against mother-in-law."

The family is a group to which one is irrevocably assigned, but in those first two units, that given grouping is negated in favor of another one open to all who wish to join it. And the reason those groups are set in stark contrast becomes more clear by the third example. A woman declares Mary blessed because of Jesus, presuming, in splendid Mediterranean fashion, that a woman's greatness derives from mothering a famous son. But that patriarchal chauvinism is negated by Jesus in favor of a blessedness open to anyone who wants it, without distinction of sex or gender, infertility or maternity.

Finally, it is in the last aphorism that the point of Jesus' attack on the family becomes most clear. Imagine the standard Mediterranean family with five members: mother and father, married son with his wife, and unmarried daughter, a nuclear extended family all under one roof. Jesus says he will tear it apart. The usual explanation is that families will become divided as some accept and others refuse faith in Jesus. But notice where and how emphatically the axis of separation is located. It is precisely *between the generations*. But why should faith split along that axis? Why might faith not separate, say, the women from the men or even operate in ways far more random? *The attack has nothing to do with faith but with power*. The attack is on the Mediterranean family's axis of power, which sets father and mother over son, daughter, and daughter-in-law. That helps us to understand all of those examples. The family is society in miniature, the place where we first and most deeply learn how to love and be loved, hate and be hated, help and be helped, abuse and be abused. It is not just a center of domestic serenity; since it involves power, it invites the abuse of power, and it is at that precise point that Jesus attacks it. His ideal group is, contrary to Mediterranean and indeed most human familial reality, an open one equally accessible to all under God. It is the Kingdom of God, and it negates that terrible abuse of power that is power's dark specter and lethal shadow.

BLESSED ARE (WE?) BEGGARS

Turning from familial to political groupings, it is hard to imagine an aphorism initially more radical but eventually more banal than Jesus' conjunction of blessed poverty and the Kingdom of God. Here are four versions of the same saying, from the *Gospel of Thomas* 54, from the Q *Gospel* in both Luke 6:20 and Matthew 5:3, and from James 2:5, respectively. The first example is in Coptic translation and the last three are in Greek. As you read from first to last you can see the process of normalization at work:

1. "Blessed are the poor, for yours is the kingdom of heaven."

2. "Blessed are you who are poor, for yours is the kingdom of God."

3. "Blessed are the poor in spirit, for theirs is the kingdom of heaven."

4. Has not God chosen those who are poor in the world to be rich in faith and heirs of the kingdom which he has promised to those who love him?

In the third example, Matthew's *in spirit* diverts interpretation from economic to religious poverty, and James's emphasis on faith and love points toward a promised rather than a present Kingdom of God. But the stark and startling conjunction of blessed poverty and divine Kingdom is still there for all to see in the first two versions. We can no longer tell, of course, whether Jesus meant *the* or *you* or *we* poor.

There is, however, a very serious problem when the Greek word *ptōchos* is translated as "poor" in the last three examples. The Greek word *penes* means "poor," and *ptōchos* means "destitute." The former describes the status of a peasant family making a bare subsistence living from year to year; the latter indicates the status of such a family pushed, by disease or debt, draught or death, off the land and into destitution and begging. One can see this distinction most clearly in the *Plutus* of Aristophanes, the last play of that great comic dramatist, produced probably in the Athens of 388 B.C.E. The key section is in *Plutus* 535–554, with Chremylus arguing for the advantages of the god *Plutus* (or Wealth) and declaring that *Penia* (or Poverty) and *Ptōcheia* (or Destitution) are both the same in any case. Poverty, appearing here as a goddess, immediately denies her equation with Destitution:

Chremylus:
Well, Poverty [*penian*] and Destitution [*ptōcheias*],
    truly the two to be sisters we always declare.

Poverty:
It's the beggar [*ptōchou*] alone who has nothing his
    own, nor even a penny possesses.
My poor [*penetos*] man, it's true, has to scrimp and to
    scrape, and his work he must never be slack in;

There'll be no superfluity found in his cot;
but then there will nothing be lacking.

The *poor* man has to work hard but has always enough to
survive, while the *beggar* has nothing at all. Jesus, in other
words, did not declare blessed the poor, a class that
included, for all practical purposes, the entire peasantry;
rather, he declared blessed the destitute—for example, the
beggars.

Now, what on earth does that mean, especially if one
does not spiritualize it away, as Matthew immediately did,
into "poor [or destitute] in spirit"—that is, the spiritually
humble or religiously obedient? Did Jesus really think that
bums and beggars were actually blessed by God, as if all
the destitute were nice people and all the aristocrats correspondingly evil? Is this some sort of naïve or romantic
delusion about the charms of destitution? If, however, we
think not just of personal or individual evil but of social,
structural, or systemic injustice—that is, of precisely the
imperial situation in which Jesus and his fellow peasants
found themselves—then the saying becomes literally, terribly, and permanently true. In any situation of oppres-
sion, especially in those oblique, indirect, and systemic
ones where injustice wears a mask of normalcy or even of
necessity, the only ones who are innocent or blessed are
those squeezed out deliberately as human junk from the
system's own evil operations. A contemporary equivalent:
only the homeless are innocent. That is a terrifying aphorism against society because, like the aphorisms against
the family, it focuses not just on personal or individual
abuse of power but on such abuse in its systemic or structural possibilities—and there, in contrast to the former

level, none of our hands are innocent or our consciences particularly clear.

If It Is a Girl, Cast It Out

Another striking conjunction is that between infant children and divine Kingdom. Once again we can move easily from aphorism to dialogue as the tradition creates situations and settings for sayings it has retained in memory. And, once again, earliest oral memory would not have been in the form of exact syntactical arrangements recalling precisely what Jesus saw or said, but rather of a startling combination, children/Kingdom, which could then be articulated as needed in various forms and versions. Although there are four independent versions of that conjunction, I give only one, for the sake of brevity. From Mark 10:13–16:

> People were bringing little children to him in order that he might touch them; and the disciples spoke sternly to them. But when Jesus saw this, he was indignant and said to them, "Let the little children come to me; do not stop them; for it is to such as these that the kingdom of God belongs. *Truly I tell you, whoever does not receive the kingdom of God as a little child will never enter it.*" And he took them up in his arms, laid his hands on them, and blessed them.

What was, first of all, the immediate connotation of children or infants to the ancient Mediterranean as distinct from the modern American mind? Read this ancient papyrus letter, discovered around the turn of the century on the west bank of the Nile about 120 miles south of

Cairo in the excavated rubbish dumps of ancient Oxyrhynchus, the modern El Bahnasa. The worker Hilarion writes to his wife, Alis, addressed in Egyptian fashion as sister, on June 18 in the year 1 B.C.E. From the Oxyrhynchus Papyri 4.744:

> Hilarion to his sister Alis many greetings, likewise to my lady Berous [his mother-in-law?] and to Apollonarion [their first and male child]. Know that we are even yet in Alexandria. Do not worry if they all come back [except me] and I remain in Alexandria. I urge and entreat you, be concerned about the child [Apollonarion] and if I should receive my wages soon, I will send them up to you. If by chance you bear a son, if it is a boy, let it be, if it is a girl, cast it out [to die]. You have said to Aphrodisias, "Do not forget me." How can I forget you? Therefore I urge you not to worry. 29 [year] of Caesar [Augustus], Payni [month] 23 [day].

Hilarion and some companions had left their home at Oxyrhynchus and traveled north to work in Alexandria. His wife, Alis, pregnant with their second child, having heard nothing nor received anything from him, transmitted her concern through Aphrodisias, who was also traveling to the capital. The letter is Hilarion's response to her concern, and, tender to his pregnant wife but terrible to his unborn daughter, it shows us with stark clarity what an infant meant in the Mediterranean. It was quite literally a nobody unless its father accepted it as a member of the family rather than exposing it in the gutter or rubbish dump to die of abandonment or to be taken up by another and reared as a slave. To be like an infant child is interpreted by Matthew 18:1–4 as meaning to have appropriate humility, by the *Gospel of Thomas* 22 as meaning to practice sexual asceticism, and by John 3:1–10 as meaning to have recently received baptism. Those three readings avoid the horrifying meaning of a child as a nothing, a nobody, a nonperson in the Mediterranean world of paternal power, absolute in its acceptance or rejection of the newly born infant.

In giving Mark's version above I italicized the core aphorism whose basic conjunction of children/Kingdom is all that certainly came from Jesus. Concentrate, for a moment, on the framing situation created by Mark himself. This indicates the situation created not from the historical Jesus but from the historical Mark. Notice those framing words: *touch, took in his arms, blessed, laid hands on.* Those are the official bodily actions of a father designating a newly born infant for life rather than death, for accepting it into his family rather than casting it out with the garbage. And the disciples do not want Jesus to act in this positive and accepting way. There must, therefore, have been a debate within the Markan community on whether it should adopt such abandoned infants, and Mark has Jesus say yes even though other authorities—the disciples themselves—say no. Once again we are forced to face ancient Mediterranean realities, and Mark's later application helps us to see more clearly what was there from Jesus in the beginning: that a Kingdom of Children is a Kingdom of Nobodies.

WHO NEEDS A MUSTARD PLANT?

There is another rather startling conjunction, but in a parable rather than in an aphorism or dialogue—the conjunction between the mustard seed and the Kingdom. The parable is, by the way, the only one attributed to Jesus that has triple independent attestation. I give only one version, from Mark 4:30–32:

> And he said, "With what can we compare the kingdom of God, or what parable shall we use for it? It is like a grain of mustard seed, which, when sown upon the ground, is the smallest of all the seeds on earth; yet when it is sown it grows up and becomes the greatest of all shrubs, and puts forth large branches, so that the birds of the air can make nests in its shade."

Once again, a word about Mediterranean mustard plants and nesting birds helps us to understand the startling nature of that conjunction. The Roman author Pliny the Elder, who was born in 23 C.E. and died when scientific curiosity brought him too close to an erupting Vesuvius in 79 C.E., wrote about the mustard plant in his encyclopedic *Natural History* 19.170–171:

> Mustard . . . with its pungent taste and fiery effect is extremely beneficial for the health. It grows entirely wild, though it is improved by being transplanted; but on the other hand when it has once been sown it is scarcely possible to get the place free of it, as the seed when it falls germinates at once.

There is, in other words, a distinction between the wild mustard and its domesticated counterpart, but even when one deliberately cultivates the latter for its medicinal or culinary properties, there is an ever-present danger that it will destroy the garden. The mustard plant is dangerous even when domesticated in the garden, and is deadly when growing wild in the grain fields. And those nesting birds, which may strike us as charming, represented to ancient farmers a permanent danger to the seed and the grain. The point, in other words, is not just that the mustard plant starts as a proverbially small seed and grows into a shrub of three, four, or even more feet in height. It is that it tends to take over where it is not wanted, that it tends to get out of control, and that it tends to attract birds within cultivated areas, where they are not particularly desired. And that, said Jesus, was what the Kingdom was like. Like a pungent shrub with dangerous take-over properties. Something you would want only in small and carefully controlled doses—if you could control it. It is a startling metaphor, but it would be interpreted quite differently by those, on the one hand, concerned about their fields, their crops, and their harvests, and by those, on the other, for whom fields, crops, and harvest were always the property of others.

OPEN COMMENSALITY

Let that title stand unexplained for a moment. Its meaning and necessity will soon become clear. At the end of the preceding chapter, a comparison was made between John and Jesus in terms of fasting and feasting. The contrast was made both in neutral terms by Jesus himself and in very inimical terms by opponents: John fasted and they called him demonic; Jesus ate and drank and they said he was "a glutton and a drunkard, a friend of tax collectors and sinners." It is obvious why John, as an apocalyptic ascetic, was fasting, but what was Jesus doing? It is not enough to say that those opponents are simply accusing him of social deviancy through nasty name-calling. That is, of course, quite true, but why precisely those names rather than any of the others easily available?

Here is another parable of Jesus, which helps answer that question and will serve to ground all of those aphorisms, dialogues, and parables concerning the Kingdom of God. It is found in the *Q Gospel*, but with widely divergent versions in Matthew 22:1–13 and Luke 14:15–24. It is also found in the *Gospel of Thomas* 64, as follows:

> Jesus said, "A person was receiving guests. When he had prepared the dinner, he sent his servant to invite the guests. The servant went to the first and said to that one, 'My master invites you.' That person said, 'Some merchants owe me money; they are coming to me tonight, I must go and give them instructions. Please excuse me from dinner.' The servant went to another and said to that one, 'My master has invited you.' That person said to the servant, 'I have bought a house and I have been called away for a day. I shall have no time.' The servant went to another and said to that one, 'My master invites you.' That person said to the servant, 'My friend is to be married and I am to arrange the banquet. I shall not be able to come. Please excuse me from dinner.' The servant went to another and said to that one, 'My master invites you.' That person said to the servant, 'I have bought an estate and I am going to collect the rent. I shall not be able to come. Please excuse me.' The servant returned and

said to his master, 'The people whom you invited to dinner have asked to be excused.' The master said to his servant, 'Go out on the streets and *bring back whomever you find* to have dinner.' Buyers and merchants [will] not enter the places of my father."

This is one of those rare cases where the Gospel of Thomas interprets a parable. It appends, as commentary: "Buyers and merchants [will] not enter the places of my father." Jesus, not the host, speaks that judgment. For my present purpose, I leave aside that interpretation to focus closely on the replacement guests, the reference to which I have italicized above. Compare how they are described by Jesus in Luke 14:21–23 and in Matthew 22:9–10, respectively:

1. "'Go out quickly to the streets and lanes of the city, and bring in the poor and maimed and blind and lame.' And the servant said, 'Sir, what you commanded has been done, and still there is room.' And the master said to the servant, 'Go out to the highways and hedges, and *compel people to come in*, that my house may be filled.'"

2. "'Go therefore to the thoroughfares, and invite to the marriage feast *as many as you find*.' And those servants went out into the streets and gathered all whom they found, both bad and good; so the wedding hall was filled with guests."

In both those cases, separate interpretations have divergently specified the replacement guests. Luke mentions the outcasts and Matthew mentions the good and the bad, but the italicized phrases indicate the more original and unspecified command to bring in whomever you can find.

I leave aside, therefore, individual interpretations inserted around or within the three texts to underline the common structural plot discernible behind them all. It tells the story of a person who gives a presumably unannounced feast, sends a servant to invite friends, but finds by late in the day that each has a quite valid and very politely expressed excuse. The result is a dinner ready and a room empty. The host replaces the absent guests with anyone off the streets, but if one actually brought in *anyone off the street*, one could, in such a situation, have classes, sexes, and ranks all mixed up together. Anyone could be reclining next to anyone else, female next to male, free next to slave, socially high next to socially low, and ritually pure next to ritually impure. And a short detour through the cross-cultural anthropology of food and eating underlines what a social nightmare that would be.

Think, for a moment, if beggars came to your door, of the difference between giving them some food to go, of inviting them into your kitchen for a meal, of bringing them into the dining room to eat in the evening with your family, or of having them come back on Saturday night for supper with a group of your friends. Think, again, if you were a large company's CEO, of the difference between a cocktail party in the office for all the employees, a restaurant lunch for all the middle managers, or a private dinner party for your vice presidents in your own home. Those events are not just ones of eating together, of simple table fellowship, but are what anthropologists call *commensality*—from *mensa*, the Latin word for "table." It means the rules of tabling and eating as miniature models for the rules of association and socialization. It means table fellowship as a map of economic discrimination, social hierarchy, and political differentiation. This is how Peter Farb and George Armelagos summarized commensality at the beginning and end of their book on the anthropology of eating:

> In all societies, both simple and complex, eating is the primary way of initiating and maintaining human relationships. . . . Once the anthropologist finds out where, when, and with whom the food is eaten, just about everything else can be inferred about the relations among the society's members. . . . To know what, where, how, when, and with whom people eat is to know the character of their society.[1]

Similarly, Lee Edward Klosinski reviewed the significant cross-cultural anthropological and sociological literature on food and eating and concluded:

> Sharing food is a transaction which involves a series of mutual obligations and which initiates an interconnected complex of mutuality and reciprocity. Also, the ability of food to symbolize these relationships, as well as to define group boundaries, surfaced as one of its unique properties. . . . Food exchanges are basic to human interaction. Implicit in them is a series of obligations to give, receive and repay. These transactions involve individuals in matrices of social reciprocity, mutuality

and obligation. Also, food exchanges are able to act as symbols of human interaction. Eating is a behavior which symbolizes feelings and relationships, mediates social status and power, and expresses the boundaries of group identity.[2]

What Jesus' parable advocates, therefore, is an open commensality, an eating together without using table as a miniature map of society's vertical discriminations and lateral separations. The social challenge of such equal or egalitarian commensality is the parable's most fundamental danger and most radical threat. It is only a story, of course, but it is one that focuses its egalitarian challenge on society's miniature mirror, the table, as the place where bodies meet to eat. Since, moreover, Jesus lived out his own parable, the almost predictable counteraccusation to such open commensality would be immediate: Jesus is a glutton, a drunkard, and a friend of tax collectors and sinners. He makes, in other words, no appropriate distinctions and discriminations. And since women were present, especially unmarried women, the accusation would be that Jesus eats with whores, the standard epithet of denigration for any female outside appropriate male control. All of those terms—tax collectors, sinners, whores—are in this case derogatory terms for those with whom, in the opinion of the name callers, open and free association should be avoided.

The Kingdom of God as a process of open commensality, of a nondiscriminating table depicting in miniature a nondiscriminating society, clashes fundamentally with honor and shame, those basic values of ancient Mediterranean culture and society. Most of American society in the twentieth century is used to *individualism*, with guilt and innocence as sanctions, rather than to *groupism*, with honor and shame as sanctions. Here is a description of Mediterranean honor and shame, from a 1965 cross-cultural anthology; Pierre Bourdieu is speaking on the basis of his field work among the Berber tribesmen of Algerian Kabylia in the late fifties:

> The point of honour is the basis of the moral code of an individual who sees himself always through the eyes of others, who has need of others for his existence, because the image he has of himself is indistinguishable from that presented to him by other people. . . . Respectability, the reverse of shame, is the characteristic of a person who needs other people in order to grasp his own identity and whose conscience is a kind of interiorization of others, since these fulfil for him the role of witness and judge. . . . He who has lost his honour no longer exists. He ceases to exist for other people, and at the same time he ceases to exist for himself.[3]

The key phrase here is "through the eyes of others," and the more we understand that process, the more radically challenging Jesus' Kingdom of God starts to appear. We might see Jesus' message and program as quaintly eccentric or charmingly iconoclastic (at least at a safe distance), but for those who take their very identity from the eyes of their peers, the idea of eating together and living together without any distinctions, differences, discriminations, or hierarchies is close to the irrational and the absurd. And the one who advocates or does it is close to the deviant and the perverted. He has no honor. He has no shame.

RADICAL EGALITARIANISM

Open commensality is the symbol and embodiment of radical egalitarianism, of an absolute equality of people that denies the validity of any discrimination between them and negates the necessity of any hierarchy among them. To all of this there is an obvious objection: you are just speaking of contemporary democracy and anachronistically retrojecting that back into the time and onto the lips of Jesus. I look, in reply and defense, both to general anthropology and to specific history during the first century.

Those who, like peasants, live with a boot on their neck can easily envision two different dreams. One is quick revenge—a world in which they might get in turn to put their boots on those other necks. Another is reciprocal justice—a world in which there would never again be any boots on any necks. Thus, for example, the anthropologist James C. Scott, moving from Europe to Southeast Asia, notes the popular tradition's common reaction to such disparate elite traditions as Christianity, Buddhism, and Islam, and argues very persuasively that peasant culture and religion are actually an anticulture, criticizing alike both the religious and political elites that oppress it. It is, in fact, a reactive inversion of the pattern of exploitation common to the peasantry *as such*:

> The radical vision to which I refer is strikingly uniform despite the enormous variations in peasant cultures and the different great traditions of which they partake. . . . At the risk of over generalizing, it

is possible to describe some common features of
this reflexive symbolism. It nearly always implies a
society of brotherhood in which there will be no
rich and poor, in which no distinctions of rank and
status (save those between believers and nonbelievers) will exist. Where religious institutions are
experienced as justifying inequities, the abolition
of rank and status may well include the elimination of religious hierarchy in favor of communities
of equal believers. Property is typically, though not
always, to be held in common and shared. All
unjust claims to taxes, rents, and tribute are to be
nullified. The envisioned utopia may also include a
self-yielding and abundant nature as well as a radically transformed human nature in which greed,
envy, and hatred will disappear. While the earthly
utopia is thus an anticipation of the future, it often
harks back to a mythic Eden from which mankind
has fallen away.[4]

That is the ancient peasant dream of radical egalitarianism. It does not deny the other dream, that of brutal
revenge, but neither does that latter negate the former's
eternal thirst for reciprocity, equality, and justice.

One instance from the first century shows both those
dreams coming together in the last days of the doomed
Temple during the First Roman-Jewish War. As Vespasian's
forces moved steadily southward and tightened the noose
around Jerusalem in the fall of 67 and winter of 68 C.E.,
groups of peasant rebels under bandit leaders were forced
repeatedly into the capital for refuge. They became known,
collectively or in coalition, as the Zealots, and one of their

first actions was to install a new High Priest. According to ancient tradition, the High Priest was chosen from the family of Zadok, as had been true since at least the time of Solomon. But when, in the second century B.C.E., the Jewish dynasty of the Hasmoneans wrested control of their country from the Syrians, they had simply appointed themselves High Priests. And thereafter, from Herod the Great to the outbreak of the revolt against Rome, the High Priests were selected from four families, likewise not of legitimate Zadokite origins. What the Zealots did was return to the legitimate high-priestly line, but within it they elected by lot rather than by choice. Josephus, telling the story in *Antiquities* 4.147–207, as an aristocratic priest is almost inarticulate with anger at what he considers an impious mockery. Here is the key section, in 155–156:

> They accordingly summoned one of the high-priestly clans, called Eniachin, and cast lots for a high priest. By chance the lot fell to one who proved a signal illustration of their depravity; he was an individual named Phanni, son of Samuel, of the village of Aphthia, a man who not only was not descended from high priests, but was such a clown that he scarcely knew what the high priesthood meant. At any rate they dragged their reluctant victim out of the country and, dressing him up for his assumed part, as on the stage, put the sacred vestments upon him and instructed him how to act in keeping with the occasion.

Lottery is what egalitarianism looks like in practice. If all members of some group are eligible for office, then the only fair human way to decide is by lot, leaving the choice up to God. That was how Saul, the first Jewish king, was elected from "all the tribes of Israel," according to 1 Samuel 10:21. And that was how the early Christians chose a replacement for the traitor apostle Judas from among "the men who have accompanied us" since the beginning, according to Acts of the Apostles 1:21–26. Obviously, of course, as in the implicit and presumed male exclusivity of the former case and the explicit and very deliberate male exclusivity of the latter one, discriminations can be present even in a lottery. They are there, too, in electing a High Priest only from a certain family. But granting that, a lottery attempts to deal equally among all candidates accepted as appropriate within a given context. Despite all of Josephus's tendentious rhetoric, what the Zealots did is quite clear and consistent. They restored the ancient Zadokite line according to selection by lot, and one presumes, of course, that such was to be the future mode of selection as well. Furthermore, this was probably more than just a new or legitimate High Priest. It was also, at least as far as the Zealots were concerned, a new and legitimate government of the city and the country. For those peasants, then, the idea of egalitarianism, even if not in its most radical form, was quite understandable and practicable.

Radical egalitarianism is not contemporary democracy. In the United States, for example, every appropriate person has a vote *in electing* the president, but although every appropriate person has also a legitimate right *to be* president, we are not yet ready for a national lottery instead of a presidential campaign. The open commensality and radical egalitarianism of Jesus' Kingdom of God are more terrifying than anything we have ever imagined, and even if we can never accept it, we should not explain it away as something else. I conclude, then, by putting Jesus' vision and program back into the matrix from which it sprang, the ancient and universal peasant dream of a just and equal world. These are the words of an unnamed peasant woman from Piana dei Greci, in the province of Palermo, Sicily, speaking to a northern Italian journalist during an 1893 peasant uprising:

> We want everybody to work, as we work. There should no longer be either rich or poor. All should have bread for themselves and for their children. We should all be equal. To have five small children and only one little room, where we have to eat and sleep and do everything, while so many lords have ten or twelve rooms, entire palaces. . . . It will be enough to put all in common and to share with justice what is produced.[5]

NOTES:

1. Peter Farb and George Armelagos, *Consuming Passions: The Anthropology of Eating* (Boston: Houghton Mifflin, 1980), pages 4 and 211.

2. Lee Edward Klosinksi, *The Meals in Mark* (Ann Arbor, Mich. University Microfilms, 1988), pages 56–58.

3. Pierre Bourdieu, "The Sentiment of Honour in Kabyle Society," in *Honour and Shame: The Values of Mediterranean Society*, ed. John G. Peristiany (Chicago: Univ. of Chicago Press, 1966; Midway Reprints, 1974), pages 211–212.

4. James C. Scott, "Protest and Profanation: Agrarian

Revolt and the Little Tradition," *Theory and Society* 4
(1977): 225–226.
5. Cited in Eric J. Hobsbawm, *Primitive Rebels: Studies in
Archaic Forms of Social Movement in the 19th and 20th
Centuries* (New York: Norton, 1965), page 183.

Building Global Justice

from *Sojourners* (6/12/04)

Jim Wallis

Good Morning.

I am grateful to the graduates for the opportunity to
address you today on this great occasion. My title is
"Building Global Justice" or "We Are the Ones We Have
Been Waiting For."

Let me begin with a story, about another occasion when
I was invited to speak—not for the Baccalaureate address
at a major university, but for the inmates at Sing Sing
Prison in upstate New York. The invitation letter came
from the prisoners themselves and it sounded like a good
idea. So I wrote back asking when they wanted me to
come. In his return letter, the young Sing Sing resident
replied, "Well, we're free most nights! We're kind of a captive audience here." Arrangements were made, and the
prison officials were very generous in giving us a room
deep in the bowels of that infamous prison facility—just
me and about eighty guys for four hours. I will never
forget what one of those young prisoners said to me that
night, "Jim, all of us at Sing Sing are from only about five

neighborhoods in New York City. It's like a train. You get on the train when you are about nine or ten years old. And the train ends up here at Sing Sing." Many of these prisoners were students too, studying in a very unique program of the New York Theological Seminary to obtain their Master of Divinity degree—behind the walls of the prison. They graduated when their sentences were up (of course, none of you feel that way). Here's what that young man at Sing Sing told me he would do upon his graduation: "When I get out, I'm going to go back and stop that train." Now that is exactly the kind of faith and hope we desperately need today from the graduates of Sing Sing, and the graduates of Stanford.

When I was growing up, it was continually repeated in my evangelical Christian world that the greatest battle and biggest choice of our time was between belief and secularism. But I now believe that the real battle, the big struggle of our times, is the fundamental choice between cynicism and hope. The choice between cynicism and hope is ultimately a spiritual choice; and one which has enormous political consequences.

More than just a moral issue; hope is a spiritual and even religious choice. Hope is not a feeling; it is a decision. And the decision for hope is based upon what you believe at the deepest levels—what your most basic convictions are about the world and what the future holds—all based upon your faith. You choose hope, not as a naïve wish, but as a choice, with your eyes wide open to the reality of the world—just like the cynics who have not made the decision for hope.

And the realities of our world are these: almost half the world, close to 3 billion people, live on less than two dollars a day; and more than 1 billion live on less than one dollar a day. And every day, thirty thousand children die needlessly due to utterly preventable causes like hunger, disease, and things like the lack of safe drinking water—things we could change if we ever decided to.

For the first time in history we have the information, knowledge, technology, and resources to bring the worst of global poverty virtually to an end. What we don't have is the moral and political will to do so. And it is becoming clear that it will take a new moral energy to create that political will.

Malcolm Gladwell in his best-selling book, *The Tipping Point*, talks of how an idea, product, or behavior moves from the edges of a society to broad acceptance, consumption, or practice. Along the way there is a "tipping point" that transforms a minority perception to a majority embrace. Today, a sizable and growing number of individuals and institutions have identified the deep chasm of global poverty as their central moral concern and have made significant commitments to overcome the global apathy that leads to massive suffering and death. But we have not yet reached the tipping point—when the world demands solutions. I believe the religious communities of the world could provide the "tipping point" in the struggle to eliminate the world's most extreme poverty.

The most astute observers of the issue now realize that only a new moral, spiritual, and even religious sensibility, in relation to the problems of global poverty, will enable us to reach that critical tipping point. Even some of the world's political leaders who are focused on this question (whether they themselves are religious or not), are coming to realize the need for a moral imperative.

In a 2004 speech to a conference of mostly faith-based development agencies in the UK, British Chancellor of the Exchequer Gordon Brown, gave a sobering report on how the world was failing to keep the promises of the United Nations Millennium Development Goals in the crucial areas of education, health, and targeted poverty reduction. Despite the commitments made by 147 nations to cut extreme poverty in half by the year 2015, global progress is significantly behind schedule. As to the causes of the thirty thousand infant deaths which still occur each day in the poorest parts of the world, Brown pointed to our moral apathy, "And let us be clear: it is not that the knowledge to avoid these infant deaths does not exist; it is not that the drugs to avoid infant deaths do not exist; it is not that the expertise does not exist; it is not that the means to achieve our goals do not exist. It is that the political will does not exist. In the nineteenth century you could say that it was inadequate science, technology and knowledge that pre-vented us saving lives. Now, with the science, technology and knowledge available, we must face the truth that the real barrier is indifference."

New options for public life, and even political policy choices, can be inspired by our best moral and religious traditions; especially when present options are failing some fundamental ethical tests. The eighth-century Micah has become my favorite prophet of national and global security. Listen to his prescriptions:

> He shall judge between many peoples, and shall arbitrate between strong nations far away; they shall beat their swords into plowshares, and their spears into pruning hooks; nation shall not lift up

sword against nation, neither shall they learn war
any more; but they shall all sit under their own
vines and under their own fig trees, and no one
shall make them afraid.

Micah is saying, you simply cannot and will not beat
"swords into plowshares" (remove the threats of war)
until people can "sit under their own vines and fig
trees" (have some share in global security). Only then
will you remove the fear that leads inextricably to conflict and violence.

Several millennia later, Pope Paul VI paraphrased
Micah when he said: "If you want peace, work for justice."
The prophet's insight is that the possibilities for peace, for
avoiding war, even for defeating terrorism, depend also
upon everyone having enough for their own security—
having a little vine and fig tree. The wisdom of Micah is
both prophetic and practical for a time like this. If the
tremendous gaps on our planet could be leveled out just a
little, nobody would have to be so afraid. Anglican Arch-
bishop Rowan Williams says it well, "There is no security
apart from common security." The developed world will
never be secure until the developing world also achieves
some economic security; America will not be safe until the
injustice and despair that fuel the murderous agendas of
terrorists has finally been addressed.

Poverty is not the only cause of terrorism; it's more
complicated than that with roots that are also religious,
cultural, and ideological. But unless we drain the swamps
of injustice in which the mosquitoes of terrorism breed,
we will never overcome the terrorist threat.

Micah is pleading with us to go deeper, to the resentments

and the angers, the insecurities and injustices embedded in the very structures of the world today.

Micah knew we will not overcome violence until everyone has their own vine and fig tree—their own little piece of the global economy, their own small stake in the world, their own share of security for themselves and their families. Because when you have a little patch upon which to build a life, nobody can make you afraid. And it is fear that leads to violence. That spiritual reality is truer today than ever before. Our weapons cannot finally protect us; only a world where most people feel secure will truly be safe for us and our children.

There are voices rising up in our world that sound like Micah. I believe they are modern day prophets, often coming from unexpected places. One is the most famous rock singer in the world, the leader of the Irish band U2. Of course, I'm speaking of Bono, who has become a serious and well-informed activist, talking always about Africa and HIV/AIDS. Bono is a spiritual man, though not a churchy person, and often comes to Washington D.C.

Bono spoke at the Africare dinner in Washington, to fifteen hundred of the capitol's leaders and media. "Excuse me if I'm a little nervous," Bono apologized, "but I'm not used to speaking to less than twenty thousand people!" Then he spoke like a preacher.

"So you've been doing God's work, but what's God working on now? What's God working on this year? Two and a half million Africans are going to die of AIDS. What's God working on now? I meet the people who tell me it's going to take an act of God to stop this plague. Well, I don't believe that. I think God is waiting for us to act. In fact, I think that God is on His knees to us. . . . waiting for us to turn around this supertanker of indifference . . . waiting for us to recognize that distance can no longer decide who is our neighbor. We can't choose our neighbors anymore. We can't choose the benefits of globalization without some of the responsibilities, and we should remind ourselves that 'love thy neighbor' is not advice: it is a command." I can hear the tones of Micah in the voice of Bono and also in Gordon Brown. Now at the beginning of a new century and millennium, I see a new generation of young activists coming of age and committing themselves to build global justice.

A rock star, a Chancellor, and young people across the world are all talking about globalization, HIV/AIDS, and reducing global poverty—and all in the prophetic voice of Micah. I am convinced that global poverty reduction will not be accomplished without a spiritual engine, and that history is changed by social movements with a spiritual foundation. That's what's always made the difference—abolition of slavery, women's suffrage, civil rights—they were social movements, but they had a spiritual foiundation.

This will be no different.

So let's turn to you, the graduates. You are a bright, gifted, and committed group of students. There are probably many people who tell you about your potential, and they are right. You are people who could make a real contribution to a movement for global justice.

In that regard, I would encourage each of you to think about your vocation more than just your career. And there is a difference. From the outside, those two tracks may look very much alike, but asking the vocational question rather than just considering the career options will take you much deeper. The key is to ask why you might take one path instead of another—the real reasons you would do something more than just because you can. The key is to ask who you really are and want to become. It is to ask what you believe you are supposed to do.

Religious or not, I would invite you to consider your calling, more than just the many opportunities presented to graduates of Stanford University. That means connecting your best talents and skills to your best and deepest values; making sure your mind is in sync with your soul as you plot your next steps. Don't just go where you're directed or even invited, but rather where your own moral compass leads you. And don't accept others' notions of what is possible or realistic; dare to dream things and don't be afraid to take risks.

You do have great potential, but that potential will be most fulfilled if you follow the leanings of conscience and the language of the heart more than just the dictates of the market, whether economic or political. They want smart people like you to just manage the systems of the world. But rather than managing or merely fitting into systems, ask how you can change them. You're both smart and talented enough to do that. That's your greatest potential. Ask where your gifts intersect with the groaning needs of the world.

The antidote to cynicism is not optimism but action. And action is finally born out of hope. Try to remember that.

One of the best street organizers I ever met was Lisa Sullivan. Lisa was a young African-American woman from Washington D.C., a smart kid from a working class family who went to Yale and earned a Ph.D. But Lisa felt called back to the streets and the forgotten children of color who

had won her heart. With unusual intelligence and entre-
preneurial skills she was in the process of creating a new
network and infrastructure of support for the best youth
organizing projects up and down the east coast. But at the
age of forty, Lisa died suddenly of a rare heart ailment.

Lisa's legacy is continuing though countless young
people who she inspired, challenged, and mentored. But
there is one thing she often said to them and to all of us
that has stayed with me ever since Lisa died. When people
would complain, as they often do, that we don't have any
leaders today, or ask where are the Martin Luther Kings
now?—Lisa would get angry. And she would declare these
words: "We are the ones we have been waiting for!" Lisa
was a person of faith. And hers was a powerful call to leadership and responsibility and a deep affirmation of hope.

Lisa's words are the commission I want to give to you.
It's a commission learned by every person of faith and
conscience who has been used to build movements of
spiritual and social change. It's a commission that is quite
consistent with the virtue of humility, because it is not
about taking ourselves too seriously; but rather taking
the commission seriously. It's a commission that can
only be fulfilled by very human beings, but people who,
because of faith and hope, believe that the world can be
changed. And it is that very belief that only changes the
world. And if not us, who will believe? If not you, who?
After all, we are the ones that we have been waiting for.

What is really possible? The eleventh chapter of the book
of Hebrews says this: "Now faith is the substance of things
hoped for, the evidence of things not seen." And my best
paraphrase of that for you is this: Hope is believing in spite
of the evidence, and then watching the evidence change.

Stanford graduates; you are the ones we have been waiting for.

Let's give Micah the last word—something to take away with you as you leave from this place and for every step of your journey.

"What does the Lord require of you, but to do justice, love kindness, and walk humbly with your God."

Thank you and God bless you.

"It must be wonderful for President Bush to deplore class warfare while making sure his class wins."

—William Sloane Coffin, from *Credo*

Americans threatened by change often seek solace in an angry version of religion. Such religion invents scapegoats, while over-looking the real forces that undermine traditional communities.

from *What's the Matter with Kansas?* (2004)
Thomas Frank

One thing unites all these different groups of Kansans, these millionaires and trailer-park dwellers, these farmers and thrift-store managers and slaughterhouse workers and utility executives: they are almost all Republicans. Meatpacking Garden City voted

FROM *WHAT'S THE MATTER WITH KANSAS?*

for George W. Bush in even greater numbers than did affluent Johnson County. The blue-collar, heavily union-ized city of Wichita used to be one of the few Democratic strongholds in the state; in the nineties it became one of the most consistently conservative places of them all, a mighty fortress in the wars over abortion, evolution, loose interpretation of the Constitution, and water fluoridation.

Not too long ago, Kansas would have responded to the current situation by making the bastards pay. This would have been a political certainty, as predictable as what happens when you touch a match to a puddle of gasoline. When business screwed the farmers and the workers—when it implemented monopoly strategies invasive beyond the Populists' furthest imaginings—when it ripped off shareholders and casually tossed thousands out of work—you could be damned sure about what would follow.

Not these days. Out here the gravity of discontent pulls in only one direction: to the right, to the right, farther to the right. Strip today's Kansans of their job security, and they head out to become registered Republicans. Push them off their land, and next thing you know they're protesting in front of abortion clinics. Squander their life savings on manicures for the CEO, and there's a good chance they'll join the John Birch Society. But ask them about the remedies their ancestors proposed (unions, antitrust, public ownership), and you might as well be referring to the days when knighthood was in flower.

The ills described here—depopulation, the rise of the food trust, the general reorganization of life to favor the wealthy—have been going on for ten to twenty years now. Nobody denies that they have happened, that they're still happening. Yet Kansas, that famous warrior for justice, how does it react? Why, Kansas looks its problems straight in the eye, sets its jaw, rolls up its sleeves—and charges off in exactly the wrong direction.

It's not that Kansas isn't angry; rage is a bumper crop here, and Kansas has produced enough fury to give every man, woman, and child in the country apoplexy. The state is in rebellion. The state is up in arms. It's just that the arms are all pointing away from the culprit.

Kansans just don't care about economic issues, gloats Republican senator Sam Brownback, a man who believes the cause of poverty is spiritual rather than "mechanistic." Kansans have set their sights on grander things, like the purity of the nation. Good wages, fair play in farm country, the fate of the small town, even the one we live in—all these are a distant second to evolution, which we will strike from the books, and public education, which we will undermine in a hundred inventive ways.

Hear as our leaders square off against the issues of the day. What afflicts us is a "crisis of the soul," wails Wichita congressman Todd Tiahrt. What motivates us, says a leader of the state's largest anti-abortion group, is disgust with the "immoral decadence in society." "We in America and we here in Kansas are in a moral crisis," thunders the state's conservative Galahad, David Miller, to his army of followers. What we need is to become "virtuous," as per the founding fathers' clear instructions; for if we fail, "our entire culture may be lost." And from the heights of Capitol Hill the great Brownback denounces gangsta rap, inveighs against stem-cell research, and proposes that the U.S. Senate hold hearings to investigate America's "cultural decline."

The state's strategy for waging this war for America's soul has been blunt and direct: Kansas has trawled its churches for the most aggressively pious individuals it could find and has proceeded to elevate them to the most prominent positions of public responsibility available, whence these saintly emissaries are then expected to bark and howl and rebuke the world for its sins. "I'm a Christian," the leader of the Wyandotte County GOP once told a reporter by way of explaining his political plans. "Primarily my goal is to build the Kingdom of God."

And thus we have, as U.S. representative from central Kansas, the legendary track star Jim Ryun, who says he ran for office because God wanted him to and is glad to tell reporters the exact date in 1972 when he "became a Christian." Ryun once thrilled his followers at a campaign event by speaking in tongues, and in 1995 he published an article describing the hyperprotective social order he imposes upon his female children:

> If a young man is interested in a young woman, he starts by praying about the relationship. With a go-ahead from the Lord and his parents, he then approaches the girl's parents. The parents pray and, if the young woman has a reciprocal interest in the young man, her father talks through courtship and its expectations with the fellow.

The young man has by now received two separate green lights from the Almighty, but it's still not enough for courtship to commence. Next he must demonstrate to Jim's satisfaction that he is "spiritually and financially prepared to marry"—evidently Ryun has to see the money up front!

From Wichita comes Todd Tiahrt, a man notable mainly for his perfectly swooping hair, who campaigns

in the city's evangelical churches and peppers his conversation with biblical references. "What it's all about,"
the triumphant Tiahrt told the *Wichita Eagle* on the
occasion of his upset victory over the district's long-
standing Democratic Representative, is "bring[ing] America
back to God." Or, more accurately, scolding America for
its insufficient godliness. On three separate occasions in
1998 Tiahrt admonished the nation from the floor of
Congress for "losing its soul" by turning its back on
God and family values.

Where Tiahrt is fiery, Sam Brownback is thoughtful and
soft-spoken, the intellectual of the Kansas conservatives. If
speaking in tongues is Ryun's trademark, Brownback's sig-
nature gesture was the time he washed the feet, in the
manner of Jesus Christ, of an assistant who was leaving his
service.* While the Kansas conservative style generally features loud, sweaty campaigning at the most energetic and
antihierarchical sort of Protestant churches—charismatic,
Pentecostal, Assemblies of God—Brownback favors the
approach of the unhurried insider, the ultramontane,
even. In 2002 he converted to Catholicism under the
supervision of the Reverend John McCloskey, a leading
light of Opus Dei, the ultraconservative prelature
renowned for its role in the Franco regime in Spain. Nor is
Opus Dei the only right-wing quasi cult with which
Brownback has chosen to link himself. When in Washington, he lives in a town house operated by a Christian
group known as the Family or the Fellowship, whose mis-

---

* One seasoned Kansas political hand I spoke to called this incident "religious harassment." When "your boss says, 'take your shoes off,' what can
you do?"

sion seems to be bringing together American lawmakers with capitalists and dictators from around the world. And studying the leadership secrets of Hitler.

However bizarre such eruptions of zealotry might be, they are not enough by themselves to discredit these men. What makes the Kansas way so remarkable—and so dysfunctional—is that in each case the state's lawmakers combine this flamboyant public piety with a political agenda that only makes the state's material problems worse. Protestant fundamentalism, remember, is not necessarily friendly to big business; after all, it once gave the world William Jennings Bryan, who was widely regarded as being only a few steps shy of an anarchist. But even though Kansas is burning on a free-market pyre, each of the state leaders described here is as dedicated an apostle of the free-market doctrine as they are of the teachings of Jesus.

Each one, for example, receives high rankings from the U.S. Chamber of Commerce for his pro-business voting records. And each one has pledged himself to the sacred conservative causes of deregulating, dismantling government, and rolling back the welfare state. Jim Ryun, for example, may have built a wall around his daughters to protect them from our lascivious culture, but there is virtually no aspect of corporate orthodoxy that he has not internalized and endorsed. He has compared American economic policy of the pre-Reagan years to the Soviet Union and supported tax cuts for the rich on the grounds that the wealthy need incentives to keep on making their superhuman contributions to society. He supported the repeal of the estate tax on the delusional pretext that removing it would help family farms;* he expressed doubt about global warming; and he blamed the California electricity crisis not on deregulation but on "the state's political establishment," which "interfered with the free market." You can go right down the list, checking off the items one after another: Ryun's earnest Christianity causes not a single deviation from the big-business agenda that I have been able to detect.

Todd Tiahrt was a manager at Boeing before going to Congress, and he may be even more ferociously committed than Ryun to the nation's corporate brass. In Washington he is known mainly for his single-minded hostility to the Department of Energy. According to Wichita's remaining Democrats, it is his hostility to organized labor that distinguishes him. In 1992 the *Wichita Eagle* dryly summarized his views on nonreligious matters: Tiahrt "dislikes government in general" despite Boeing's massive reliance on government defense spending; he calls for "privatization of prisons, says that some people are poor because they are determined to be poor and describes social-welfare programs as inefficient." Four years later,

---

*The Republican push to repeal the estate tax was often presented as a way to help small farmers in a difficult time. But by far the greatest beneficiaries of the tax's repeal have been the very rich. Only a tiny percentage of the assets taxed each year under the estate tax were farm properties, and one agricultural economist from Iowa State declared in 2001 that, even after studying the subject for thirty-five years, he had encountered not a single case in which a family had lost its farm due to the estate tax. "The problem is farm income and corporate concentration," wrote one Missouri farmer in an eloquent essay on the subject. "The estate tax isn't even on the radar screen of farm policy fixes that family farmers are fighting for."

the paper noted that this moral crusader had become the toast of corporate Wichita. When Koch Industries, a Wichita oil and gas concern that funds right-wing magazines and think tanks in addition to politicians, held a fund-raiser for Tiahrt, the newspaper seemed surprised at how far this young man with the common touch had come. "He's one of the new style of Republican conservatives," the paper pointed out. "His social views are what most people talk about. But his thinking on economics is what company officials are more interested in. Tiahrt is stridently pro-business, deeply suspicious of government, convinced Big Brother is lurking behind volumes and volumes of government regulations."

Of the bunch, though, it is Sam Brownback, a member of one of the wealthiest families in the state, who has done the most distinguished service to God and mammon both. Admirers of Saint Sam will tell you about the much-publicized frugality of his D.C. lifestyle and refer you to his high-profile wars against human cloning and in support of persecuted Christians in third-world countries. They would also do well to examine the peculiar series of events that propelled Brownback into public life back in 1993. At the time Brownback was laboring in obscurity as Kansas secretary of agriculture, a position of little note but considerable power that he had held since 1986. Which is not to say that Brownback was elected agriculture secretary, or even appointed agriculture secretary by someone who was elected. At the time, the state's Department of Agriculture was a curious nineteenth-century throwback that did not answer to the people at all; Brownback had been chosen for the post by the state's largest agricultural interests—by the heads of the very industry he was charged with overseeing. For example, when he made limits on dangerous herbicides voluntary, Brownback was acting as a government regulator, but the kind of regulator conservatives approve of, the kind who answers to private industry instead of the public. Unfortunately, the cozy world of Kansas agriculture was turned on its head by a lawsuit pointing out the unconstitutionality of the whole arrangement, and Brownback was forced to make his way in the world by other means.

As a leader of the "freshman class" of Republican congressmen elected in 1994, Brownback played the role of the principled outsider, working out of a tiny office where he had scrawled the amount of the national debt on a whiteboard, and endlessly, tirelessly denouncing the role of big PAC money in politics. He even wrote a pious meditation distinguishing ambition of the spiritual variety from the sinful, worldly ambition that often tempted members of Congress.

Before long, though, Brownback found that the two varieties of ambition could complement each other nicely. In his 1996 campaign for the U.S. Senate, he was materially assisted by a shadowy corporate front-group called Triad Management Services, which poured sufficient last-minute money into the race to drown out the messages of his foe. Brownback celebrated the resulting victory at a reception sponsored by the U.S. Telecom Association, a powerful lobbying group for an industry whose deregulatory agenda the senator would advance diligently in the years to come. Along the way he learned to appreciate the virtue of big PAC money in politics, even finding a reason to vote against the McCain-Feingold campaign finance reform measure.

FROM *WHAT'S THE MATTER WITH KANSAS?*

So it is with Sam Brownback right down the line: a man of sterling public principle, he seems to take the side of corporate interests almost regardless of the issues at hand. This is true even when the corporate interests in question are industries whose products Brownback considers the source of all evil. Such, at least, was the case in 2003, when one of Brownback's Senate committees was called upon to consider the growing problem of monopoly ownership in radio since the industry's deregulation seven years previously. Brownback, of course, has made a career out of denouncing the culture industry for its vulgarity, its bad values, presumably for the damage it has done to America's soul. Taking this opportunity to rein it in should have been a no-brainer. After all, as the industry critic Robert McChesney points out, the link between media ownership, the drive for profit, and the media's insulting content should be obvious to anyone with ears to hear. "Vulgarity is linked to corporate control and highly concentrated, only semi-competitive markets," McChesney says. And for many conservatives, "the radio fight was the moment of truth. If people are seriously concerned about vulgarity, this was their chance to prove it." For that reason, McChesney notes, certain right-wing culture warriors were happy to join the fight against further relaxation of radio ownership rules. But Brownback was not one of them. Faced with a choice between protecting corporate profits and actually doing something about the open cultural sewer he has spent his career deploring, Brownback chose the former. Deregulation is always for the better, he insisted, and he even proceeded to scold the witnesses *criticizing* the industry for acting out of—get this—*self-interest*. The free-market system is inviolable, in other words, even when it's that branch of the system that you spend all your time campaigning against for coarsening our lives and leading us away from God. In Kansas, mammon always comes first.

Mixing culture war and capitalism is not just a personal quirk shared by these three individuals; it is writ in the very manifesto of the Kansas conservative movement, the platform of the state Republican Party for 1998. Moaning that "the signs of a degenerating society are all around us," railing against abortion and homosexuality and gun control and evolution ("a theory, not a fact"), the document went on to propound a list of demands as friendly to plutocracy as anything ever dreamed up by Monsanto or Microsoft. The platform called for:

- A flat tax or national sales tax to replace the graduated income tax (in which the rich pay more than the poor).
- The abolition of taxes on capital gains (that is, on money you make when you sell stock).
- The abolition of the estate tax.
- No "governmental intervention in health care."
- The eventual privatization of Social Security.
- Privatization in general.
- Deregulation in general and "the operation of the free market system without government interference."
- The turning over of all federal lands to the states.
- A prohibition on "the use of taxpayer dollars to fund any election campaign."

Along the way the document specifically endorsed the disastrous Freedom to Farm Act, condemned agricultural

price supports, and came out in favor of making soil con-
servation programs "voluntary," perhaps out of nostalgia
for the Dust Bowl days, when Kansans learned a healthy
fear of the Almighty.

Let us pause for a moment to ponder this all-American dys-
function. A state is spectacularly ill-served by the Reagan-
Bush stampede of deregulation, privatization, and
laissez-faire. It sees its countryside depopulated, its towns
disintegrate, its cities stagnate—and its wealthy enclaves
sparkle, behind their remote-controlled security gates. The
state erupts in revolt, making headlines around the world
with its bold defiance of convention. But what do its rebels
demand? More of the very measures that have brought
ruination on them and their neighbors in the first place.

This is not just the mystery of Kansas; this is the mystery of America, the historical shift that has made it all
possible.

In Kansas the shift is more staggering than elsewhere,
simply because it has been so decisive, so extreme. The
people who were once radical are now reactionary.
Though they speak today in the same aggrieved language
of victimization, and though they face the same array of
economic forces as their hard-bitten ancestors, today's
populists make demands that are precisely the opposite.
Tear down the federal farm programs, they cry. Privatize
the utilities. Repeal the progressive taxes. All that Kansas
asks today is a little help nailing itself to that cross of gold.

JESUS IS NOT A SINGLE-ISSUE VOTER

An Open Letter to Religious Leaders
on Abortion as a Moral Decision
BY THE RELIGIOUS INSTITUTE FOR SOCIAL MORALITY,
JUSTICE, AND HEALING—229

We don't have his views on abortion, but we know he hoped to reduce human suffering. We also know that there are some 46 million abortions around the world each year. Roe v. Wade isn't the reason: Most abortions are in fact illegal. Anyone who truly hopes to reduce the number of abortions should try to reduce the number of unwanted pregnancies, using every tool at hand.

The most effective tools include condoms and sex education—which many opponents of legal abortion in this country oppose. Other tools include economic development and social justice programs aimed at lifting people out of poverty, with its attendant miseries such as illness, hunger and sexual exploitation. Many Republicans who rail against legal abortion refuse to support such programs.

Abortion poses important moral questions. We are wise to debate them carefully, bearing in mind that any policy we pursue may cause suffering.

An Open Letter to Religious Leaders on Abortion as a Moral Decision (2005)

by The Religious Institute on Sexual Morality, Justice, and Healing

A s religious leaders, we are committed to supporting people's efforts to achieve spiritual, emotional, and physical well-being, including their reproductive and sexual health. We assist women and families confronted with unintended pregnancies or pregnancies that can no longer be carried to term. We are committed to social justice, mindful of the 46 million women worldwide who have an abortion each year, almost half in dangerous and illegal situations. We seek to create a world where abortion is safe, legal, accessible, and rare.

Millions of people ground their moral commitment to the right to choose in their religious beliefs. While there are strong public health and human rights arguments for supporting the right of women to safe and legal abortion, here we invite you to consider the religious foundations for affirming abortion as a morally justifiable decision.

AFFIRMING WOMEN'S MORAL AGENCY

Abortion is always a serious moral decision. It can uphold and protect the life, health, and future of the woman, her partner, and the family. We affirm women as moral agents who have the capacity, right and responsibility to make the decision as to whether or not abortion is justified in their specific circumstances. That decision is best made when it includes a well-informed conscience, serious reflection, insights from her faith and values, and consultation with a

JESUS IS NOT A SINGLE-ISSUE VOTER

caring partner, family members, and spiritual counselor. Men have a moral obligation to acknowledge and support women's decision-making.

RESPECT FOR LIFE

Our religious traditions affirm that life is sacred. Our faiths celebrate the divinely bestowed blessings of generating life and assuring that life can be sustained and nurtured. Religious traditions have different beliefs on the value of fetal life, often according greater value as fetal development progresses. Science, medicine, law, and philosophy contribute to this understanding. However, we uphold the teaching of many religious traditions: the health and life of the woman must take precedence over the life of the fetus. The sanctity of human life is best upheld when we assure that it is not created carelessly. It is precisely because life and parenthood are so precious that no woman should be coerced to carry a pregnancy to term. We support responsible procreation, the widespread availability of contraception, prenatal care and intentional parenting.

SCRIPTURE

Scripture neither condemns nor prohibits abortion. It does, however, call us to act compassionately and justly when facing difficult moral decisions. Scriptural commitment to the most marginalized means that pregnancy, childbearing, and abortion should be safe for all women. Scriptural commitment to truth-telling means women must have accurate information as they make their decisions.

MORAL IMPERATIVE FOR ACCESS

The ability to choose an abortion should not be compromised by economic, educational, class or marital status, age, race, geographic location or inadequate information. Current measures that limit women's access to abortion services—by denying public funds for low-income women; coercing parental consent and notification as contrasted with providing resources for parental and adolescent counseling; denying international family planning assistance to agencies in developing countries that offer women information about pregnancy options; and banning medical procedures—are punitive and do nothing to promote moral decision-making. When there is a conflict between the conscience of the provider and the woman, the institution delivering the services has an obligation to assure that the woman's conscience and decision will be respected and that she has access to reproductive health care, either directly or through referral. We condemn physical and verbal violence and harassment directed against abortion clinics, their staffs, and their clients.

We must work together to reduce unintended and unwanted pregnancies and address the circumstances that result in the decision to have an abortion. Poverty, social inequities, ignorance, sexism, racism, and unsupportive relationships may render a woman virtually powerless to choose freely. We call for a religious and moral commitment to reproductive health and rights; there must be access to comprehensive sexuality education and contraception, including emergency contraception.

RELIGIOUS PLURALISM
No government committed to human rights and democracy can privilege the teachings of one religion over another. No single religious voice can speak for all faith traditions on abortion, nor should government take sides on religious differences. Women must have the right to apply or

reject the principles of their own faith without legal restrictions. We oppose any attempt to make specific religious doctrine concerning abortion the law for all Americans or for the women of the world.

A Call to Religious Leaders

Religious leaders have been in the forefront of the movement for abortion rights for more than fifty years. We call on leaders of all faiths to prepare themselves to offer counsel compassionately, competently, and justly to individuals and families faced with pregnancy decisions. We urge them to:

- advise and assist adolescent women in involving parents and family members in their decisions, while acknowledging that not every family can offer this support;
- provide age-appropriate faith-based sexuality education that underscores the importance of planned childbearing and responsible sexual decision-making, including abstinence;
- encourage parents to talk openly and honestly about sexuality with their own children;
- counsel women facing pregnancy decisions to reflect, pray, examine their own conscience and faith, and talk with partners and family members;
- support with love to those who choose adoption or termination of their pregnancies, including providing worship opportunities for those who seek them to mourn losses from miscarriages, stillbirths, and abortions;

- provide financial and emotional support for those women who carry their pregnancies to term and provide loving community for them after birth;
- publicly advocate for reproductive rights— including sexuality education, contraception, prenatal care, adoption, and abortion—through sermons, public witness, and involvement in the political process.

IN CLOSING

More than thirty years ago, many religious denominations passed courageous resolutions in support of women's moral agency and their right to a safe and legal abortion. Despite numerous legal challenges and social, scientific and medical advances, we reaffirm this theological commitment: women must be able to make their own moral decisions based on conscience and faith. We call for increased dialogue and respectful listening with those who disagree with us. With them, we share the vision of a world where all children are loved and wanted. We renew our own call for relational and reproductive justice for all.

JESUS IS NOT A THEOCRAT

*with quotations from Randall Terry, William Sloane Coffin,
George H. W. Bush and Jerry Falwell;
and cartoons by Pat Oliphant*

Jesus offered a model of how to govern our lives as individuals. He did not leave a coherent model of political governance. Anyone who invents a Christian government must draw upon scraps of religious dogma—and there is no telling which scraps he or she will stress. Theocrats among us back up their agendas with Gospel passages that portray a self-important and intolerant Jesus. Their Jesus is an invention of the early Christians, who had their own emotional and political agendas.

Bush Plays Pope on Gay Marriage

from *The Nation* (8/7/03)

Robert Scheer

I agree with the president and the pope: Marriage is a very serious endeavor, not to be trifled with. Just ask any of the tens of millions of divorced parents who are tied together for life in a precarious, often combative attempt to raise their kids well in separate households.

Done right, marriage—or "civil unions" if the M word is too loaded—can be a bridge to loyalty, sexual stability, shared financial responsibility and the more efficient rearing of children. All the more reason, then, to support anybody, gay or straight, who wants to commit to a lifelong union. Whether you are united in "holy matrimony" or simply trying to build a lasting relationship should be of no concern to the state, nor should your sexual orientation.

Where I differ from the president and the pope is in defining marriage in religious terms. Under the U.S. Constitution, after all, church is clearly separated from state, and thus marriage is a civic institution not in any way requiring the participation of religious organizations. Government policies favor the family unit. If the state is offering special rights and benefits for those couples who marry, then to exclude gays is simply unconstitutional.

In Germany, France, Canada and Vermont, state-sanctioned unions help gay couples clarify the legal status and rights of their partnership in everything from bank accounts to hospital visitation to child custody. For gays seeking these rights elsewhere, this is primarily a practical struggle, and it is wrong for the president to exploit it for political purposes.

The drive for gay marriage is also an affirmation of responsible love, and it is bizarre that this honorable impulse could be blocked on the basis of someone else's religious views. The desire of two people to commit to some shared order in their lives, presumably reinforcing notions of sexual monogamy, has particular relevance in the gay community, which has paid an enormous price for promiscuity. It is also a community riven by the loss of loved ones in which a partner's rights to share in managing grief have been painfully challenged when a mate faces death.

It is one thing for the pope, a religious leader, to oppose gay marriage based on the theology that "homosexual acts go against the natural moral order." But the president of the United States, as the highest official in our secular government, is overstepping his bounds mightily when he lectures about "sin" and "the sanctity of marriage."

"I believe a marriage is between a man and a woman. And I think we ought to codify that one way or another," Bush said last week, seizing upon a question about homosexuality that didn't mention marriage. "And we've got lawyers looking at the best way to do that."

Well, lawyers can do just about anything with the law to make their case, but it is hoped that most judges will have read the Constitution and seen that it says nothing about merging church and state.

What the president didn't mention was that the U.S. high court finally has acknowledged that homosexuality is not a threat to public order, striking down discriminatory anti-sodomy laws in Texas.

BUSH PLAYS POPE ON GAY MARRIAGE

If homosexual sex is legal, it doesn't matter if our born-again president believes it's a sin on the grounds that it offends his or anyone else's interpretation of Christian Scripture.

Ironically, in the same press session in which Bush acted as if our nation is a Christian theocracy, he applauded Iraq's faltering steps toward a secular society that would break with Islamic dictates. He even mentioned the prospect of an Iraqi Thomas Jefferson emerging to show those folks how to go about building a free society.

But Jefferson was an awkward choice for Bush because he was as responsible as any of the founders for the very notion of the separation of church and state. As a public man, Jefferson even resisted identifying himself as Christian, being, as he wrote, "averse to the communication of my religious tenets to the public because it would seduce public opinion to erect itself into that inquisition over the rights of conscience, which the laws have so justly proscribed."

And, as the Supreme Court has clearly stated, being gay, even in Bush's home state of Texas, is one of those rights of conscience.

*"I want you to just let a wave of intoler-
ance wash over you. I want you to let a
wave of hatred wash over you. Yes, hate is
good . . . Our goal is a Christian nation. We
have a biblical duty, we are called on by
God to conquer this country. We don't want
equal time. We don't want pluralism."*
—Randall Terry, founder of the militant anti-
abortion group Operation Rescue, as quoted
by the Fort Wayne, Indiana *News Sentinel*,
8/16/93

W.'s Christian Nation
from *The American Prospect* (6/1/03)
Chris Mooney

In November of 1992, shortly after Bill Clinton was
elected president, a telling controversy arose at a
meeting of the Republican Governors Association. When a
reporter asked the governors how their party could both
satisfy the demands of Christian conservatives and also
maintain a broad political coalition, Mississippi's Kirk
Fordice took the opportunity to pronounce America a
"Christian nation." "The less we emphasize the Christian
religion," Fordice declared, "the further we fall into the

abyss of poor character and chaos in the United States of America." Jewish groups immediately protested Fordice's remarks; on CNN's *Crossfire*, Michael Kinsley asked whether Fordice would also call America a "white nation" because whites, like Christians, enjoy a popular majority. The incident was widely seen as exposing a rift between the divisive Pat Robertson wing of the GOP and the more moderate camp represented by then-president George Herbert Walker Bush.

Fast-forward a decade. Republicans have solved their internal problems, and the party is united under our most prayerful of presidents, the born-again believer George W. Bush. Though not originally the favored candidate of the religious right—John Ashcroft was—Bush has played the part well. Virtually his first presidential act was to proclaim a National Day of Prayer and Thanksgiving; soon he appointed Ashcroft to serve as attorney general. Since then the stream of religiosity from the White House has been continuous. With the help of evangelical speechwriter Michael Gerson, Bush lards his speeches with code words directed at Christian conservatives. In this year's State of the Union address, Bush mentioned the "wonder-working power" of the American people, an allusion to an evangelical Christian song whose lyrics cite the "power, wonder-working power, in the blood of the Lamb"—i.e., Jesus.

Bush also uses his office to promote marriage, charitable choice and school vouchers as conservative Christian policy objectives. Yet he has never endorsed, at least not explicitly, the time-honored religious-right claim that the United States is a Christian nation. Nor has he seconded Pat Robertson's cry that the separation of church and state is "a lie of the left." "There are a lot of libertarian

Republicans and business-oriented Republicans who would be really turned off by that sort of rhetoric," explains John C. Green, a political scientist at the University of Akron who specializes in religion and politics. Bush strategist Karl Rove, a political-history buff, presumably remembers the Fordice debacle.

But could Rove and Bush, through their diligent courting of the Christian right, be moving us toward a form of Christian nationhood anyway? To see what's new and dangerous about Bush's approach to religion, you have to look beyond the president's copious prayers and exhortations, which are legally meaningless. Clinton also showed immense political sympathy for religion, but he didn't nominate a slate of right-wing judges who could give the law a decidedly majoritarian, pro-Christian bent. And Bush has gone further than that. From school-prayer guidelines issued by the Department of Education to faith-based initiatives to directives from virtually every federal agency, there's hardly a place where Bush hasn't increased both the presence and the potency of religion in American government. In the process, the Bush administration lavishly caters to the very religious-right groups that gave us the dubious Christian-nation concept to begin with.

Consider Bush's faith-based initiative. In October 2002, the Department of Health and Human Services doled out $30 million to twenty-one religious and community groups as part of the faith-based program. Sure enough, $500,000 went to Pat Robertson's religious charity Operation Blessing. In addition, according to Americans United for Separation of Church and State, a grant of $700,000 went to the National Center for Faith-Based Initiative, founded by Bishop Harold Calvin Ray, who has declared church-state separation "a fiction." Another $2.2 million went to Dare Mighty Things, a group affiliated with Chuck Colson, a Watergate felon turned evangelist who tries to convert prison inmates to Christianity and has the ear of the Bush administration. All of the religious recipients of Health and Human Services grants were connected to Christian ministries, mostly evangelical ones.

These grant allocations suggest that while Bush may not say he's forging a Christian nation, at the very least he's blending church and state to fund Christianity. And Health and Human Services is just one government agency now engaged in promoting faith-based initiatives. Under Bush, notes Americans United Executive Director Barry Lynn, the departments of Justice, Housing and Urban Development, Health and Human Services and Education all "are issuing regulations, guidelines and other directives that promote religion." Bush has also placed influential religious-right figures in his administration. Consider a few little-noticed examples. David Caprara, the head of AmeriCorps* VISTA, directed the American Family Coalition, a faith-based social-action group affiliated with Sun Myung Moon's Unification Church. Kay Coles James, a staunch anti-abortionist who was formerly a dean at Pat Robertson's Regent University and senior vice president of the Family Research Council, is now director of the U.S. Office of Personnel Management, which monitors the federal workforce.

But the nexus of the religious right in the administration may be Ashcroft's Justice Department, which is well positioned to effect pro-Christian legal changes. Until recently, Carl Esbeck, who helped to draft the charitable-choice provisions of the 1996 welfare-reform legislation and directed the Center for Law and Religious Freedom at the conservative Christian Legal Society, headed the department's faith-based office. Over the years, Esbeck has been a leading lawyer and legal thinker involved in laying the intellectual groundwork for the Bush administration's current merging of church and state.

Something similar can be said of Eric Treene, formerly litigation director at the conservative Becket Fund for Religious Liberty, who was appointed in June 2002 to serve as the Justice Department's special counsel for religious discrimination, a newly created position. According to Yeshiva University law professor and church-state specialist Marci Hamilton, Treene has been "in the trenches of trying to get religious entities special privileges under the law." No wonder the conservative Christian group Faith and Action, which seeks to remind legislators about the "prominent role that the word of God played in the creation of our nation and its laws," celebrated Treene's appointment as "a new day for Christians in Washington."

So far Treene has proved responsive to groups seeking to amplify legal protections for Christians. For example, following a complaint by the archconservative Liberty Legal Institute of Plano, Texas, Treene headed an investigation of Texas Tech University biology professor Michael Dini, who had promulgated a policy requiring that students seeking medical-school letters of recommendation from him be able to "truthfully and forthrightly affirm a scientific answer" to the question, "How do you think the human species originated?" Despite the fact that recommendation writing is a voluntary activity, this was deemed discrimination against creationists. After Treene and the Justice Department opened their investigation, Dini changed his policy.

Treene also recently helped file a brief in a Massachusetts

district court case arguing that a high school had engaged in "viewpoint discrimination" when it refused to allow Christian students to pass out candy canes distributed with religious messages. This time the Justice Department drew upon work by the Alliance Defense Fund, a "unique Christian legal organization" based in Scottsdale, Arizona, that was founded by Focus on the Family's James Dobson and other religious-right leaders. So forget about counting the mentions of God in Bush's speeches; it's legal coordination between the Bush administration and the religious right that could truly cause Thomas Jefferson's wall of separation between church and state to crumble.

Even when working in the federal government and responding to Christian-right legal groups, however, lawyers can only go so far to make America more hospitable to Christianity. To achieve their objectives, Christian conservatives have long realized they need sympathetic judges on the bench as well—judges whose worldviews are suffused with religiosity. Judges, in short, such as Antonin Scalia.

In a January 2002 speech at the University of Chicago Divinity School, Scalia cited his religious views in order to defend the death penalty. He further argued that democracy has a tendency to "obscure the divine authority behind government"—a situation that people of faith should approach with "the resolution to combat it as effectively as possible." As Princeton University historian Sean Wilentz wrote in a *New York Times* critique, Scalia "seeks to abandon the intent of the Constitution's framers and impose views about government and divinity that no previous justice, no matter how conservative, has ever embraced."

Bush has explicitly stated that he sees Scalia and

Clarence Thomas as models for his judicial nominees. And
most of them do fit the mold. On the church-state front, the
most outrageous example is the nomination of Alabama
Attorney General Bill Pryor for a seat on the Eleventh U.S.
Circuit Court of Appeals. Pryor is notorious for his defense
of Alabama Chief Justice Roy Moore, who has steadily
fought to post the Ten Commandments in his courthouse.
Almost as troubling is University of Utah law professor
Michael McConnell, one of the intellectual giants behind
the "accommodationist" approach to the First Amendment's religion clauses, who was confirmed for a post on
the Tenth U.S. Circuit Court of Appeals. McConnell's exaggerated notion of religious free exercise led him to criticize
a 1983 U.S. Supreme Court ruling revoking Bob Jones University's tax-exempt status because of its ban on interracial
dating, which he dubbed a failure "to intervene to protect
religious freedom from the heavy hand of government."

Many of Bush's other judicial nominees, such as Miguel
Estrada and Priscilla Owen, have also been resolutely
championed by religious conservatives. "A few of [the
nominees] have specific histories on religion issues,"
explains People for the American Way legal director Elliot
Mincberg. But the religious right, he adds, is "smart
enough" to realize that conservative legal positions tend
to come together in one package.

Granted, in some sense the Bush administration is only
building upon previous legal and social trends that have
brought church and state closer. Despite our thoroughly
"godless" Constitution, as Cornell University scholars
Isaac Kramnick and R. Laurence Moore have put it, these
aren't very good days for strict church-state separation.
Over the past fifteen years, explains Vanderbilt University

law professor and First Amendment specialist Thomas McCoy, the Supreme Court has gradually modified its church-state jurisprudence, especially when it comes to whether government money can go to individuals who then choose whether to distribute it to religious organizations. Last term, the court used this "neutral aid" approach to uphold an Ohio voucher scheme, a ruling that would have been unthinkable three decades ago.

Simultaneously, religion has seeped into American political life, often on a bipartisan basis. Clinton, after all, signed into law a version of charitable choice as part of the 1996 welfare-reform bill. He held prayer meetings regularly and declared that an atheist could not be president of the United States (despite the Constitution's ban on religious tests for public office). Clinton's views on religion were shaped by Yale University law professor Stephen Carter's 1993 book, *The Culture of Disbelief*, which argued that American society had come to exclude the religious from public life, a wrong that required remedying. In a 2000 legal article, Yeshiva University's Marci Hamilton called Clinton "the most religiously activist President in history"—up until that point, anyway—and accused him of being "oblivious to [James] Madison's warnings that all entities, including religious entities, are likely to abuse their power in the political process."

Still, there were limits to Clinton's attempt to make government friendlier to religion. Consider Clinton's and Bush's starkly opposed approaches to the contentious issue of school prayer. In 1995, Clinton's Department of Education released a set of school-prayer guidelines based on a consensus document drafted by groups covering the political spectrum, from the liberal People for the American Way to the conservative Christian Legal Society. The guidelines sought a balance between the free exercise and establishment clauses of the First Amendment, noting that students may engage in private religious speech, including prayer, but cannot harass other students or direct speech at a captive audience. School employees, meanwhile, should neither discourage nor encourage such speech.

The Clinton guidelines were legally accurate and had a reputation for helping school districts. Nevertheless, this February the Bush Department of Education—headed by Rod Paige, who recently stumbled into a Fordice-style church-state brouhaha when he suggested that Christian schools instill better values than public ones—released a new set of school-prayer guidelines. This time liberal and moderate groups weren't consulted. But two leading religious-right figures, Jay Sekulow of Pat Robertson's American Center for Law and Justice and Ken Connor of the Family Research Council, claimed involvement in the drafting process.

The new guidelines advance a skewed picture of the law that favors the religious right. As the American Jewish Congress' Marc Stern protested in a letter to Paige, the guidelines "make no concession whatsoever to the rights of the captive audience" when it comes to school prayer, in the process misrepresenting the state of court rulings on the question. When it comes to church and state, "The Clinton people reached out to all segments, and really did attempt to work on consensus issues," says People for the American Way's Mincberg, who was involved in drafting the consensus statement that led to the Clinton prayer guidelines. "The Bush people are reaching out to their political allies only."

How much damage could Bush do in the long term? When it comes to the separation of church and state, one is always dealing with a slippery slope—the notion that government involvement with religion will make it easier for more government involvement with religion to occur. That is, after all, what the framers were trying to prevent. But provided that you're willing to think in these terms, the picture is fairly clear. "The goal here," says American United's Lynn, "is to erode the vitality of the church-state separation principle, to get a lot of judges in place who have trouble distinguishing between that which is illegal and that which is sinful, and to put in place regulations—and perhaps later statutes—that make it easier to require Americans to pay for the Christianization of the country."

That's the goal of Christian conservatives, anyway. Yet it may not be Bush's conscious objective. Although religiously devout, his highest calling is re-election. And as a source of fundraising, grassroots manpower and sheer votes, the religious right is crucial to that push. Karl Rove has explicitly stated that when it comes to turning out the white, evangelical Republican base in 2000, "There should have been 19 million of them, and instead there were 15 million of them. So 4 million of them did not turn out to vote."

"I don't think Bush has set out to reshape church and state relationships, but by doing the kind of politics that he's been doing, there are some strong implications," says the University of Akron's Green. Those implications were summarized, in their most radical form, by Pat Robertson in his 1992 book, *The New World Order*. There, Robertson wrote, "There will never be world peace until God's house and God's people are given their rightful place of leadership at the top of the world." America is certainly on top of the world, and with George W. Bush in the White House, religious conservatives are standing there with him.

11/5

"Did it turn out that by reason of the separation of church and state, the Jews were safer in Europe than they were in the United States of America? I don't think so." —Supreme Court Justice Antonin Scalia on the Holocaust, 11/04

VS.

"The National Government . . . regards Christianity as the foundation of our national morality, and the family as the basis of national life." —Adolf Hitler, 2/1/33

"History warns that the best is always a hair's breadth from the worst, and that heartless moralists in the corridors of power are those who start inquisitions."
—William Sloane Coffin, from *Credo (2003)*

Stacked Decalogue
from *The Nation* (9/22/03)
Katha Pollitt

The 5,300-pound hunk of granite carved with the Ten Commandments has been rolled out of Alabama Chief Justice Roy Moore's Montgomery courtroom to gather moss in an unspecified back room. According to a Gallup poll, 77 percent of Americans think the rock should have been allowed to remain; many are hopping mad at Alabama Attorney General William Pryor, only yesterday the darling of the religious right and the object of an ongoing Senate filibuster against his nomination to an appellate court, because Pryor reluctantly agreed to do his job and enforce a federal court order to have the monument removed. As *New York Times* columnist Nicholas Kristof loves to remind his readers, Americans are big believers— the virgin birth (83 percent), creationism (48 percent), the devil (68 percent). Forty-seven percent think the Antichrist is on earth *right now*. How many of these devotees, though, have actually read the Ten Commandments lately? There's a reason the laws inscribed on those stone tablets are often represented by Roman numerals or squiggles. As a vague wave in the direction of law and order, the Decalogue pops up in thousands of public places, including the Supreme Court building, where Moses shares a frieze with Hammurabi and Justinian. Spelled out in all their ancient splendor, though, the commandments are a decidedly odd set of directives to be looming, physically or spiritually, over an American courtroom.

Consider Commandment One: God identifies himself

as God—as if you didn't know! Who else crashes about with thunder and lightning? He reminds the Jews that he brought them out of Egypt and orders that "thou shalt have no other gods before me." What does that mean, exactly? No other gods, period, or no other gods come first? No other gods because they don't exist, or no other gods because they are minor and inferior and God doesn't like them? His need for constant reassurance is one of God's more perplexing characteristics. If you had created the universe and everything in it down to the seven-day week, would you care if people believed in you? Wouldn't it be enough that you knew you existed? Why can't God give anonymously? So what if people give Baal or Ishtar the credit?

In any case, God's status anxiety has precious little to do with the civil and criminal codes of the state of Alabama, where worshiping Baal and Ishtar is legal. Commandments Two, Three and Four continue God's preoccupation with himself. No graven images, indeed, no "likeness" of anything in nature, to which he holds the copyright; no taking his name in vain; no work on the Sabbath. Representational art and sculpture, swearing a blue streak and working on Saturday (or, in Alabama, Sunday) are all legal; nor does the law require that we honor our fathers and mothers as enjoined in the Fifth Commandment, despite God's barely veiled threat of death and/or exile if we sass them. Adultery is legal (well, actually, not in Alabama), as is coveting your neighbor's house, wife, servants, livestock—or husband, a possibility God seems either not to have considered or not to have minded. In fact, the only activities banned by the Ten Commandments that are also crimes under American law are murder, theft and perjury. But those are illegal (I'm guessing) under just about every civil and religious code. Even Baal and Ishtar presumably took a dim view of them.

What sets the Ten Commandments apart is not content but style: that gloomy, vengeful, obsessive, insecure authorial voice, alternately vulnerable (he confesses he's "jealous") and dissociated (he talks about himself in the third person, like an American celebrity). As elsewhere in the Bible, God looks constantly over his shoulder at the competition, threatens to visit the sins of the father on generations yet unborn, raves against those who hate him. He is equally disturbed by killing and cursing, and is incredibly possessive (I made that tree! no copying!). Granted we all know people like this, but would you want them presiding over your trial?

When you consider that God could have commanded anything he wanted—anything!—the Ten have got to rank as one of the great missed moral opportunities of all time. How different history would have been had he clearly and unmistakably forbidden war, tyranny, taking over other people's countries, slavery, exploitation of workers, cruelty to children, wife-beating, stoning, treating women—or anyone—as chattel or inferior beings. It's not as if God had nothing more to say. The minute he's through with the Decalogue, he gives Moses a long list of legal minutiae that are even less edifying: what happens if you buy a Hebrew slave and give him a wife who has children (he goes free after six years, but you keep the rest of the family); what should happen if a man sells his daughter as a "maidservant" and her master decides he doesn't fancy her after all (he can give her to his son). God enjoins us to kill witches, Sabbath violators, disrespectful children, and people who have sex with animals, but not masters who beat their slaves to death, especially if the death takes place a day or two after the beating, because the slave is the master's "money." No wonder the good white Christians of Alabama believed the Bible permitted slavery! It does! After several chapters in this vein, with much tedious discussion of oxen and more inveighing against other gods and their benighted followers, God finally settles down to the subject closest to his heart: the precise mode in which he would like to be worshiped. He drones on for pages and pages about the tabernacle, the ark and the ephod, like a demented Bronze Age interior decorator—*golden* candlesticks, mind you, and *ten* linen curtains twenty-eight cubits long and four cubits wide, and loops around the edges, and *eleven* goat-hair curtains, maybe a little wider, and loops around their edges too. He specifies down to the last beryl the ostentatious get-up he wants his priests to wear and what animals they should sacrifice and when, and which parts of the burnt offering he likes best (the fat around the tail and liver—well, that's everyone's favorite, isn't it?); he even gives recipes for incense and priestly perfume.

Has anyone checked out Judge Moore's aftershave?

"I don't know that atheists should be considered citizens, nor should they be considered patriots. This is one nation under God."

—George H. W. Bush, as quoted in *Free Inquiry* magazine, Fall 1988

Under God and Over

from *The New Republic* (4/12/04)

by Leon Wieseltier

It was the first time that William Rehnquist ever put me in mind of Søren Kierkegaard. As I watched the Supreme Court discuss God with Michael A. Newdow, the atheist from California who was defending his victory in a lower court that had concurred with his view that the words "under God" should be stricken from the Pledge of Allegiance because it is a religious expression, and was therefore responding to the Bush administration's petition to protect the theism in the Pledge, I remembered a shrewd and highly un-American observation that was included among the aphorisms in *Either/Or*: "The melancholy have the best sense of the comic, the opulent often the best sense of the rustic, the dissolute often the best sense of the moral, and the doubter often the best sense of the religious." The discussion that morning fully vindicated the majesty of the chamber, as legal themes gave way to metaphysical themes and philosophy bewitched the assembly. But something strange happened. Almost as soon as philosophy was invited, it was disinvited. It seemed to make everybody anxious, except the respondent. I had come to witness a disputation between religion's enemies and religion's friends. What I saw instead, with the exception of a single comment by Justice Souter, was a disputation between religion's enemies, liberal and conservative. And this confirmed me in my conviction that the surest way to steal the meaning, and therefore the power, from religion is to deliver it to politics, to enslave it to public life.

Some of the individuals to whom I am attributing a hostility to religion would resent the allegation deeply. They regard themselves as religion's finest friends. But what kind of friendship for religion is it that insists that the words "under God" have no religious connotation? A political friendship, is the answer. And that is precisely the kind of friendship that the Bush administration exhibited in its awful defense of the theistic diction of the Pledge. The solicitor general stood before the Court to argue against the plain meaning of ordinary words. In the Pledge of Allegiance, the government insisted, the word "God" does not refer to God. It refers to a reference to God. The government's argument, as it was stated in the brief filed by Theodore B. Olson, was made in two parts. The first part was about history, the second part was about society. "The Pledge's reference to 'a Nation under God,'" the solicitor general maintained, "is a statement about the Nation's historical origins, its enduring political philosophy centered on the sovereignty of the individual." The allegedly religious words in the Pledge are actually just "descriptive"—the term kept recurring in the discussion—of the mentality of the people who established the United States. As Olson told the Court, they are one of several "civic and ceremonial acknowledgments of the indisputable historical fact that caused the framers of our Constitution and the signers of the Declaration of Independence to say that they had the right to revolt and start a new country."

This is, for a start, an imprecise understanding of American origins. The American revolutionaries appealed not only to God, but also to reason; and their appeal to reason was animated by more than their feeling that reason was divine. It is historical and intellectual nonsense to believe that the concept of the sovereignty of the individual rests exclusively, or even mainly, upon religious foundations. Modernity was not merely the most recent era in the history of religion. The American order was a new idea, not a new version of an old idea. Moreover, a ceremony is not a museum. There are many notions that filled the heads of our eighteenth-century heroes that we do not reproduce in our civic life. Our reverence toward the Founders, which is eternally justified by what they wrought, is not a curatorial attitude. This is the case also with regard to their religious convictions. They were, many of them, Deists—which is to say, the United States was created in the very short period in history when it was theologically respectable to believe in a God that never intervenes in the world that He (the pronoun is ridiculous) created. In the matter of our religious origins, then, we were freakishly fortunate. No theology more convenient for a secular democracy ever existed. But there are no Deists in America anymore. This is why it was exceedingly odd to hear the controversial words in the Pledge described at the Court with Eugene Rostow's phrase "ceremonial deism." Ceremonial theism, perhaps; but that is a more highly charged activity. If there were still Deists in America, we would enjoy more cultural peace. Why do the God-inebriated opponents of the separation of church and state in America, the righteous citizens who see God's hand in everything that Fox News reports, insult the Founders by revising and even rejecting their God?

The second part of Olson's argument was a rather candid appeal to the expediency of religion. The Pledge is "a patriotic exercise and a solemnizing ceremony," which serves "the secular values of promoting national unity, patriotism, and an appreciation of the values that defined the Nation." The brief further notes that the introduction of God into the Pledge in 1954 had "a political purpose," which was to "highlight the foundational difference between the United States and Communist nations." (The brief does not cite some of the embarrassingly sectarian expostulations in that congressional debate.) It is certainly correct that the materialism of communist ideology offended many Americans; but the American dispensation differed from the Soviet dispensation in many significant ways, and it is foolish to impute all the evils of the Soviet Union to its godlessness. The record of religious states in the matter of mass persecution and mass murder does not support the political complacency of many American believers. In contemporary America, however, it seems forever necessary to repeat the elementary admonition that there is a distinction between religion and morality. At the Christian demonstration outside the Supreme Court that

morning, one of the speakers remarked, as she reminded
her listeners that "the Soviet Union was definitely not a
nation under God," that "I guess it's not a surprise that if
you don't acknowledge God you don't care about lying."
Are there no religious liars? Not if you hold that religion
and morality are the same; or if you deem a statement to
be true because it includes a mention of God. This same
silly woman went on to suggest that in the inner city "children are killing children because they have not heard
'Thou Shalt Not Kill.'" Surely the situation is more complicated and more disturbing. Surely some of those young
people with guns have heard the Sixth Commandment,
but it has had no effect on their ethics. Faith is not a
promise of goodness, as the Bible frequently shows.

The distinction between religion and morality was
championed by religious thinkers in all the monotheistic
faiths, who worried that religion would be reduced to
morality. Now we must worry that for many Americans
morality is being reduced to religion. Newdow was right
when he insisted that there is nothing paradoxical about a
godless patriotism, when he ringingly concluded with the
hope that "we can finally go back and have every American want to stand up, face the flag, place their hand over
their heart, and pledge to one nation, indivisible, not
divided by religion, with liberty and justice for all." Patriotism is certainly a mark of a polity's moral soundness,
and the Pledge is one of many splendid instruments for
making patriots; but patriotism, as even the solicitor general notes, is a secular value. To cherish religion for its
political utility is to cherish it narrowly, selfishly, conse-
quentially, because it allows you to accomplish one of
your objectives, because it works. American conservatives

love to chant Richard Weaver's old slogan that ideas have consequences; but if you are chiefly interested in the consequences, then you are not chiefly interested in the ideas. If you care primarily about patriotism or "national unity" or "civilization," then you will concern yourself with the practical impact of the phrase "under God" and not with its theoretical implication. You will neglect religion even as you denounce others for doing the same.

But the conservatives were not the only ones at the Supreme Court who denied religion by the manner in which they defended it. Justice Breyer wondered, in a challenge to Newdow, whether the words "under God" referred only to a "supreme being." Citing *United States v. Seeger* from 1965, though he might have illustrated his speculation more vividly with the historical precedent of the Cult of the Supreme Being in revolutionary Paris, Breyer proposed that such a faith "in any ordinary person's life fills the same place as belief in God fills in the life of an orthodox religionist," and so "it's reaching out to be inclusive"—so inclusive, in fact, that it may satisfy a non-believer such as Newdow. Breyer suggested that the God in "under God" is "this kind of very comprehensive supreme being, *Seeger*-type thing." And he posed an extraordinary question to Newdow: "So do you think that God is so generic in this context that it could be that inclusive, and if it is, then does your objection disappear?"

Needless to say, Newdow's objection did not disappear, because it is one of the admirable features of atheism to take God seriously. Newdow's reply was unforgettable: "I don't think that I can include 'under God' to mean 'no God,' which is exactly what I think. I deny the existence of God." The sound of those words in that room gave me what I can only call a constitutional thrill. *This* is freedom. And he continued: "For someone to tell me that 'under God' should mean some broad thing that even encompasses my religious beliefs sounds a little, you know, it seems like the government is imposing what it wants me to think in terms of religion, which it may not do. Government needs to stay out of this business altogether." So the common ground that Breyer depicted was not quite as common as he thought it was. In fact, Breyer was advocating the Lockean variety of toleration, according to which it would be based on a convergence of conviction, a consensus about the truth, among the overwhelming majority of the members of a society. The problem with such an arrangement is that the convergence is never complete and the consensus is never perfect. Locke himself instructed that "those are not at all to be tolerated who deny the Being of a God." The universal absolute is never quite universal. And there is another problem. It is that nobody worships a "very comprehensive supreme being, *Seeger*-type thing." Such a level of generality, a "generic" God, is religiously senseless. Breyer's solution was another attempt to salvage religious expression by emptying it of religious content. But why should a neutralized God be preferred to a neutral government? The preference is attractive only if religion is regarded primarily from the standpoint of politics.

There are two words in the phrase "under God." Each of them is indeed descriptive—but it is not our history that they describe. They describe our cosmos. Or rather, they purport to describe our cosmos. They make a statement about the universe, they paint a picture of what exists. This statement and this picture is either true or false. Either there is a God and we are under Him—the spatial metaphor, the image of a vertical reality, is one of the most ancient devices of religion—or there is not a God and we are not under Him. Since 1954, in other words, the Pledge of Allegiance has conveyed metaphysical information, and therefore it has broached metaphysical questions. I do not see how its language can be read differently. During the deliberations at the Court, only Justice Souter conceded that a cosmological claim, a worldview, is being advanced by the allusion to God in the Pledge. "I will assume that if you read the Pledge carefully, the reference to 'under God' means something more than a mere description of how somebody else once thought," he told Newdow. "The republic is then described as being under God, and I think a fair reading of that would be: I think that's the way the republic ought to be conceived, as under God. So I think there's some affirmation there. I will grant you that."

To recognize the plain meaning of the words "under God," and the nature of the investigation that they enjoin, is to discover the philosophical core of religion. This is not at all obvious to the modern interpretation of religion, and not to the American interpretation of it. After Kant explained that we can have no direct knowledge of the thing itself, and certainly not of God, religious statements have tended to be not propositions of fact, but propositions of value—expressions of inner states that are validated by the intensity of the feeling with which they are articulated. Certainty weirdly became an accomplishment of subjectivity. Kant thought that he secured religion by placing it beyond the bounds of knowledge. But this was a false security, because the vocabulary of theism continues to point to more than emotion or experience or tribe or culture. Prayer in particular remains, at least at the level of its language, an address in the second-person singular to an entity that is not oneself. Theology, if it wishes to be regarded as more than a cerebral fantasy, cannot be content to have its basis in the imagination; it must appeal to the authority of philosophy if it is to continue to speak about what is true.

Many modern believers, and modern commentators on religion, resent this. A recent historian of atheism, a Jesuit scholar, laments that in modern theology "religion was treated as if it were theism," as if it had no resources of its own to guarantee anything generally binding and true. But if religion is not theism, if its ground is not an intellectually supportable belief in the existence of God, then all the spiritual exaltation and all the political agitation in the world will avail it nothing against the skeptics and the doubters, and it really is just a beloved illusion. Others denounce the abstraction of the God of the philosophers, and the impersonality. Before such a deity, Heidegger demagogically complained, "man can neither fall to his knees in awe nor can he play music and dance." But this is not philosophy's problem, or even religion's problem, if by religion you mean something other than an excuse to fall to your knees or to dance with your feet. If the impersonal God does not exist, I do not see how the personal God can exist.

There is no greater insult to religion than to expel strictness of thought from it. Yet such an expulsion is one of the traits of contemporary American religion, as the discussion at the Supreme Court demonstrated. Religion in America is more and more relaxed and "customized," a jolly affair of hallowed self-affirmation, a religion of a holy whatever. Speaking about God is prized over thinking about God. Say "under God" even if you don't mean under God. And if you mean under God, don't be tricked into giving an account of what you mean by it. Before too long you have arrived at a sacralized cynicism: In his intervention at the Court, Justice Stevens recalled a devastating point from the fascinating brief submitted in support of Newdow by thirty-two Christian and Jewish clergy, which asserted that "if the briefs of the school district and the United States are to be taken seriously," that is, if the words in the Pledge do not allude to God, "then every day they ask schoolchildren to violate [the] commandment" that "Thou shalt not take the Name of the Lord in vain." Remember, those are not the Ten Suggestions. It is a very strange creed indeed that asks its votaries not to reflect too much about itself.

For this reason, American unbelief can perform a great quickening service to American belief. It can shake American religion loose from its cheerful indifference to the inquiry about truth. It can remind it that religion is not only a way of life but also a worldview. It can provoke it into remembering its reasons. For the argument that a reference to God is not a reference to God is a sign that American religion is forgetting its reasons. The need of so many American believers to have government endorse their belief is thoroughly abject. How strong, and how wise, is a faith that needs to see God's name wherever it looks? (His name on nickels and dimes is rather damaging to His sublimity.) I do not mean to exaggerate the virtues of Michael Newdow: There was something too shiny about him, too dogmatic about his opposition to other people's dogmas. Atheists can be as mindless as theists. From his comments at the Supreme Court, there was no way to tell how thoughtful Newdow's arguments against theism are, or even what they are. And when Newdow insisted that there is some injury to him when his daughter "is asked every morning to say that her father is wrong" by praying in class, because "the government says there is a God and her dad says there isn't," he failed to grasp one of the ends of education, which is to make children unlike their parents. And yet Newdow's appearance at the Supreme Court was terrifically stirring. *Elk Grove Unified School District v. Michael A. Newdow* exposed a spiritual poverty, and honored an American tradition, and cautioned an entire country about the consequences of a smug and sloppy entanglement of religion with politics, for politics and for religion. It is never long before one nation under God gives way to one God under a nation.

"The idea that religion and politics don't mix was invented by the Devil to keep Christians from running their own country."
—Jerry Falwell, 7/4/76

10/27

James Madison Rebukes
the Religious Right

Rob Boston

Right-wing fundamentalist Christians love to quote the Founding Fathers. Through selective culling of quotations, taking phrases out of context and sometimes simply making stuff up, they try to convince Americans that the founders of the United States really wanted to establish a "Christian nation"—but just forgot to mention that in the Constitution.

One framer they don't quote that often is James Madison. That's probably because Madison stands in rebuke to everything the Religious Right believes and desires. If Madison we're alive today, he'd go on CNN and demolish Jerry Falwell. It would be quite a sight to see.

A little perspective on Madison's accomplishments is useful. Madison is the father of the Constitution. He penned some of the Federalist Papers and he helped draft the Bill of Rights. Jefferson's Statute for Religious Freedom, a piece of legislation that many scholars believe inspired the First Amendment, is eloquently worded—but it would have remained merely nice words on paper if James Madison hadn't pushed it through the Virginia legislature and made it law.

The Declaration of Independence is a stirring document of enduring greatness. But Madison's Constitution is an actual governance document. It has withstood the assaults of time and the incredible changes in American society in more than two centuries and still remains in use. Likewise, Madison's Bill of Rights continues to inspire the oppressed all over the world.

Despite these accomplishments, Madison is often overlooked in the public mind, overshadowed even by his own wife, who is invariably described as "vivacious." When he is remembered, it's all too often for the bad things, not the good. Some people might dimly recall that Madison was president during the War of 1812—when the British burned our capital. "Mr. Madison's war," the critics lampooned. Even here Madison is the victim of bad PR. That war, looked at more than two hundred years later, marked a turning point for the United States. It is sometimes called the Second War of Independence, and there's more than a little truth to that. After the war, the European powers grudgingly accepted that the United States meant to truly be an independent nation, not merely the pawn of larger and more powerful countries.

What Madison needs is a full-fledged revival. It shouldn't be too hard to start one. John Adams became popular thanks to David McCullough's book, so why not Madison? If John Adams, a man derided as "His Rotundity" by contemporaries, a man who gave us the oppressive Alien and Sedition Acts, can be cast as a hero, why not Madison—whose accomplishments are much more meaningful and enduring?

One of those accomplishments is Madison's pioneering work in defense of the separation of church and state. When people think of separation of church and state, the figure of Jefferson comes to mind. Jefferson, after all, coined the metaphor of a "wall of separation between church and state."

But Madison was probably the more consistent advocate

of that cause, even if he did it in a mostly low-key manner. In February of 1811, a bill reached his desk that would have officially incorporated an Episcopal church in the District of Columbia. Madison vetoed it, and in a message to Congress explained that it "exceeds the rightful authority to which governments are limited by the essential distinction between civil and religious functions."

About a week later, Congress struck again, sending Madison a bill that would have given some surplus federal land to a Baptist church in Mississippi. Again Madison reached for his veto pen. This time he wrote that the bill "comprises a principle and precedent for the appropriation of funds of the United States for the use of and support of religious societies, contrary to the article of the Constitution which declares that 'Congress shall make no law respecting a religious establishment.'"

Robert J. Morgan, a Madison scholar and author of *James Madison on the Constitution and the Bill of Rights*, stated recently, "You can see the sum of his thinking in those veto messages. People need to read them to understand Madison's thinking on the separation of church and state."

Yet there are those who argue that Madison was inconsistent in his support of the principle of church-state separation. They point out that Madison issued proclamations calling for days of prayer and fasting. That's true, but after Madison left the presidency he wrote a long essay in which he concluded that his actions were wrong and explained why he undertook them: because Congress had asked him to. In that same essay, Madison outlined his opposition to chaplains in the Congress and in the military.

Here's how hardcore Madison was on the separation of

church and state: During his presidency, Congress proposed undertaking a census. One of the things they
wanted to do was count people by profession. Madison
said no. He told Congress that counting the clergy would
be a church-state violation.

But, the Religious Right sputters, Madison once said
that the Ten Commandments should be the foundation of
our government. The answer to that one is simple: Prove
it. There is a quotation attributed to Madison floating
around on the Internet that makes this claim, but no one
has been able to cite an original source for it.

Here is the alleged quotation: "We have staked the
whole future of American civilization upon the capacity of
each of us to govern ourselves according to the Ten Commandments of God." This quotation, attributed to
Madison, appears in dozens of Religious Right books. But
the footnotes never refer to an original document; they
always refer to some other book.

A few years ago the curators of the Madison Papers at
the University of Virginia were asked to look into the
matter. They were skeptical of the quotation, saying it did
not look like something Madison would say. Their search
came up empty. They could not confirm Madison ever
said it.

Can anyone prove Madison didn't say it? No, that's
impossible. But available evidence indicates that there is
no good reason for believing that Madison ever made
this statement. Some Religious Right leaders have finally
admitted that the quotation is probably bogus and have
advised their followers to stop using it.

When you are an opponent of church-state separation,
and your efforts to distort the views of a Founding Father

have failed, your phony quotes stand unmasked as specious, what's left? That's when you go to ridicule. You say
something like, "Well, Madison's views were kind of
extreme. The other framers didn't think that way."

Some have tried this line of argument. They assert, for
example, that Madison's rhetoric was sometimes over the
top. For example, in his famous "Memorial and Remonstrance Against Religious Assessments," Madison asserted
that in Europe "torrents of blood have been spilt by vain
attempts of the secular arm to extinguish religious discord
by proscribing all difference in religious opinion."

Is this extreme or just accurate? We are hundreds of
years removed from the Middle Ages. Madison was a lot
closer to that age. He was also much better versed on the
history of that period than most Americans are today.
And, of course, we all know that torrents of blood are still
being spilt around the world because of differences in religious opinion and efforts by governments to impose
orthodoxy. Madison spoke not in extremism but with
insight.

How did it happen? How did Madison get to that place
where he could champion religious liberty and usher in a
freedom that marks and defines our country more than
two hundred years later?

It was an odd role for him to take on. As a young man,
Madison was frail and frequently of ill health. He didn't
expect to live long. He was never what you would call vigorous. When he took the oath of office as president in 1809,
he looked so wan and physically taxed that some feared he
would not make it through the ceremony. One of his contemporaries called him, "a withered little applejohn."

Lacking physical stamina, Madison turned to intellectual

pursuits. He considered studying to become a clergyman. His father had been a minister, and there is some evidence that Madison, as a young man, had a brief flirtation with intense religiosity. For whatever reason, this rather quickly cooled, and Madison's personal beliefs in this area remain to this day something of a mystery. He was nominally an Episcopalian, but Ralph Ketcham, his leading biographer, believes Madison is best described as a Deist.

Madison attended the College of New Jersey, now Princeton. Employing what he later called a "minimum of sleep and the maximum of application," he was able to earn his degree in just under three years. Madison didn't really have a major like we know them today, and he studied what might best be described as a classical-studies curriculum.

He studied under the direction of college president John Witherspoon, an enlightened Scotch Presbyterian with a commitment to what we would later call democratic thought. Madison had a wide range of instruction, much of it defined by Witherspoon. Along with the religious tradition of the Scottish enlightenment, Madison was introduced to the study of the great philosophers and scientists.

It's easy to see how this form of education influenced Madison and how it equipped him with the intellectual tools he carried forth into adulthood. He returned home in 1772, where he continued his studies under private tutors while keeping up an active correspondence with his friend William Bradford.

One letter shows Madison's state of mind at this time. "I am too dull and infirm now," he wrote, "to look out for any extraordinary things in this world for I think my sensations for many months past have intimated to me not to expect a long or healthy life."

What Madison needed, it seemed, was a cause. He soon found one in the struggle for religious freedom. And when he did, his melancholy lifted.

It's important to remember what colonial Virginia was like at this time. The colony maintained strict laws regulating religious expression. The Anglican Church was established by law. The statutes were so extreme that other religious groups were not even allowed to meet.

As early as 1642, a group of Congregationalist ministers who had settled in the state were forced to leave. Baptists were fined or imprisoned for their religious views. Preachers had to receive a license from the state. All citizens were forced, through taxation, to support the established church.

Young Madison's life was profoundly changed after he saw what he called several "well meaning men" languishing in prison merely because they had challenged the state orthodoxy and insisted on worshipping their own way. Madison, a perceptive man with a razor-sharp intellect, could sense the growing undercurrent in colonial society—an undercurrent of agitation for religious liberty. Madison would later tap this source and turn it into a great battering ram for religious freedom. That battering ram would topple state-established churches in Virginia and spark the beginnings of religious freedom in the United States—and rebuke the Religious Right until this very day.

It may be hard for us in the twenty-first century to grasp what religious life was like more than two hundred years ago. Before the First Amendment, people were actually put in jail for their religious beliefs. Everyone had to pay taxes to support the official church—no matter what their own religious views were. If they refused, they were either imprisoned or kicked out of the state.

In a famous letter dated January 24, 1774, Madison told his friend Bradford about his displeasure with the reigning church-state partnership in Virginia. Madison spoke of a desire to visit Bradford in Philadelphia, where he could "breathe your free air." He remarked upon the "pride, ignorance and knavery among the priesthood and vice and wickedness among the laity."

Wrote Madison:

> This is bad enough. But it is not the worst. I have to tell you That diabolical Hell conceived principle of persecution rages among some, and to their eternal Infamy the Clergy can furnish their Quota of Imps for such business. This vexes me the most of any thing whatever. There are at this [time] in the adjacent County not less than 5 or 6 well meaning men in close Goal for publishing their religious Sentiments, which in the main are very orthodox. I have neither patience to hear talk or think of any thing relative to this matter, for I have squabbled and scolded, abused, and ridiculed so long about it, to so little purpose, that I am without common patience. So I leave you to pity me and pray for Liberty of Conscience to revive among us.

As Madison's outburst shows, religious freedom—a concept we take for granted today—was a radical idea in Madison's day. And Madison was definitely ahead of the curve in this regard. When, at the tender age of twenty-five, Madison—then a delegate to the Virginia Convention drafting a new state constitution—proposed an amendment guaranteeing religious freedom, his idea was roundly dismissed.

But Madison had put into motion a series of events that could not be stopped. Elected to the Continental Congress, Madison continued to press for complete religious liberty. His formerly "radical" idea gained support, and years later he returned to Virginia as a member of the House of Delegates to demand the disestablishment of the Anglican Church and to fight a bill proposed by Patrick Henry that would have levied a "general assessment" on all citizens to support "teachers of the Christian religion."

This was an epic struggle and one that in many ways would define what religious freedom would mean for the entire nation. It was during this battle that Madison penned his great "Memorial and Remonstrance," an essay that is essentially a list of fifteen reasons why the government should not be expected to support religion.

Madison begins the document with a bang. Why is government-supported religion so bad? Point one lays it all out: "Because we hold it for a fundamental and undeniable truth that religion or the duty which we owe to our Creator and the manner of discharging it, can be directed only by reason and conviction, not by force or violence. The Religion then of every man must be left to the conviction and conscience of every man; and it is the right of every man to exercise it as these may dictate. This right is in its nature an unalienable right."

Point three is also well stated: "The same authority which can establish Christianity, in exclusion of all other

religions, may establish with the same ease, any particular sect of Christians in exclusion of all other sects, and
the same authority which can force a citizen to contribute three pence only of his property for the support
of any one establishment, may force him to conform to
any other establishment in all cases whatsoever."

To put it bluntly, the "Memorial and Remonstrance" is
a grand slam. And it had the desired effect. The Remonstrance, aided by a little backdoor political wheeling and
dealing, defeated Henry's "general assessment bill."

But Madison didn't stop there. He went on to see the
Virginia legislature pass Jefferson's Statute for Religious
Freedom. This was a radical measure for the time because
it guaranteed all men the right to worship as they saw fit.
Efforts to limit its protections exclusively to Christians
were rejected. Many scholars believe the Virginia Statute
laid the philosophical foundation for the First Amendment's religion clauses.

Madison went on to play a pivotal role in the drafting
of the Bill of Rights. He drafted several versions of the First
Amendment's religious freedom clauses before settling on
the language we know today: "Congress shall make no law
respecting an establishment of religion, or prohibiting the
free exercise thereof . . ."

Jefferson's "wall of separation between church and
state" phrase is well known, but what Madison had to say
about church-state separation is probably more interesting and more relevant.

In an 1819 letter to Robert Walsh, Madison com-
mented on the state of religious freedom in his native
Virginia. He was feeling pretty optimistic about it, chiefly
because an official distance had been put between religion

and government. He wrote, "The number, the industry
and the morality of the priesthood and the devotion of
the people have been manifestly increased by the total
separation of the church from the state."

In his "Detached Memoranda," an essay scholars
believe was written between 1817 and 1832, Madison
called on states to do away with any religious establishments they might still retain. He called on "ye states of
America" that retained these establishments to "purify
your systems and make the example of your country as
pure and complete in what relates to the freedom of the
mind and its allegiance to its maker, as in what belongs to
the legitimate objects of political and civil institutions."

The next sentence reads, "Strongly guarded . . . is the
separation between religion and government in the Constitution of the United States." There's that term again,
that reference to separation.

And of course we know what Madison did in office and
in his public life—the vetoes of legislation that favored
churches, the regret he later expressed for issuing prayer
proclamations during the War of 1812.

Now consider what the Religious Right has to say. On
January 22, 1995, TV preacher Pat Robertson said this
about church-state separation: "That was never in the
Constitution. However much the liberals laugh at me for
saying it, they know good and well it was never in the
Constitution. Such language only appeared in the constitution of the communist Soviet Union."

More recently, House Majority Leader Tom DeLay told
the *Washington Times* that separation of church and state is
found "nowhere in the Constitution."

So who's right about what the First Amendment was

intended to do? Madison, one of the primary authors of
the First Amendment, or Robertson, a modern-day television evangelist, and DeLay? Who pioneered the separation
ideal—Madison, or Lenin?

Since Robertson and DeLay obviously do not like
Madison's handiwork, it's worthwhile to answer some of
their objections to it. Religious Right arguments against
church-state separation boil down to a few. They are:

• **Separation of church and state leads to a decline
in religion's influence on society.** Really? This
would surprise Madison. Madison saw the concept
as the best guarantor of a vibrant religious community. In his view, separation would lead to more religious activity, not less. Time has proven him right.
Compare U.S. church attendance rates to the United
Kingdom, which has an established church, or Germany, which has a system of church taxes. It's no
contest. In America, more people believe in God,
more people attend houses of worship and more
people say religion is important to them.

Madison speaks to this objection quite powerfully. In an 1823 letter to Edward Everett, Madison
reflected that prior to the revolution, most of the
colonies had established churches. Many began to
wither away after independence. "Prior to the revolution, the Episcopal Church was established by
law in this state," Madison wrote. "On the Declaration of Independence it was left with all other sects,
to a self support. And no doubt exists that there is
much more of religion among us now than there
ever was before the change; and particularly in the

sect which enjoyed the legal patronage. This proves rather more than, that the law is not necessary to the support of religion."

• **Separation of church and state means that children cannot pray in school.** Simply not true. The Supreme Court banned mandatory, school-sponsored forms of religious activity in public schools in 1962 and 1963. Prior to these rulings, young people could be forced to recite the Lord's Prayer or engage in Bible-reading every day. The Court said it is not the appropriate role of government to inculcate religion. Madison would have agreed. He did not favor force in matters of religion.

Public school students have the right to pray on their own time before, during, or after school. They can meet with fellow students for prayer. They can read the Bible or any other religious book during free time. They can invite their friends to go to church with them. All of this is protected activity. It is protected by the First Amendment. Coercive, state-sponsored programs of prayer are not.

• **The lack of formal religious activity in public schools has spawned undesirable social consequences.** Robertson and his ideological soulmates often assert that the removal of mandatory prayer from schools has led to increased rates of crime, juvenile delinquency, alcohol and drug abuse, high rates of teen pregnancy, and lower SAT scores, among other things.

There are people in the Religious Right who

make a living trying to prove that the quality of life in the United States has declined since those rulings were handed down. A classically trained scholar like Madison could have debunked this argument handily. The Latin phrase *post hoc, ergo propter hoc* translates as "after this, therefore on account of this." It's one of the common fallacies of logic—assuming that if two things occur in sequence they must be related.

• **Separation of church and state means that religion is accorded second-class status in society**. Again, Madison would have known why this assertion is specious.

Separation of church and state protects religion. It puts it out of the government's reach. Houses of worship routinely receive exemptions from laws that other organizations must follow, and rightly so. Houses of worship can discriminate in hiring. No on else can. And that's as it should be.

Religious groups are free to influence the political system and do so all of the time. Pastors and religious groups speak out on every imaginable issue, from same-sex marriage and gun control to health care and the minimum wage.

Think about our political campaigns. How many times do you see candidates appearing in houses of worship seeking votes? One can argue about the propriety of that action, but the fact that it occurs is a good sign that the politicians do not consider religion to be a taboo subject. Quite the opposite. They are well aware that in a nation that is overwhelmingly religious, appearing in church on Sunday can have a real payoff at the polls.

Turn on your TV on Sunday morning. How many of the channels are occupied by television preachers? Think of the Jehovah's Witnesses who go door-to-door or the Mormons who approach you in public places, seeking a conversion. Our society, unlike others in the world today, makes no attempts to place curbs on this type of activity, nor should it. Any such curbs would be clearly unconstitutional and unacceptable.

Arguments advanced by the Religious Right attacking church-state separation simply are not convincing. In fact, Madison demolished them all with one single letter he wrote back in 1833.

In the spring of that year, Jasper Adams, the president of the College of Charleston, sent Madison a copy of a pamphlet he had written titled "The Relations of Christianity to Civil Government in the United States." Adams believed that it was impossible for a government to survive without the prop of religion. And since Adams was a Christian, he naturally believed that the prop should be Christian. He probably knew of Madison's record in this area and was interested in finding out if Madison's views had changed any since he left the White House.

They hadn't. Madison wrote back, thanking Adams for the pamphlet but essentially saying that he did not accept its argument. He pointed out that the question boils down to this: which system works better in protecting the right of conscience—separation of church and state or combinations of the two.

"In the papal system," Madison wrote, "government and religion are in a manner consolidated and that is found to be the worst of government. In most of the governments of the Old World, the legal establishment of a particular religion and without or with very little toleration of others makes a part of the political and civil organization, and there are few of the most enlightened judges who will maintain that the system has been favorable either to religion or to government."

In 1985, William H. Rehnquist, who is now the chief justice, wrote in a dissent to a case dealing with "moments of silence" in public schools, "The wall of separation between church and state is a metaphor based on bad history, a metaphor which has proved useless as a guide to judging. It should be frankly and explicitly abandoned."

Rehnquist reserved most of his fire for Jefferson. He didn't take aim at Madison, probably because he realized the futility of the exercise.

How do we know that Rehnquist was wrong and Madison right? Take a look around you.

We can see the evidence of Madison's vision all around us. In the cities and towns of America, where houses of worship representing hundreds of different denominations—from mega-churches with thousands of members to storefront churches with just a handful—not only exist but in many cases flourish.

We can see the evidence in the public opinion polls that routinely show that the United States is among the most religious nations in the world. We see the statistical data that proves that, far from hindering religion, separation of church and state gives it vitality.

Compare the United States to Great Britain, which

retains a state church and other trappings of government support for religion. London is full of impressive cathedrals, but most sit nearly empty on Sundays. In Great Britain, polls routinely show that as much as 35 percent of the population or more expresses doubts about the existence of God. In the United States, that number is in the single digits. In Great Britain and in many European nations, the idea of religion playing a political role is absurd. For better or for worse, the concept of religion playing a political role is common here; yes, it is controversial—but it happens—and the fact that it happens is a further sign of religion's vitality.

What really bothers many supporters of the Religious Right is not that so many Americans are irreligious or atheistic—because not many are—but that many Americans refrain from adopting the extreme, fundamentalist interpretation of religion embraced by the Religious Right.

Americans are a spiritual people, but they are not necessarily a dogmatic people. Most Americans believe that great truths can be found in different religions and reject that idea that one faith has a lock on truth.

Americans also like the idea of blending religious traditions. Polls show that on any given Saturday or Sunday, about 40 percent of the population attends a religious service. Does that mean the other 60 percent are nonbelievers? Not at all. Many of these people have created a personal spirituality that may be uniquely their own or may be a blend of religious traditions they have been exposed to over the years. People feel comfortable creating this type of spiritual expression only in an atmosphere of religious freedom. Where the state imposes orthodoxy, it simply is not possible.

The idea of a home-grown spirituality infuriates the Religious Right. They don't like to see people make decisions about religion outside of rigid, hierarchical frameworks. They insist that the Bible holds all of the answers and that people cannot deviate from that system and expect salvation.

But here's the problem with that view, and here also is the genius of the separation of church and state: Ultimately, the Religious Right and those who espouse the doctrine of so-called biblical inerrancy are not advocating for a system of religion based on the Bible. They are advocating for a system based on *their interpretation* of the Bible. And their interpretation of the Bible can differ from ones held even by other self-proclaimed inerrantists.

Virginia is home to two famous TV preachers—Jerry Falwell and Pat Robertson. Falwell and Robertson both claim to be proponents of biblical inerrancy. That is, they believe the Bible is without error and speaks authoritatively on all issues. Yet Falwell and Robertson do not interpret the Bible in the same way, even though both men are Baptists.

Consider one example: Robertson is a Pentecostal Christian. He speaks in tongues, practices faith healing, and gets "words of knowledge" that he says come directly from God. These practices can be traced to the New Testament Book of Acts, Chapter 2, which described how "cloven tongues like as of fire" descended upon Jesus' apostles. "And they were all filled with the Holy Ghost and began to speak with other tongues, as the Spirit gave them utterance."

Falwell argues that these gifts of the Holy Spirit were intended only for those living at the time of the Pentecost and that they are not accessible for people today. Robertson would strongly disagree.

JESUS IS NOT A THEOCRAT

Who is right? Possibly they are both right, possibly they are both wrong. Let them thrash it out in their private arenas. Nothing would be more dangerous than for the government to take sides in that theological debate or any other.

In the end, despite all of their proof-texting, and for all of their hoisting of large Bibles with the words of Jesus in red, neither Falwell or Robertson can prove that he is right. The best they can do is say, "My interpretation of the Bible leads me to believe I am correct."

Down the street lives someone else who says, "My interpretation of the Bible leads me to believe that you are wrong, and my view is the correct one." A little further down the block lives someone else who says, "Your arguments are incomplete because you have neglected to take into account the Book of Mormon." A few more doors down lives a Jew who says, "What New Testament? We're still waiting for the Messiah." Across the street is a Roman Catholic who asserts, "You need to augment your interpretation of the Scriptures with the teaching magesterium of the Church of Rome." And houses down from there is a Muslim who says, "We recognize Jesus as a moral teacher, but there is no God but Allah, and Mohammed is his prophet."

And what of the Hindus, the Buddhists, the Wiccans, the Pagans, the atheists, the Scientologists, the Unification Church members, the Zoroastrians, etc.? All of these adherents are probably convinced that their system offers truth, that their path is the right one. They have their inspired writings, their moral leaders, their important figures. They believe these doctrines with great passion and zeal. Their sincerity is real, which is all the more reason why none must be permitted to claim the imprimatur of the state.

One thing Falwell and Robertson have never understood

—but that Madison did understand—is that separation of church and state does not weaken our nation; it gives it strength. A nation that is secure enough to allow complete religious freedom is mature, confident, and ready to take on all challenges.

A nation that realizes that government and religion do not need a mutual dependence severs that tie and in the process strengthens both institutions. In the United States, we see the results of that every day. We are the oldest, most stable democracy in the world and a nation of unparalleled religious freedom and diversity.

Madison left us a real legacy. At times like this—when we face uncertainty, when we try to deal with no small amount of fear, when we strive for meaning in unsettled times—his timeless wisdom is a kind of comfort. His words call out to us and ring down through the ages, reminding us that the promise of America isn't just airy words for Fourth of July parades, but real, concrete freedoms that we can take advantage of every day. Primary among these is our religious freedom, something that could not exist without the protective wall of separation between church and state.

In 1823, Edward Everett, a professor at Harvard, wrote to Madison to complain that one religious denomination had monopolized all of the theological positions at that school.

Madison replied a few weeks later. He took pride in the fact that the University of Virginia, a school his colleague Jefferson had founded, had avoided this type of unpleasantness.

"I am not surprised at the dilemma produced at your University by making theological professorships an integral part of the system," Madison wrote. "The anticipation of such one led to the omission in ours; the Visitors being merely authorized to open a public Hall for religious occasions, under impartial regulations; with the opportunity to the different sects to establish Theological schools so near that the Students of the University may respectively attend the religious exercises in them. The village of Charlottesville also, where different religious worships will be held, is also so near that resort may conveniently be had to them."

Madison continued, "A University with sectarian professorships, becomes, of course, a Sectarian Monopoly; with professorships of rival sects, it would be an Arena of Theological Gladiators. Without any such professorships, it may incur for a time at least, the imputation of irreligious tendencies, if not designs. The last difficulty was thought more manageable then either of the others."

Madison then moved on the big picture, tying it all together in that way he had of turning his argument into a type of rhetorical blunderbuss:

The settled opinion here is that religion is essentially distinct from Civil Govt and exempt from its cognizance; that a connextion between them is injurious to both; that there are causes in the human breast which ensure the perpetuity of religion without the aid of the law; that rival sects, with equal rights, exercise mutual censorships in favor of good morals; that if new sects arise with absurd opinions or overheated maginations, the proper remedies lie in time, forbearance and example; that a legal establishment of religion without a toleration could not be thought of, and with a toleration, is no security for public quiet & harmony, but rather a source itself of discord & animosity; and finally that these opinions are supported by experience, which has shewn that every relaxation of the alliance between Law & religion, from the partial example of Holland, to its consummation in Pennsylvania, Delaware, N.J. etc. has been found as safe in practice as it is sound in theory.

No need to say any more. Madison laid down the best arguments for separation of church and state that the world has ever known. His assertions are just as relevant today and just as powerful—if only we will listen.

"*A Christian nation.* That is the phrase that drives the liberals mad. That is the concept that infuriates them all. It is infuriating because it is true. Primary source documents will simply not allow humanists or atheists to declare with any kind of intellectual integrity that our Founding Fathers were either unreligious or irreligious."
—from an article on the Web site of the American Family Association, July 4, 2001

REALLY?

"Congress shall make no law respecting an establishment of religion, or prohibiting the free exercise thereof . . ."
—First Amendment

"The United States is in no sense founded upon the Christian doctrine."
—George Washington

JESUS IS NOT A THEOCRAT

"As the government of the United States of America is not in any sense founded on the Christian Religion . . ."
—from the Treaty of Tripoli, signed by John Adams, June 10, 1797

"Believing with you that religion is a matter which lies solely between man and his God; that he owes account to none other for his faith or his worship; that the legislative powers of the government reach actions only, and not opinions, I contemplate with sovereign reverence that act of the whole American people which declared that their legislature should 'make no law respecting an establishment of religion, or prohibiting the free exercise thereof,' thus building a wall of separation between church and State."
—Thomas Jefferson, January 1, 1802

"Who does not see that the same authority which can establish Christianity, in exclusion of all other Religions, may establish with the same ease any particular sect of Christians, in exclusion of all other Sects?"
—James Madison, in "Memorial and Remonstrance," 1785

"The number, the industry, and the morality of the priesthood, and the devotion of the people have been manifestly increased by the total separation of church and state."
—James Madison, March 2, 1819

JESUS IS LOVE

with quotations from Thomas Jefferson and Leo Tolstoy

The Gospels offer us more than one Jesus. If we are angry, we can find a Jesus who will support us in our rage. We find the real Jesus when we find ourselves.

"The whole history of these books [the Gospels] is so defective and doubtful that it seems vain to attempt minute enquiry into it: and such tricks have been played with their text, and with the texts of other books relating to them, that we have a right, from that cause, to entertain much doubt what parts of them are genuine. In the New Testament there is internal evidence that parts of it have proceeded from an extraordinary man; and that other parts are of the fabric of very inferior minds. It is as easy to separate those parts, as to pick out diamonds from dunghills."

—Thomas Jefferson in a letter to John Adams, 1/24/1814

Jesus Was Not A Republican, but St. Paul Probably Was

By J. M. Berger

George W. Bush likes to tell people he embraced evangelical Christianity after reading the famous story of St. Paul's conversion on the road to Damascus. In reality, the two men couldn't be more different. After all, Paul was a reactionary, power-crazed conservative who believed that God was giving him the exclusive power to set moral absolutes for everyone else, and George Bush is a reactionary . . . uh . . . Well, maybe there is some common ground after all.

To understand the story of Paul, you must first understand this: Nearly everything you've been told about the birth of the institutional Christian Church is wrong. No authentic record remains to inform us about Christianity's first four or five decades.

Many scholars believe the religion that goes by the name of Christianity today would be more accurately called "Paulinism."[1] The distinction matters. Jesus taught a liberal creed, while Paul preached a right-wing screed. When Paul usurped Christianity from its namesake founder, he twisted the social values of Jesus so profoundly that the consequences are still plainly visible today.

Modern scholars believe that the teachings of Jesus were first recorded in a "sayings gospel," often referred to as Q. The writers of the "official" gospels derived their stories from this collection of quotes, supplemented by oral traditions about the life of Christ and a few eyewitness accounts.

But before the canonical gospels were even written, there was this guy named Paul.

Tradition holds that the artist formerly known as Saul was a Pharisee tool who spent his waking hours persecuting the followers of Jesus, usually with extreme prejudice.

One day, as Saul was traveling to Damascus to indulge this hobby, a vision of Jesus literally knocked him off his horse. According to the account preserved in the Acts of the Apostles:

> Now as he journeyed he approached Damascus, and suddenly a light from heaven flashed about him. And he fell to the ground and heard a voice saying to him, "Saul, Saul, why do you persecute me?"[2]

Saul was naturally quite alarmed by this event, which left him blind as a syphilitic bat. The voice told him to continue to Damascus, where he would receive help from the followers of Jesus.

The followers of Jesus were less than enthralled with the idea of helping Saul. Although they had a reputation for being team players, they stalled and dithered until God Himself had to step in and overrule their objections. After miraculously regaining his sight, Saul did an abrupt 180 and began stridently preaching the virtues of Christ.

You might expect this experience—being struck down by God for murdering upright people—would have a humbling effect. Instead, Saul's megalomania grew by leaps and bounds. Changing his name to Paul, he started preaching new doctrines to anyone who would listen. Despite the fact that he had not known Jesus in the flesh, Paul felt free to embellish Christ's teachings with his own visionary insights.

According to the Acts of the Apostles and Paul's own accounts, he immediately alienated most traditional Jews and many of his fellow Christians as well.

Paul's friends found themselves fully occupied evacuating him from town after town when he invariably incited the locals to rise up against him—a good trick, since the early Christians were pacifists like their founder. When Paul traveled to Jerusalem for a visit with the apostles Peter and James (two men who had actually known Jesus during his life), they warned him he was treading on thin ice:

> You can see, brother, how many tens of thousands there are among the Jews who have come to believe, and all of them are zealots for the law [i.e., followers of the Torah]. And they have been told concerning you that you are teaching all the Jews who live among the Gentiles to turn away from Moses, telling them not to circumcise their children, and not to follow his customs.[3]

The Torah was the main point of contention between Paul and the original apostles. As Acts makes clear, members of the Jerusalem Christian Church had continued to obey traditional Jewish laws, including dietary restrictions and the practice of circumcision.

But Paul preached that Jesus had come to eliminate the Torah entirely. Paul replaced the Old Law with an entirely new set of moral guidelines, which had allegedly been dictated by the voices in Paul's head.

Divinely inspired or not, Paul's new approach was extremely pragmatic. His self-appointed mission was to convert the Gentiles to Christianity, after all, and few adult male converts were willing to offer up their foreskins for the sake of salvation. Later, Paul simply started telling people that the Torah's shelf life had expired.[4]

Paul never heard Jesus teach firsthand. The religious principles he promoted were not based on the teachings of the historical Jesus but instead derived from his own visions. You are perfectly entitled to believe these visions came from God—but regardless, they did not reflect what Jesus appears to have presented during his lifetime.

There are dozens of examples of this disconnect, and many of Paul's revisions contain distinctly political overtones from a modern viewpoint. Take the following example:

> **Jesus:** Consider the lilies of the field, how they grow; they neither toil nor spin; yet I tell you, even Solomon in all his glory was not arrayed like one of these. But if God so clothes the grass of the field, which today is alive and tomorrow is thrown into the oven, will he not much more clothe you, O men of little faith?[5]

> **Paul:** [K]eep away from any brother who is living in idleness and not in accord with the tradition that you received from us. For you yourselves know how you ought to imitate us; we were not idle when we were with you, we did not eat any one's bread

> without paying, but with toil and labor we worked
> night and day, that we might not burden any of you.
> [. . .] If any one will not work, let him not eat.[6]

Jesus delivers one of his most memorable and beautiful lines here, the eternal metaphor of the lilies of the field. God will take care of you, he promises. Focus on the real things, the spiritual life.

Paul's message stands in sharp contrast. Industry is good, capitalism is good. In direct contradiction to the teachings of Christ, Paul commands Christians to toil and labor "night and day." While Jesus taught that God would "give us this day our daily bread," Paul believed the private sector was better equipped for the job.

Now it's easy to play textual games with the Bible. The book is loaded with contradictions and paradoxes. But there's something more at work here. Inconsistencies between Paul's epistles and the four gospels are expected. What's interesting is the fact that the inconsistencies are themselves so consistent.

Early Christianity consisted of a group of small, communal sects patiently awaiting the end of the world. The first Christians were religious and ethnic Jews, an oppressed class living under an imperial occupation.

It's no secret that leftism runs rampant among demographic groups whom The Man is keeping down. Right-leaning views tend to be embraced by people who are interested in obtaining or consolidating power.

As the New Testament tells us on several occasions, Paul was a Roman citizen, regardless of his status as a Jew.[7] As such, he was a member of the privileged elite. On more than one occasion, Paul exploits the power associated with his status as a Roman citizen.[8] Correspondingly, Paul preached that political power is ordained by God, once again undermining a view expressed by Jesus.

> **Jesus:** You know that those who are supposed to rule over the Gentiles lord it over them, and their great men exercise authority over them. But it shall not be so among you; but whoever would be great among you must be your servant, and whoever would be first among you must be slave of all.[9]

> **Paul:** Let every person be subject to the governing authorities. For there is no authority except from God, and those that exist have been instituted by God. Therefore he who resists the authorities resists what God has appointed, and those who resist will incur judgment. For rulers are not a terror to good conduct, but to bad. Would you have no fear of him who is in authority? Then do what is good, and you will receive his approval, for he is God's servant for your good.[10]

Time and again, Paul embraces doctrines which are designed to reinforce the status quo, whether it be class distinctions, "law and order," slavery, or male supremacy.

Paul is particularly notorious on the subject of women. During his life, Jesus consistently treated women with respect, and they responded by joining his movement in droves. Some early church traditions teach that Mary Magdalene (later accused of being a prostitute by the church "fathers") was one of his most prominent disciples. Jesus consistently reached out to women, including those who had been accused of immoral behavior, much to the reported consternation of his apostles.

According to New Testament scholar Karen L. King:

> Certainly, the New Testament Gospels, written toward the last quarter of the first century C.E., acknowledge that women were among Jesus' earliest followers. From the beginning, Jewish women disciples, including Mary Magdalene, Joanna, and Susanna, had accompanied Jesus during his ministry and supported him out of their private means (Luke 8:1–3). He spoke to women both in public and private, and indeed he learned from them. According to one story, an unnamed Gentile woman taught Jesus that the ministry of God is not limited to particular groups and persons, but belongs to all who have faith (Mark 7:24–30; Matthew 15:21–28). A Jewish woman honored him with the extraordinary hospitality of washing his feet with perfume. Jesus was a frequent visitor at the home of Mary and Martha, and was in the habit of teaching and eating meals with women as well as men. When Jesus was arrested, women remained firm, even when his male disciples are said to have fled, and they accompanied him to the foot of the cross. It was women who were reported as the first witnesses to the resurrection, chief among them again Mary Magdalene. Although the details of these gospel stories may be questioned, in general they reflect the prominent historical roles women played in Jesus' ministry as disciples.[11]

Paul did not hold women in the same esteem. Although the Acts of the Apostles and his own epistles prominently mention female disciples, Paul laid out rules explicitly curtailing the role of women in the church:

> As in all the churches of the saints, the women should keep silence in the churches. For they are not permitted to speak, but should be subordinate, as even the law says. If there is anything they desire to know, let them ask their husbands at home. For it is shameful for a woman to speak in church.[12]
>
> I desire then that in every place the men should pray, lifting holy hands without anger or quarreling; also that women should adorn themselves modestly and sensibly in seemly apparel, not with braided hair or gold or pearls or costly attire but by good deeds, as befits women who profess religion. Let a woman learn in silence with all submissiveness. I permit no woman to teach or to have authority over men; she is to keep silent.[13]

And, in perhaps his most infamous line:

> Wives, be subject to your husbands, as to the Lord. For the husband is the head of the wife as Christ is the head of the church, his body, and is himself its Savior. As the church is subject to Christ, so let wives also be subject in everything to their husbands.[14]

The list goes on and on. Paul laid out extensive rules for behavior which form the basis of Roman Catholic ideology as well as the moral guidelines embraced by the fundamentalist Christian sects that are today adjuncts to the Republican Party—everything from gay-baiting to an outright endorsement of slavery. Paul's epistles are a gold-mine for religiously motivated political conservatives like George W. Bush, the man who was so moved by the tale of the apostle's conversion on the road to Damascus.

Ironically, these same conservatives who gleefully quote Paul on homosexuality[15] also argue that America is a nation based on Christian values, because the founding fathers were presumably Christians.

The foundingest father of them all was surely Thomas Jefferson, the author of the Declaration of Independence, a primary architect of the Constitution, and the third president of the United States.

Jefferson was very interested in Christianity, and he spent many years studying the religion and writing about its contents. He spent a great deal of time dissecting the New Testament, and he felt that its "groveling" authors had "feeble minds."[16] Jefferson wrote:

Among the sayings and discourses imputed to [Jesus] by his biographers, I find many passages of fine imagination, correct morality, and of the most lovely benevolence; and others, again, of so much ignorance, so much absurdity, so much untruth, charlatanism and imposture, as to pronounce it impossible that such contradictions should have proceeded from the same being. I separate, therefore, the gold from the dross; restore to him the former, and leave the latter to the stupidity of some, and roguery of others of his disciples. Of this band of dupes and impostors, Paul was the great Coryphaeus,* and first corruptor of the doctrines of Jesus.[17]

Jefferson, like many modern scholars, believed that Paul's influence had shaped the gospel narratives. Jefferson felt so strongly about Paul's corruption of the Jesus teachings that he made an effort to reconstruct Q, the hypothetical "sayings gospel" on which the New Testament Gospels were based.[18]

Scientist Carl Sagan summarized the result: "Thomas Jefferson attempted to excise the Pauline parts of the New Testament. There wasn't much left when he was done, but it was an inspiring document."[19]

And perhaps, in the end, that's the point.

Religion is a sticky, messy, inconsistent business. From a historical perspective, we can barely prove Jesus of Nazareth lived at all, and we certainly have no clue what he did or said during his presumably short life. What little genuine tradition survives is buried in the words of Jesus as recorded in the gospels and the scattered records of the earliest Christian sects.

The word "Christianity" encompasses a wide diversity of beliefs. American conservatives have tried to claim that their lifestyle choices were mandated by Christ himself. Even if you believe the words of the four gospels are unimpeachably true, there is no basis for this claim.

Jesus never spoke a single word about homosexuality, nor did he confine the concept of marriage to a union

---

*The leader of a Greek chorus. Jefferson and many others suspected Paul of Hellenizing the early church.

between a man and a woman. Only one person in the New Testament expresses an opinion about the evils of the gay lifestyle, and that's Paul.[20]

Jesus never made a single comment about whether life begins in the womb, but Paul makes a glancing reference that serves as the primary New Testament basis for conservative Christian opposition to abortion (although even this reference is frankly not sufficient for any reasonable person to use as the basis of a moral imperative).[21]

Jesus praised a life lived in poverty. Paul ordered Christians to toil night and day. Jesus dismissed political power with contempt—"Render unto Caesar what is Caesar's, and unto God what is God's."[22] Paul urged Christian submission to political power and claimed the privileges of wealth and political power—which he himself employed liberally—were ordained by God.

There's just no way to get around it.

Jesus was a bleeding heart liberal, protector of the weak and downtrodden, enemy of the status quo and friend to sinners everywhere. Paul was a Republican—a moral and political right-winger who inspired the hell out of George W. Bush but earned the contempt of Thomas Jefferson.

So the next time you find yourself standing in a voting booth, remember the real history that truly defines your choice.

Will you vote for George Bush or Thomas Jefferson?

Will you vote for Paul or Jesus?

Some decisions are tough.

Some are not.

NOTES

1. J. Gresham Machen, *The Origin of Paul's Religion*, (Grand Rapids, Mich: Eerdman's Publishing Company, 2002).

2. Acts 9:3–6, Revised Standard Version.

3. Acts 21.

4. Hyam Maccoby, *The Mythmaker: Paul and the Invention of Christianity*, (New York: HarperCollins, 1987). Maccoby's overall premise is quite compelling, despite the author's distracting tendency to present gigantic speculative leaps as if they were inevitable conclusions born from inescapable logic.

5. Matthew 6:28–30.

6. 2 Thessalonians 3:6–10.

7. See Maccoby, among others, for a fuller discussion of Paul's supposed Judaism.

8. Acts 16, Acts 22, just for instance.

9. Mark 10:42–45.

10. Romans 13.

11. Essay written for PBS *Frontline*, www.pbs.org/wgbh/pages/frontline/shows/religion/first/women.html

12. 1 Corinthians 14:33–35

13. 1 Timothy 2:8–12

14. Ephesians 5:22–24

15. "[M]en likewise gave up natural relations with women and were consumed with passion for one another, men committing shameless acts with men and receiving in their own persons the due penalty for their error." Romans 1:26–27, among others. Some researchers speculate that Paul was a repressed homosexual himself.

16. John E. Remsberg, *Six Historic Americans*, (The Truth Seeker Company, 1908).

17. Thomas Jefferson, Letter to W. Short, 1820.

18. Jefferson eventually published his findings as *The Life and Morals of Jesus of Nazareth: Extracted Textually from the Gospels Greek, Latin, French, and English.*
19. Carl Sagan to Ken Schei, author of *Christianity Betrayed.*
20. Romans 1:27, among several others.
21. Galatians 1:15.
22. Luke 20:25.

"When, at the age of 50, I first began to study the Gospels seriously, I found in them the spirit that animates all who are truly alive. But along with the flow of that pure, life-giving water, I perceived much mire and slime mingled with it; and this had prevented me from seeing the true, pure water. I found that, along with the lofty teachings of Jesus, there are teaching bound up which are repugnant and contrary to it. I thus felt myself in the position of a man to whom a sack of garbage is given, who, after long struggle and wearisome labor, discovers among the garbage a number of infinitely precious pearls."

—Leo Tolstoy

from *The Gospel According to Jesus Christ* (1991)
Stephen Mitchell

W hat *is* the gospel according to Jesus? Simply this: that the love we all long for in our innermost heart is already present, beyond longing. Most of us can remember a time (it may have been just a moment) when we felt that everything in the world was exactly as it should be. Or we can think of a joy (it happened when we were children, perhaps, or the first time we fell in love) so vast that it was no longer inside us, but we were inside it. What we intuited then, and what we later thought was too good to be true, isn't an illusion. It is real. It is realer than the real, more intimate than anything we can see or touch, "unreachable," as the Upanishads say, "yet nearer than breath, than heartbeat." The more deeply we receive it, the more real it becomes.

Like all the great spiritual Masters, Jesus taught one thing only: presence. Ultimate reality, the luminous, compassionate intelligence of the universe, is not somewhere else, in some heaven light-years away. It didn't manifest itself any more fully to Abraham or Moses than to us, nor will it be any more present to some Messiah at the far end of time. It is always right here, right now. That is what the Bible means when it says that God's true name is *I am.*

There is such a thing as nostalgia for the future. Both Judaism and Christianity ache with it. It is a vision of the Golden Age, the days of perpetual summer in a world of straw-eating lions and roses without thorns, when human

life will be foolproof, and fulfilled in an endlessly pro-
longed finale of delight. I don't mean to make fun of the
messianic vision. In many ways it is admirable, and it has
inspired political and religious leaders from Isaiah to
Martin Luther King, Jr. But it is a kind of benign insanity.
And if we take it seriously enough, if we live it twenty-four
hours a day, we will spend all our time working in anticipation, and will never enter the Sabbath of the heart. How
moving and at the same time how ridiculous is the story
of the Hasidic rabbi who, every morning, as soon as he
woke up, would rush out his front door to see if the Messiah had arrived. (Another Hasidic story, about a more
mature stage of this consciousness, takes place at the
Passover seder. The rabbi tells his chief disciple to go outside and see if the Messiah has come. "But Rabbi, if the
Messiah came, wouldn't you know it in here?" the disciple
says, pointing to his heart. "Ah," says the rabbi, pointing
to his own heart, "but in here, the Messiah has already
come.") Who among the now-middle-aged doesn't
remember the fervor of the sixties, when young people
believed that love could transform the world? "You may
say I'm a dreamer," John Lennon sang, "but I'm not the
only one." The messianic dream of the future may be
humanity's sweetest dream. But it is a dream nevertheless,
as long as there is a separation between inside and outside, as long as we don't transform ourselves. And Jesus,
like the Buddha, was a man who had awakened from all
dreams.

When Jesus talked about the kingdom of God, he was
not prophesying about some easy, danger-free perfection
that will someday appear. He was talking about a state of
being, a way of living at ease among the joys and sorrows

of *our* world. It is possible, he said, to be as simple and beautiful as the birds of the sky or the lilies of the field, who are always within the eternal Now. This state of being is not something alien or mystical. We don't need to earn it. It is already ours. Most of us lose it as we grow up and become self-conscious, but it doesn't disappear forever; it is always there to be reclaimed, though we have to search hard in order to find it. The rich especially have a hard time reentering this state of being; they are so possessed by their possessions, so entrenched in their social power, that it is almost impossible for them to let go. Not that it is easy for any of us. But if we need reminding, we can always sit at the feet of our young children. They, because they haven't yet developed a firm sense of past and future, accept the infinite abundance of the present with all their hearts, in complete trust. Entering the kingdom of God means feeling, as if we were floating in the womb of the universe, that we are being taken care of, always, at every moment.

All spiritual Masters, in all the great religious traditions, have come to experience the present as the only reality. The Gospel passages in which "Jesus" speaks of a kingdom of God in the future can't be authentic, unless Jesus was a split personality, and could turn on and off two different consciousnesses as if they were hot- and cold-water faucets. And it is easy to understand how these passages would have been inserted into the Gospel by disciples, or disciples of disciples, who hadn't understood his teaching. Passages about the kingdom of God as coming in the future are a dime a dozen in the prophets, in the Jewish apocalyptic writings of the first centuries B.C.E., in Paul and the early church. They are filled with passionate hope, with a desire for universal justice, and also, as Nietzsche so correctly insisted, with a festering resentment against "them" (the powerful, the ungodly). But they arise from ideas, not from an experience of the state of being that Jesus called the kingdom of God.

The Jewish Bible doesn't talk much about this state; it is more interested in what Moses said at the bottom of the mountain, than in what he saw at the top. But there are exceptions. The most dramatic is the Voice from the Whirlwind in the Book of Job, which I have examined at length elsewhere. Another famous passage occurs at the beginning of Genesis: God completes the work of creation by entering the Sabbath mind, the mind of absolute, joyous serenity; contemplates the whole universe and says, "Behold, it is very good."

The kingdom of God is not something that will happen, because it isn't something that *can* happen. It can't appear in a world or a nation; it is a condition that has no plural, but only infinite singulars. Jesus spoke of people "entering" it, said that children were already inside it, told one particularly ardent scribe that he, the scribe, was not "far from" it. If only we stop looking forward and backward, he said, we will be able to devote ourselves to seeking the kingdom of God, which is right beneath our feet, right under our noses; and when we find it, food, clothing, and other necessities are given to us as well, as they are to the birds and the lilies. Where else but here and now can we find the grace-bestowing, inexhaustible presence of God? In its light, all our hopes and fears flitter away like ghosts. It is like a treasure buried in a field; it is like a pearl of great price; it is like coming home. When we find it, we find ourselves, rich beyond all dreams, and we realize that we can afford to lose everything else in the world, even (if we must) someone we love more dearly than life itself.

The portrait of Jesus that emerges from the authentic passages in the Gospels is of a man who has emptied himself of desires, doctrines, rules—all the mental claptrap and spiritual baggage that separate us from true life—and has been filled with the vivid reality of the Unnamable. Because he has let go of the merely personal, he is no one, he is everyone. Because he allows God *through* the personal, his personality is like a magnetic field. Those who are drawn to him have a hunger for the real; the closer they approach, the more they can feel the purity of his heart.

What is purity of heart? If we compare God to sunlight, we can say that the heart is like a window. Cravings, aversions, fixed judgments, concepts, beliefs—all forms of selfishness or self-protection—are, when we cling to them, like dirt on the windowpane. The thicker the dirt, the more opaque the window. When there is no dirt, the window is by its own nature perfectly transparent, and the light can stream through it without hindrance.

Or we can compare a pure heart to a spacious, light-filled room. People or possibilities open the door and walk in; the room will receive them, however many they are, for as long as they want to stay, and will let them leave when they want to. Whereas a corrupted heart is like a room cluttered with valuable possessions, in which the owner sits behind a locked door, with a loaded gun.

One last comparison, from the viewpoint of spiritual practice. To grow in purity of heart is to grow like a tree. The tree doesn't try to wrench its roots out of the earth and

plant itself in the sky, nor does it reach its leaves down-
ward into the dirt. It needs both ground and sunlight, and
knows the direction of each. Only because it digs into the
dark earth with its roots is it able to hold its leaves out to
receive the sunlight.

For every teacher who lives in this way, the word of God
has become flesh, and there is no longer a separation
between body and spirit. Everything he or she does pro-
claims the kingdom of God. (A visitor once said of the
eighteenth-century Hasidic rabbi Dov Baer, "I didn't travel
to Mezritch to hear him teach, but to watch him tie his
shoelaces.")

People can feel Jesus' radiance whether or not he is
teaching or healing; they can feel it in proportion to their
own openness. There is a deep sense of peace in his presence, and a sense of respect for him that far exceeds what
they have felt for any other human being. Even his silence
is eloquent. He is immediately recognizable by the quality
of his aliveness, by his disinterestedness and compassion.
He is like a mirror for us all, showing us who we essentially are.

> The image of the Master:
>   one glimpse
> and we are in love.

He enjoys eating and drinking, he likes to be around
women and children; he laughs easily, and his wit can cut
like a surgeon's scalpel. His trust in God is as natural as
breathing, and in God's presence he is himself fully
present. In his bearing, in his very language, he reflects
God's deep love for everything that is earthly: for the sick

and the despised, the morally admirable and the morally repugnant, for weeds as well as flowers, lions as well as lambs. He teaches that just as the sun gives light to both wicked and good, and the rain brings nourishment to both righteous and unrighteous, God's compassion embraces all people. There are no pre-conditions for it, nothing we need to do first, nothing we have to believe. When we are ready to receive it, it is there. And the more we live in its presence, the more effortlessly it flows through us, until we find that we no longer need external rules or Bibles or Messiahs.

> For this teaching which I give you today is not hidden from you, and is not far away. It is not in heaven, for you to say, "Who will go up to heaven and bring it down for us, so that we can hear it and do it?" Nor is it beyond the sea, for you to say, "Who will cross the sea and bring it back for us, so that we can hear it and do it?" But the teaching is very near you: it is in your mouth and in your heart, so that you can do it.

He wants to tell everyone about the great freedom: how it feels when we continually surrender to the moment and allow our hearts to become pure, not clinging to past or future, not judging or being judged. In each person he meets he can see the image of God in which they were created. They are all perfect, when he looks at them from the Sabbath mind. From another, complementary, viewpoint, they are all imperfect, even the most righteous of them, even he himself, because nothing is perfect but the One. He understands that being human *means* making mistakes.

When we acknowledge this in all humility, without wanting anything else, we can forgive ourselves, and we can begin correcting our mistakes. And once we forgive ourselves, we can forgive anyone.

He has no ideas to teach, only presence. He has no doctrines to give, only the gift of his own freedom.

> *Tolerant like the sky,*
> *all-pervading like sunlight,*
> *firm like a mountain,*
> *supple like a branch in the wind,*
> *he has no destination in view*
> *and makes use of anything*
> *life happens to bring his way.*
>
> *Nothing is impossible for him.*
> *Because he has let go,*
> *he can care for the people's welfare*
> *as a mother cares for her child.*

A *Jesus Is Not A Republican* Timeline:

Nate Hardcastle

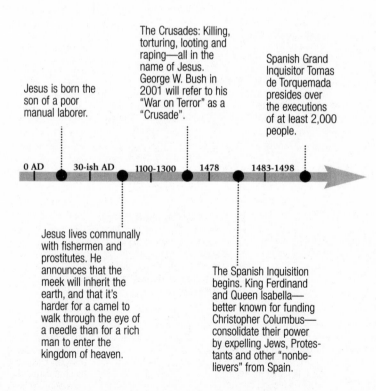

The Crusades: Killing, torturing, looting and raping—all in the name of Jesus. George W. Bush in 2001 will refer to his "War on Terror" as a "Crusade".

Spanish Grand Inquisitor Tomas de Torquemada presides over the executions of at least 2,000 people.

Jesus is born the son of a poor manual laborer.

0 AD   30-ish AD   1100-1300   1478   1483-1498

Jesus lives communally with fishermen and prostitutes. He announces that the meek will inherit the earth, and that it's harder for a camel to walk through the eye of a needle than for a rich man to enter the kingdom of heaven.

The Spanish Inquisition begins. King Ferdinand and Queen Isabella— better known for funding Christopher Columbus— consolidate their power by expelling Jews, Protestants and other "nonbelievers" from Spain.

The Pilgrims land at Plymouth, determined to build a society based upon their interpretation of the Bible.

Galileo uses a telescope to observe two of Jupiter's moons. Leading Catholic priests condemn his findings as heretical; some refuse to look through the telescope, while others declare Galileo's findings to be illusions created by the devil.

The so-called "Great Awakening" begins. Religious leaders in the American colonies, their power vulnerable to the ideas of the Enlightenment, invoke visions of hell to scare millions into abandoning logic and reason.

1610   1616   1620   1692   1730   1776

The Salem Witch Trials occur in Salem, Massachusetts. Puritan leaders and infighting townspeople accuse hundreds of their neighbors of witchcraft. Twenty people, most of them unpopular with local elites, are executed.

Under threat of imprisonment, Galileo agrees to recant his assertion that the earth revolves around the sun.

The Founding Fathers, a liberal group of Enlightenment-inspired Christians and Deists, declare the American colonies' independence from Britain.

The United States adopts the Bill of Rights, including the first Amendment to the Constitution: "Congress shall make no law respecting an establishment of religion . . ."

Congress, in the year of the Army-McCarthy hearings, adds the words "under God" to the Pledge of Allegiance in order to underline the differences between Americans and Godless communists.

Tennessee authorities charge high school biology teacher John Scopes with illegally teaching evolution. His defense team, led by Clarence Darrow, shreds the fundamentalist interpretation of the Bible, making a mockery of lead prosecutor William Jennings Bryan.

1789   1802   1925   1954   1966

H. L. Mencken's observation about the Scopes trial resonates today: "It serves notice on the country that Neanderthal man is organizing in these forlorn backwaters of the land, led by a fanatic, rid of sense and devoid of conscience. Tennessee, challenging him too timorously and too late, now sees its courts converted into camp meetings and its Bill of Rights made a mock of by its sworn officers of the law."

Jim Bakker founds his TV ministry, the PTL Club.

Thomas Jefferson coins the phrase "a wall of separation between church and state."

A *JESUS IS NOT A REPUBLICAN* TIMELINE

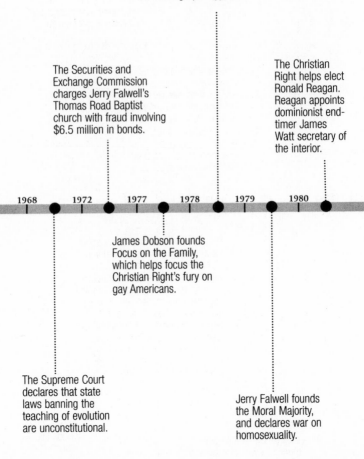

John Birch Society member Timothy LaHaye publishes *The Unhappy Gays*, which labels gay people "vile." Two decades later, LaHaye will become rich and famous as co-author of the stupendously lurid and horrifyingly popular *Left Behind* book series, which caters to fundamentalists' obsession with the coming Apocalypse.

The Securities and Exchange Commission charges Jerry Falwell's Thomas Road Baptist church with fraud involving $6.5 million in bonds.

The Christian Right helps elect Ronald Reagan. Reagan appoints dominionist end-timer James Watt secretary of the interior.

| 1968 | 1972 | 1977 | 1978 | 1979 | 1980 |

James Dobson founds Focus on the Family, which helps focus the Christian Right's fury on gay Americans.

The Supreme Court declares that state laws banning the teaching of evolution are unconstitutional.

Jerry Falwell founds the Moral Majority, and declares war on homosexuality.

Jimmy Swaggart's disgruntled former colleague Martin Gorman publicizes photos showing Swaggart visiting a motel with a prostitute. The woman in question says Swaggart regularly paid to watch her undress, and inquired whether he could have sex with her nine-year-old daughter. Swaggart tearfully resigns from his TV ministry. The long-time anti-porn crusader also confesses an addiction to pornography.

Jim Bakker is convicted of defrauding PTL's contributors. His trial reveals the depth of his corruption: Among other things, the organization once paid $100,000 for a private plane to carry the Bakkers' clothing across the country.

Televangelist Jimmy Swaggart helps defrock Assemblies of God preacher Martin Gorman after Gorman has an affair with a parishioner.

1984   1986   1987   1988   1989

Jerry Falwell pays $5,000 to gay activist Jerry Sloan. Falwell had denied saying that the gay-oriented Metropolitan Community Churches were "a vile and Satanic system," saying they would "one day be utterly annihilated and there will be a celebration in heaven." Falwell also had offered $5,000 if Sloan could produce a tape. Sloan produced a tape. Falwell later based an appeal on the notion that the Jewish judge in the case was biased.

Jerry Falwell is found guilty of illegally transferring $6.7 million intended for his religious ministries to his political action committees.

Jim Bakker resigns from the PTL club after revelations that he had an affair with parishioner Jessica Hahn. Jimmy Swaggart calls him "a cancer in the body of Christ."

A *JESUS IS NOT A REPUBLICAN* TIMELINE

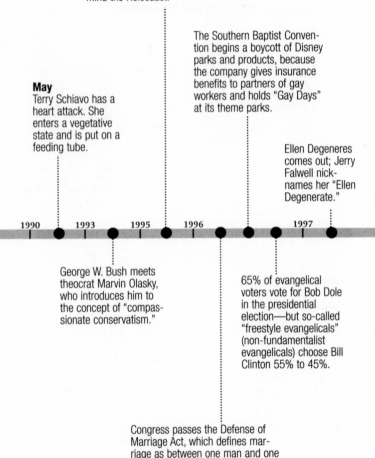

Christian-right activists Scott Lively and Kevin Abrams publish *The Pink Swastika: Homosexuality in the Nazi Party*, which claims that gay leaders helped mastermind the Holocaust.

The Southern Baptist Convention begins a boycott of Disney parks and products, because the company gives insurance benefits to partners of gay workers and holds "Gay Days" at its theme parks.

May
Terry Schiavo has a heart attack. She enters a vegetative state and is put on a feeding tube.

Ellen Degeneres comes out; Jerry Falwell nicknames her "Ellen Degenerate."

1990   1993   1995   1996   1997

George W. Bush meets theocrat Marvin Olasky, who introduces him to the concept of "compassionate conservatism."

65% of evangelical voters vote for Bob Dole in the presidential election—but so-called "freestyle evangelicals" (non-fundamentalist evangelicals) choose Bill Clinton 55% to 45%.

Congress passes the Defense of Marriage Act, which defines marriage as between one man and one woman, after intense lobbying by an anti-gay consortium called the National Pro-Family Forum.

A *JESUS IS NOT A REPUBLICAN* TIMELINE

The South Carolina Republican Primary offers clues about the ethical values of the Bush-Christian Right alliance. Bush begins his campaign at Bob Jones University, where interracial dating is banned. Later, anonymous "push-polls" spread the lie that the McCains' adopted Bangladeshi daughter is the Senator's illegitimate black child. Evangelical groups that support Bush promote this story, which helps sink McCain's campaign in the state. The episode is crucial to Bush's eventual nomination as the Republican presidential nominee.

George W. Bush as governor of Texas presides over the execution of Carla Faye Tucker—just one of a record-setting 152 executions during his tenure. Bush mocks her pleas for clemency.

Jerry Falwell's *National Liberty Journal* outs Teletubby Tinky Winky.

Judge Roy Moore runs for Alabama chief justice. He campaigns as "the Ten Commandments judge," and wins the election.

1998   1999   2000

Alabama circuit court judge Roy Moore posts in his courtroom a wooden plaque featuring the Ten Commandments, and becomes famous fighting a lawsuit to remove the plaque.

Vermont legalizes same-sex unions; Gary Bauer calls the move "worse than terrorism."

George W. Bush says that he believes God has chosen him to run for president.

Michael Schiavo petitions Florida courts to authorize removal of his wife's feeding tube, saying she would not have wanted to be kept alive without hope of recovery. His request is approved. Terry Schiavo's parents launch a legal battle to keep their daughter alive.

A *JESUS IS NOT A REPUBLICAN* TIMELINE

November
George W. Bush is elected president, despite a tepid turnout from Christian Right voters. (It helps that thousands of Florida Jews vote for . . . Pat Buchanan.) Bush and political advisor Karl Rove spend the next four years shoring up support among the fundamentalist base.

Bush announces a dishonest and restrictive policy on stem-cell research, designed to appeal to the Christian Right at the expense of Americans who suffer from a variety of ailments, including Alzheimer's, Parkinson's and ALS.

September
Jerry Falwell blames the terrorist attacks on "the Pagans, and the abortionists, and the feminists and the gays and lesbians who are actively trying to make that an alternative lifestyle." And here we thought the attacks were the work of religious zealots.

The Supreme Court declines to review the Terry Schiavo case.

2000   2001   2002

Bush names as attorney general fundamentalist ex-Missouri governor John "I think all we should legislate is morality" Ashcroft. Bush also establishes the Office of Faith-Based Initiatives, cuts off funds for organizations providing abortions overseas, and appoints Kay Coles James, former dean at Pat Roberton's Regent University, to the position of director of the U.S. Office of Personnel Management.

September
The 9/11 attacks convince Bush's fundamentalist supporters that he is chosen by God to lead America. General William Boykin later explains: "Why is this man in the White House? The majority of America did not vote for him. He's in the White House because God put him there for a time such as this."

January
Reverend and abortion-clinic bomber Michael Bray commends Saudi Arabia for beheading three gay men.

Roy Moore installs a granite monument of the Ten Commandments in the Alabama Supreme Court building.

323

A *JESUS IS NOT A REPUBLICAN* TIMELINE

April
A British intelligence officer writes a memo to Prime Minister Tony Blair about Bush's stance on Iraq. He writes, "Bush wanted to remove Saddam, through military action, justified by the conjunction of terrorism and WMD. But the intelligence and facts were being fixed around the policy . . . There was little discussion in Washington of the aftermath after military action."

George Bush finally gets his wish: The U.S. invades Iraq. Thousands of soldiers and civilians are killed.

September
Jerry Falwell says "I think Muhammad was a terrorist."

November
Pervert and sex deviant Jimmy Swaggart calls the prophet Muhammed a "pervert" and "sex deviant."

Bush signs a ban on late-term abortions, then celebrates with Religious-Right leaders who include Jerry Falwell, radio host Janet Parshall, SBC leader Richard Land and National Association of Evangelicals (NAE) president Ted Haggard.

2003

November
Republicans dominate midterm elections, largely thanks to the get-out-the-vote efforts of the Christian Right.

Alan Sears, leader of the Alliance Defense Fund, outs the cartoon sponge SpongeBob SquarePants.

November
Terri Schiavo's parents claim that Michael Schiavo may have abused their daughter, and that his abuse may have led to her condition. They provide no evidence to support this contention.

August
A Justice Department memo approved by White House Chief Council Alberto Gonzales sets the machinery of torture into motion. It opines that laws prohibiting torture do not apply to suspects in the "War on Terror," and that interrogation techniques can only be defined as torture if they cause pain equal to "injury such as death, organ failure, or serious impairment of body functions."

A *JESUS IS NOT A REPUBLICAN* TIMELINE

July
The *Atlantic Monthly* reviews memos about death-penalty cases written by Alberto Gonzales, chief legal counsel to then-Texas governor Bush. The magazine's conclusion: "Gonzales repeatedly failed to apprise the governor of crucial issues in the cases at hand . . . The memoranda seem attuned to a radically different posture, assumed by Bush from the earliest days of his administration—one in which he sought to minimize his sense of legal and moral responsibility for executions."

October
Florida Governor Jeb Bush files a federal court brief on behalf of Terri Schiavo's parents. The court quickly rules that it has no authority in the matter, and the feeding tube is removed. The Florida legislature, pandering to the Christian Right, passes "Terri's Law," giving Governor Bush the authority to interfere in the case—which he does, ordering the tube reinserted. George W. Bush praises his brother's handling of the matter.

November
Alabama's judicial ethics panel removes Chief Justice Roy Moore from office after he refuses to move his Ten Commandments monument out of the state Supreme Court building.

2003 — 2004

August
A reporter asks Christian Coalition President Roberta Combs whether she is concerned about the lack of Religious-Right speakers at the Republican Convention. Her reply: "We still own the president."

October
Lightning strikes James Caviezel, the actor playing Jesus, during filming of Mel Gibson's new picture *The Passion of the Christ*.

February
George W. Bush announces his support for a constitutional amendment to ban gay marriage.

August
Charles Taylor, president of Liberia, mass-murderer, born-again Christian and friend and business partner of Christian Broadcasting Network Pat Robertson, resigns.

February
Mel Gibson's *The Passion of the Christ* hits theatres. It goes on to gross nearly $400 million during the next 18 months. The *New York Times*' A.O. Scott reports, "*The Passion of the Christ* is so relentlessly focused on the savagery of Jesus' final hours that this film seems to arise less from love than from wrath, and to succeed more in assaulting the spirit than in uplifting it."

A *JESUS IS NOT A REPUBLICAN* TIMELINE

September
Jimmy Swaggart tells his audience, "I've never seen a man in my life I wanted to marry. And I'm gonna be blunt and plain; if one ever looks at me like that, I'm gonna kill him and tell God he died."

January
Education Secretary Margaret Spellings blasts PBS for its "Sugartime!" episode of the program *Postcards From Buster*, in which cartoon character Buster goes to Vermont to make maple syrup and meets a child with two moms.

August
Colorado bishop Michael Sheridan announces that voting for Kerry would jeopardize Catholics' chances at salvation (Translation: Vote for Kerry, go to hell).

December
The Senate holds hearings on torture of Iraqi detainees at Abu Ghraib prison. No senior official is held responsible.

February
Republican lawmakers circulate a memo about the benefits of intervening in the Schiavo case. It says ". . . the pro-life base will be excited that the Senate is debating this important issue," and "This is a great political issue . . ."

2005

September
The Florida Supreme Court declares "Terri's Law" unconstitutional.

November
Bush wins reelection, thanks largely to 80% support among evangelical Christians.

January
The U.S. Supreme Court declines to review the Florida Supreme Court's decision declaring "Terri's Law" unconstitutional.

January
Polls show deposed Alabama chief justice Roy Moore leading in a hypothetical race for governor of the state. Moore announces that he is weighing his options.

March
Terri Schiavo's feeding tube is removed for the third time. Her parents mount a last-ditch legal battle to reinsert the tube.

March
Tom DeLay calls Michael Schiavo a murderer. The *L.A. Times* later reports that DeLay in 1988 joined in a family decision to remove his comatose father's feeding tube, allowing him to die.

April
Florida's department of children and families releases 89 abuse reports filed against Michael Schiavo. The agency's investigations found no merit to any of the accusations.

March 20
Tom DeLay says "Terri Schiavo is not brain dead. She talks and she laughs, and she expresses happiness and discomfort. Terri Schiavo is not on life support."

June
Representative John Hostettler, R-Ind., accuses Democrats of "denigrating and demonizing Christians" on the House floor. Democrats had introduced an amendment to prevent "coercive and abusive religious proselytizing" at the Air Force Academy.

March
Jeb Bush reports that neurologist Dr. William Cheshire, a headache specialist who has not examined Mrs. Schiavo, claims that she is not in a persistent vegetative state.

March 31
Terri Schiavo dies. Tom Delay issues a thinly-veiled threat to the judges involved in the case, saying "the time will come for the men responsible for this to answer for their behavior."

2005

March
Senate Majority Leader Bill Frist, a heart surgeon (not a neurologist), says that he has seen video of Terri Schiavo which leads him to believe that she is not in a vegetative state.

March
Schiavo's parents file a brief claiming that they heard her try to say "I want to live."

March
Richard Alan Meywes is arrested for offering $250,000 to anyone who murders Michael Schiavo, and $50,000 to anyone who kills presiding judge George Greer.

June
Florida medical examiner Dr. John Thogmartin issues the autopsy report for Terri Schiavo. He reports that her brain had shrunk by half, leaving her blind and in a persistent vegetative state, and that "no amount of treatment or therapy would have regenerated the massive loss of neurons." He also reports that he found no evidence of abuse.

March
Congress passes a bill which purports to give the federal government authority to intervene in the Terri Schiavo case. President Bush—who took three days to respond to the devastating Asian tsunami—immediately interrupts his Easter vacation in Texas to fly to Washington, where he signs the bill at 1:11 a.m. Repeated court rulings at both the state and federal level uphold Michael Schiavo's right to have his wife's feeding tube removed.

Acknowledgments

Many people made this anthology.

At Thunder's Mouth Press and Avalon Publishing Group: Thanks to Will Balliett, John Oakes, Mike Walters, Maria Fernandez, Michael O'Connor, Cathelíne Jean-François, Nate Knaebel, Linda Kosarin, Susan Reich, David Riedy and Don Weise for their support, dedication and hard work.

We are especially grateful to J. M. Berger and Rob Boston, who contributed original writing to this anthology. Thanks also are due to the many people who helped us with research and permissions, particularly Jeffrey Sharlet at *The Revealer* and Mimi Ross at Henry Holt.

Finally, we are grateful to the writers and artists whose work appears in this book.

Permissions

J. Gomes. Copyright © 2003 by Peter J. Gomes. Reprinted with permission of the author. • "Memo to Mel Gibson" by J.M. Berger. Copyright 2005 by J.M. Berger. • "We're All Damned" by George Monbiot. Copyright © Guardian Newspapers Limited 1996. Reprinted with permission. • "The Only King We Have Is Jesus" by Calvin Trillin. Copyright © 2001 by Calvin Trillin. Reprinted by permission of the author. • Excerpt from *Jesus: A Revolutionary Biography* by John Dominic Crossan. Copyright © 1994 by John Dominic Crossan. Reprinted by permission of Harper-Collins Publishers Inc. • "Building Global Justice" by Jim Wallis. Copyright © 2004 by Jim Wallis. Reprinted with permission of Sojourners. • "God, Meet Mammon" from *What's the Matter with Kansas? How Conservatives Won the Heart of America* by Thomas Frank, © 2004 by Thomas Frank. Reprinted by permission of Henry Holt and Company, LLC. • "Open Letter to Religious Leaders" reprinted courtesy of The Religious Institute on Sexual Morality, Justice and Healing. • "Bush Plays Pope on Gay Marriage" by Robert Scheer. Reprinted with permission from the August 7, 2003 issue of the *Nation*. For subscription information, call 1-800-333-8536. Portions of each week's *Nation* magazine can be accessed at http://www.thenation.com. • "W.'s Christian Nation" by Chris Mooney. Copyright © 2003 by Chris Mooney. Reprinted with permission from the *American Prospect*, www.prospect.org. • "Stacked Decalogue" by Katha Pollitt. Copyright © 2003 by Katha Pollitt. Reprinted by permission of the author. • "Under God and Over" by Leon Wieseltier. Reprinted by permission of *The New Republic*, © 2004, The New Republic, LLC. • "James Madison Rebukes the Religious Right" by Rob Boston. Copyright © 2005 by Rob Boston. • "Jesus Was Not a

Bibliography

Boehlert, Eric. "The Grinch Who Saved Christmas." Originally published by *Salon*, www.salon.com, December 16, 2004.

Carroll, James. *Crusade: Chronicles of an Unjust War.* New York: Henry Holt, 2004.

Crossan, John Dominic. *Jesus: A Revolutionary Biography.* New York: HarperCollins, 1994.

Domke, David. "Just Another Word for Everything Left to Lose." Originally published by the *Revealer*, www.the revealer.org, January 21, 2005.

Domke, David and Kevin Coe. "How Bush's God-Talk is Different." Originally published by *Beliefnet*, www. beliefnet.com, 2004.

Dowell, William Thatcher. "American Wahabbis and the Ten Commandments." Originally published by *Mother Jones*, March 8, 2005.

Frank, Thomas. *What's the Matter with Kansas? How Conservatives Won the Heart of America.* New York: Henry Holt, 2004.

Frazier, Ian. "Here to Tell You." Originally published by the *New Yorker*, February 28, 2005.

Goldberg, Michelle. "The New Monkey Trial." Originally published by *Salon*, www.salon.com, January 12, 2005.

Gomes, Peter J. "Patriotism is Not Enough." Originally published by *Sojourners*, www.sojo.net, January/February 2003.

Leonard, Andrew. "This Has Nothing To Do With the Sanctity of Life." Originally published by *Salon*, www.salon.com, March 22, 2005.

Lobe, Jim. "Leo Strauss's Philosophy of Deception." Originally published by *Alternet*, www.alternet.org, December 7, 2004.

Mitchell, Stephen. *The Gospel According to Jesus Christ.* New York: HarperCollins, 1991.

Monbiot, George. "Apocalypse, Please." Originally published by the *Guardian*, April 20, 2004.

Monbiot, George. "We're All Damned." Originally published by the *Guardian*, November 19, 1996.

Mooney, Chris. "W.'s Christian Nation." Originally published by the *American Prospect*, www.prospect.org, June 1, 2003.

Moyers, Bill. "Battlefield Earth." Originally published by *Alternet*, www.alternet.org, December 8, 2004.

Pollitt, Katha. "Stacked Decalogue." Originally published by the *Nation*, September 22, 2003.

Posner, Sarah. "Leading Like Jesus." Originally published by the *Gadflyer*, www.gadflyer.com, December 3, 2004.

Prejean, Helen. *The Death of Innocents.* New York: Random House, 2005.

Rich, Frank. "The God Racket: From DeMille to DeLay." Originally published by the *New York Times*, March 24, 2005.

Rutledge, Fleming. "Unfair Treatment." Originally published by Church Folks for a Better America, www.cfba.org, June 28, 2004.

Scheer, Robert. "Between Religion and Morality." Originally published by *Salon*, www.salon.com, May 27, 2002.

Scheer, Robert. "Bush Plays Pope on Gay Marriage." Originally published by the *Nation*, August 7, 2003.

Trillin, Calvin. "The Only King We Have Is Jesus." Originally published by the *Nation*, February 5, 2001.

Waldman, Paul. "You're Nothing but Dirty, Dirty Sinners, Boys and Girls." Originally published by the *Gadflyer*, www.gadflyer.com, December 3, 2004.

Wallis, Jim. "Building Global Justice." Originally published by *Sojourners*, www.sojo.net, June 12, 2004.

Wieseltier, Leon. "Under God and Over." Originally published by the *New Republic*, April 5, 2004.

Williams, Patricia J. "Taking the Hospital." Originally published by the *Nation*, November 29, 2004.

Willimon, William H. "No More of This." Originally published by Church Folks for a Better America, www.cfba.org, April 4, 2004.

"Open Letter to Religious Leaders." Published by The Religious Institute on Sexual Morality, Justice, and Healing, www.relgiousinstitute.org, January 17, 2005.

CLINT WILLIS has edited more than thirty anthologies, including *The I Hate Republicans Reader; We Are the People: Stories from the Other Side of American History* (with Nathaniel May); and *Son of Man: Great Writings About Jesus Christ.* He lives in Maine.

NATE HARDCASTLE has edited and contributed to dozens of anthologies, including *The I Hate Republicans Reader* and *The I Hate Corporate America Reader.* He lives with his wife in rural Maine.